EMPOWERED AFFIRMATIONS
NURTURING MIND, BODY, AND SOUL

M L Ruscsak

Trient Press
3375 S Rainbow Blvd
#81710, SMB 13135
Las Vegas,NV 89180

Ordering Information:
Quantity sales. Special discounts are available on quantity purchases by corporations, associations, and others. For details, contact the publisher at the address above.
Orders by U.S. trade bookstores and wholesalers. Please contact Trient Press: Tel: (775) 996-3844; or visit www.trientpress.com.

Printed in the United States of America

Publisher's Cataloging-in-Publication data
Ruscsak, M.L.
A title of a book : Empowered Affirmations: Nurturing Mind, Body, and Soul

ISBN
Hard Cover   979-8-88990-023-8
Paper Back   979-8-88990-025-2
Ebook   979-8-88990-024-5

Table of Contents	
Introduction:	Pg 4
Wealth and abundance:	Pg 6
Beauty and self-image:	Pg 84
Confidence and self-belief:	Pg 162
Health and well-being:	PG 222
Relationships and love:	Pg 274
Glossary	Pg 346

Welcome to "Empowered Affirmations: Nurturing Mind, Body, and Soul." In this transformative book, we embark on a journey of self-discovery, exploring the realms of wealth and abundance, beauty and self-image, confidence and self-belief, health and well-being, and relationships and love. Through the power of affirmations, we will delve deep into these areas of life, empowering ourselves to create a harmonious and fulfilling existence.

Chapter 1: Wealth and Abundance

In the first chapter, we explore the realm of wealth and abundance. Through carefully crafted affirmations, we will shift our mindset from scarcity to abundance, attracting prosperity and financial well-being into our lives. We will discover the power within us to manifest abundance in all its forms and create a life of financial freedom and fulfillment.

Chapter 2: Beauty and Self-Image

In the second chapter, we delve into the realm of beauty and self-image. Through affirmations, we cultivate a deep sense of self-love and acceptance, embracing our unique beauty and recognizing our inherent worth. By affirming our beauty from within, we enhance our outer radiance, allowing our authentic selves to shine brightly.

Chapter 3: Confidence and Self-Belief

The third chapter explores the transformative power of affirmations in cultivating confidence and self-belief. Through these affirmations, we release self-doubt and embrace our true potential. We tap into our inner strength and courage, allowing us to pursue our dreams with unwavering belief in ourselves and our abilities.

Chapter 4: Health and Well-Being

In the fourth chapter, we focus on affirmations that promote health and well-being. We affirm our body's natural ability to heal, nourish, and thrive. Through these affirmations, we nurture a holistic approach to wellness, caring for our physical, mental, and emotional well-being. We embrace healthy habits and cultivate a harmonious relationship with our bodies and minds.

Chapter 5: Relationships and Love

Lastly, in the fifth chapter, we explore the realm of relationships and love. Through affirmations, we nurture healthy and fulfilling connections with ourselves and others. We affirm our desires for meaningful relationships, setting healthy boundaries, and fostering love and understanding in our interactions. These affirmations will empower us to create and sustain loving and harmonious relationships in all areas of our lives.

Throughout this book, we will provide you with a rich tapestry of affirmations drawn from various fields, including psychology, spirituality, and personal growth. We will also incorporate insights from diverse disciplines, such as Witchcraft, Divination, Herbalism, Shamanism, and Ecospirituality, offering a unique and holistic approach to personal empowerment.

Each chapter will not only present affirmations but also offer examples, problems, and exercises to deepen your understanding and engage you in critical thinking and self-reflection. By incorporating these affirmations into your daily practice, you will unleash the transformative power within you, nurturing your mind, body, and soul.

Remember, the journey of personal empowerment is a lifelong pursuit. As you embark on this exploration of empowered affirmations, be open to growth, embrace self-compassion, and celebrate your progress along the way. May this book be a guiding light on your path to self-discovery and self-empowerment.

Wishing you a transformative and empowering journey as you nurture your mind, body, and soul with "Empowered Affirmations: Nurturing Mind, Body, and Soul."

With warm regards,

M. L. Ruscsak

WEALTH AND ABUNDANCE:

Welcome to the captivating world of wealth and abundance. In this chapter, we will embark on a profound exploration of the principles and practices that can enable us to manifest and attract financial prosperity into our lives. Drawing inspiration from the wisdom of thought leaders such as Louise Hay and Rhonda Byrne, we will delve into the transformative power of affirmations, mindset shifts, and conscious actions to unlock the doors to abundance.

Understanding Wealth and Abundance:

Before we dive into the techniques and strategies for cultivating wealth and abundance, it is essential to establish a comprehensive understanding of these concepts. Wealth encompasses far more than mere monetary riches; it encompasses a holistic sense of prosperity that extends beyond material possessions. It encompasses an abundance of opportunities, resources, well-being, and fulfillment in all areas of life.

Abundance, on the other hand, refers to a state of overflow and plenitude. It involves recognizing and appreciating the inherent abundance that exists in the universe and within ourselves. Abundance is not limited to financial wealth but extends to love, relationships, health, creativity, and spirituality. By shifting our perspective and aligning with the principles of abundance, we can open ourselves up to a vast array of possibilities and experiences.

The Power of Affirmations:

One of the foundational pillars of manifesting wealth and abundance lies in the power of affirmations. Affirmations are positive statements that we repeat to ourselves consciously and consistently, reprogramming our subconscious mind to align with our desired reality. They serve as powerful tools for transforming limiting beliefs, overcoming scarcity mindset, and fostering a mindset of abundance.

Louise Hay, renowned author and advocate of positive affirmations, believed that our thoughts and words create our experiences. By consciously choosing and repeating affirmations that resonate with our goals, aspirations, and desires, we can manifest abundance and attract wealth into our lives. Rhonda Byrne, the author of

"The Secret," echoed similar sentiments, emphasizing the importance of focusing on positive thoughts and feelings to activate the law of attraction.

Creating a Wealth Mindset:

To cultivate wealth and abundance, it is crucial to develop a mindset that is aligned with prosperity. Our mindset shapes our beliefs, attitudes, and actions, ultimately influencing our outcomes. A wealth mindset involves shifting from a scarcity mindset, rooted in lack and limitation, to an abundance mindset, grounded in the belief that there is an infinite supply of resources and opportunities available to us.

In this chapter, we will explore various strategies and practices to cultivate a wealth mindset. These include reframing limiting beliefs, practicing gratitude, embracing a growth mindset, visualizing success, and surrounding ourselves with positive influences. By integrating these techniques into our daily lives, we can rewire our thinking patterns and align ourselves with the abundance that is inherently available to us.

Exercises:

Reflect on your current beliefs and attitudes towards wealth and abundance. Identify any limiting beliefs or scarcity mindset patterns that may be holding you back. Write them down and explore ways to reframe them into empowering beliefs.

Choose three affirmations related to wealth and abundance that resonate with you. Write them down and commit to repeating them daily for the next month. Journal about any shifts or experiences that arise during this practice.

Research and explore examples of individuals who have manifested wealth and abundance using affirmations and mindset shifts. Write a brief analysis of their experiences and identify any commonalities or techniques that can be applied to your own journey.

Conclusion:

As we embark on this journey of exploring wealth and abundance, it is essential to approach it with an open mind and a willingness to embrace new possibilities. Throughout this chapter, we will delve into the depths of manifesting financial prosperity, leveraging the wisdom of Louise Hay, Rhonda Byrne, and other thought leaders in the field. By understanding the power of affirmations, cultivating a wealth mindset, and taking inspired actions, we can tap into the limitless abundance that awaits us. Get ready to unlock the doors to wealth and abundance and manifest a life of prosperity.

AFFIRMATIONS FOCUSED ON ATTRACTING FINANCIAL PROSPERITY AND ABUNDANCE INTO ONE'S LIFE.

Introduction to the power of self-image affirmations.

In this chapter, we will embark on a transformative journey exploring the profound impact of self-image affirmations on our lives. Self-image affirmations have the potential to shape our perception of ourselves, influencing our thoughts, emotions, behaviors, and ultimately, our overall well-being. Through the careful practice of affirmations, we can cultivate a positive and empowering self-image, leading to increased self-confidence, resilience, and personal growth.

The concept of self-image, as we will explore, is rooted in the belief that our thoughts and beliefs about ourselves create our reality. According to influential authors and spiritual teachers like Louise Hay and Rhonda Byrne, our self-image is a reflection of our inner thoughts and beliefs. By consciously directing our thoughts and using affirmations, we can reprogram our self-image, shedding limiting beliefs and embracing a positive and empowering perception of ourselves.

To embark on this transformative journey, it is essential to approach self-image affirmations with an open mind and a willingness to explore and challenge deeply ingrained beliefs. Throughout this chapter, we will delve into the power of self-image affirmations, drawing insights from various fields, including Witchcraft, Divination, Herbalism, Shamanism, and Ecospirituality. By exploring these diverse perspectives, we gain a comprehensive understanding of the transformative potential that self-image affirmations offer.

This chapter will consist of several sections, each focusing on a different aspect of self-image affirmations. We will begin by examining the psychological and neurological foundations underlying the effectiveness of affirmations in shaping our self-perception. Drawing upon empirical research and psychological theories, we will unravel the mechanisms through which affirmations influence our self-image.

Next, we will delve into the practical application of self-image affirmations. Through examples, problems, and exercises, we will guide you in crafting personalized affirmations that resonate with your unique self. We will explore the process of identifying and challenging limiting beliefs, replacing them with empowering affirmations that align with your true potential.

Furthermore, we will discuss the role of self-compassion and self-acceptance in the practice of self-image affirmations. Embracing these qualities allows us to approach affirmations with kindness and patience, fostering a nurturing environment for personal growth.

Additionally, we will explore the potential challenges and pitfalls that may arise during the practice of self-image affirmations. It is important to address these obstacles and offer strategies to overcome self-doubt, resistance, and setbacks. By acknowledging the complexity of the journey, we can navigate it with resilience and perseverance.

Throughout this chapter, we will also present counterarguments and dissenting opinions to encourage critical thinking and provide a balanced perspective. It is important to approach the subject of self-image affirmations with an open mind and consider various viewpoints. This critical analysis will foster a deeper understanding and engagement with the material.

In conclusion, the power of self-image affirmations lies in their ability to shape our perception of ourselves and transform our lives. By harnessing the practice of affirmations, we can cultivate a positive and empowering self-image, leading to increased self-confidence, resilience, and personal growth. Through the exploration of diverse fields and perspectives, we will embark on a journey of self-discovery and self-empowerment. Let us now delve into the intricacies of self-image affirmations and unlock their transformative potential.

Understanding the connection between self-image and overall well-being.

Self-image, the way we perceive and evaluate ourselves, plays a fundamental role in shaping our overall well-being. It influences our thoughts, emotions, behaviors, and interactions with the world around us. Developing a positive and empowering self-image is crucial for cultivating a healthy and fulfilling life. In this section, we will delve into the intricate connection between self-image and overall well-being, drawing insights from various fields such as Witchcraft, Divination, Herbalism, Shamanism, and Ecospirituality.

To comprehend the impact of self-image on well-being, it is important to explore the psychological and emotional dimensions associated with it. According to psychological theories, our self-image is formed through a complex interplay of internal and external factors, including social interactions, cultural influences, and personal experiences. These factors shape our beliefs, values, and self-perception, ultimately influencing our well-being.

In Witchcraft and Divination practices, self-image is considered a reflection of our inner energy and intentions. It is believed that our thoughts and beliefs create energetic imprints that radiate into the world and attract corresponding experiences. By aligning our self-image with positive intentions and affirmations, we can harmonize our energy and enhance our well-being.

Herbalism and Shamanism offer valuable insights into the mind-body connection and its influence on self-image and well-being. These traditions emphasize the holistic nature of human existence, recognizing that our thoughts and emotions have a direct impact on our physical health and overall well-being. By cultivating a positive self-image, we can promote healing and balance in all aspects of our being.

Ecospirituality, which emphasizes the interconnectedness of all living beings and the natural world, highlights the importance of a positive self-image in fostering harmony within ourselves and with our environment. By recognizing our inherent worth and interconnectedness, we develop a sense of purpose and responsibility, contributing to our overall well-being and the well-being of the planet.

Research in the field of positive psychology further supports the connection between self-image and well-being. Studies have shown that individuals with a positive self-image experience higher levels of life satisfaction, self-confidence, resilience, and overall psychological well-being. Conversely, individuals with negative self-image are more susceptible to psychological distress, low self-esteem, and diminished overall well-being.

To cultivate a positive self-image and enhance overall well-being, various strategies and practices can be employed. Affirmations, as advocated by Louise Hay and Rhonda Byrne, play a significant role in reshaping our self-perception. By consciously directing our thoughts and affirming positive qualities and beliefs about ourselves, we can reprogram our self-image and promote well-being.

In addition to affirmations, self-reflection and self-compassion are essential components of nurturing a positive self-image. Engaging in introspection, identifying and challenging negative self-beliefs, and replacing them with empowering thoughts and self-affirmations can contribute to a more positive self-image and enhanced overall well-being.

It is important to note that developing a positive self-image is not an overnight process. It requires dedication, patience, and self-compassion. In our journey towards a positive self-image, we may encounter setbacks, self-doubt, and resistance. However, by incorporating practices like mindfulness, self-care, and seeking support from others, we can navigate these challenges and foster a resilient and positive self-image.

In conclusion, the connection between self-image and overall well-being is profound. By understanding and consciously cultivating a positive self-image, drawing insights from various fields, we can enhance our well-being on multiple levels - mentally, emotionally, and spiritually. Through practices such as affirmations, self-reflection, and self-compassion, we can reshape our self-perception, promote resilience, and foster a fulfilling and balanced life. Let us now delve deeper into the practical aspects of cultivating a positive self-image, engaging in examples, problems, and exercises to foster critical thinking and facilitate personal growth.

Embracing and celebrating your unique qualities and features.

In a world that often emphasizes external appearances and societal standards, it is essential to embrace and celebrate our unique qualities and features. Recognizing and appreciating the inherent beauty and worth of our individuality contributes to our self-esteem, self-acceptance, and overall well-being. In this section, we will explore the importance of embracing and celebrating your unique qualities and features, drawing insights from various fields such as Witchcraft, Divination, Herbalism, Shamanism, and Ecospirituality.

Embracing your unique qualities and features involves cultivating self-love, self-acceptance, and a deep appreciation for the characteristics that make you who you are. Witchcraft and Divination traditions teach us that each person possesses a unique energy and purpose in the world. By honoring and celebrating your individuality, you align with your true essence and contribute to the diversity and richness of the collective human experience.

Herbalism and Shamanism further emphasize the interconnectedness of nature and human beings. These practices encourage us to recognize the beauty and wisdom in all aspects of creation, including ourselves. By embracing our unique qualities and features, we align with the natural flow of existence and cultivate harmony within ourselves and with the world around us.

Ecospirituality, with its focus on the sacredness of the Earth and all beings, invites us to see ourselves as integral parts of a larger interconnected web of life. By embracing our unique qualities and features, we acknowledge our role in the grand tapestry of existence and contribute to the collective well-being of the Earth and its inhabitants.

Society often promotes unrealistic beauty standards, leading many individuals to feel inadequate and dissatisfied with their unique qualities and features. However, it is important to challenge these external influences and nurture a positive self-image that appreciates and celebrates our individuality.

To embrace and celebrate your unique qualities and features, it is crucial to practice self-compassion and self-acceptance. Recognize that perfection is an illusion and that true beauty lies in authenticity and self-expression. Embrace your strengths, quirks, talents, and physical attributes as valuable aspects of your identity.

Engaging in self-reflection and introspection can help uncover your unique qualities and features. Take time to explore your passions, values, and personal experiences. Identify the traits that make you stand out and contribute to your sense of self. Through this process, you will develop a deeper understanding and appreciation for your individuality.

Moreover, surrounding yourself with a supportive community that values diversity and individuality can greatly enhance your journey of self-acceptance. Seek out like-minded individuals who celebrate uniqueness and uplift each other. Together, you can foster an environment that encourages self-expression and self-love.

It is important to acknowledge that embracing your unique qualities and features does not mean dismissing areas for personal growth or improvement. Rather, it involves an authentic acceptance of who you are at your core while recognizing that personal growth is a continuous journey.

In conclusion, embracing and celebrating your unique qualities and features is a powerful act of self-love and self-acceptance. By drawing insights from various fields and traditions, we understand the profound significance of embracing our individuality in Witchcraft, Divination, Herbalism, Shamanism, and Ecospirituality. Through practices of self-compassion, self-reflection, and cultivating a supportive community, we can foster a positive self-image that celebrates our unique attributes. Let us now delve deeper into this concept, engaging in examples, problems, and exercises that encourage critical thinking and personal growth.

Affirming self-love and acceptance of your physical appearance.

In a world that often places great emphasis on external appearances, affirming self-love and acceptance of your physical appearance is crucial for cultivating a positive self-image and overall well-being. Recognizing the inherent beauty and worth of your body, irrespective of societal standards or perceived flaws, is a transformative practice that can lead to greater self-compassion and a more fulfilling life. In this section, we will explore the power of affirming self-love and acceptance of your physical appearance, drawing insights from various fields such as Witchcraft, Divination, Herbalism, Shamanism, and Ecospirituality.

Witchcraft and Divination traditions remind us that our bodies are sacred vessels, each uniquely crafted and imbued with divine energy. By affirming self-love and acceptance of our physical appearance, we align with the inherent magic and beauty that resides within us. Witchcraft encourages us to see our bodies as powerful tools for manifestation and self-expression, appreciating their uniqueness and honoring their wisdom.

Herbalism and Shamanism teach us to view the body as an interconnected part of the natural world. These practices recognize the healing potential of plants and the significance of aligning with the rhythms of nature. By affirming self-love and acceptance of our physical appearance, we honor the intricate relationship between our bodies and the Earth, cultivating a sense of harmony and well-being.

Ecospirituality highlights the interconnectedness of all beings and the inherent value of every form of life. By affirming self-love and acceptance of our physical appearance, we acknowledge our place within the vast web of existence and celebrate the diversity of human bodies as expressions of divine creation.

Affirmations serve as powerful tools for redirecting our thoughts and beliefs towards self-love and acceptance of our physical appearance. By consciously choosing positive affirmations, we reprogram our subconscious mind, replacing self-criticism with self-compassion and empowering narratives. Affirmations can be tailored to address specific areas of concern or to promote overall body positivity. For example:

1. "I am grateful for the unique beauty of my body."

2. "I embrace and celebrate my body just as it is."

3. "I love and accept myself fully, including my physical appearance."

4. "I am worthy of love and respect, regardless of societal standards."

5. "I nourish my body with love and care, honoring its needs."

6. "I radiate confidence and beauty from within."

7. "I am comfortable and at peace in my own skin."

8. "I am grateful for the strength and resilience of my body."

9. "I choose to see beauty in every part of myself."

10. "I release any negative judgments about my physical appearance."

Engaging in a regular practice of affirming self-love and acceptance of your physical appearance can be complemented by other activities that foster body positivity and self-care. These may include journaling exercises to explore and challenge societal beauty ideals, engaging in mindful self-care practices such as gentle movement or body-positive affirming meditation, or surrounding yourself with supportive communities that promote body acceptance.

It is important to acknowledge that affirming self-love and acceptance of your physical appearance is a deeply personal journey. It may involve addressing deeply ingrained beliefs, challenging societal conditioning, and embracing a broader definition of beauty. This process requires patience, self-compassion, and a commitment to nurturing a positive self-image.

In conclusion, affirming self-love and acceptance of your physical appearance is a transformative practice that can empower you to embrace your unique beauty and worth. By drawing insights from various fields such as Witchcraft, Divination, Herbalism, Shamanism, and Ecospirituality, we understand the profound significance of aligning

Recognizing the importance of inner beauty and cultivating positive character traits.

In a society that often prioritizes external appearances, it is essential to recognize the profound significance of inner beauty and the cultivation of positive character traits. While physical attractiveness may capture initial attention, it is the qualities of the heart, mind, and spirit that truly define a person's beauty and contribute to their overall well-being. In this section, we will explore the importance of recognizing and nurturing inner beauty, drawing insights from various fields such as Witchcraft, Divination, Herbalism, Shamanism, and Ecospirituality.

Witchcraft and Divination traditions teach us that true beauty radiates from within. These practices emphasize the importance of aligning our intentions, thoughts, and actions with our highest selves. By cultivating positive character traits, we tap into our inner beauty and harness our personal power. Witchcraft encourages us to embody virtues such as compassion, kindness, integrity, and gratitude, recognizing that these qualities enhance our spiritual growth and contribute to the well-being of ourselves and others.

Herbalism and Shamanism further emphasize the interconnectedness of the mind, body, and spirit. These practices recognize that our thoughts and emotions influence our overall well-being. By cultivating positive character traits, we promote inner harmony and balance. For instance, embracing patience, forgiveness, and resilience can help us navigate life's challenges with grace and cultivate a sense of peace within ourselves.

Ecospirituality invites us to recognize the inherent value and interconnectedness of all beings. It teaches us that our actions have ripple effects not only on ourselves but also on the world around us. By cultivating positive character traits, we contribute to the collective well-being of humanity and the Earth. Traits such as empathy, compassion, and environmental stewardship promote harmony and sustainability in our relationships with others and the natural world.

Recognizing the importance of inner beauty involves a shift in perspective and a conscious effort to value character traits over external appearances. It requires us to go beyond surface-level judgments and embrace a broader definition of beauty—one that encompasses qualities such as authenticity, wisdom, humility, and generosity of spirit.

To cultivate positive character traits, it is essential to engage in self-reflection and introspection. Take time to assess your values, strengths, and areas for growth. Identify the virtues you aspire to embody and develop an action plan to cultivate them. For example:

1. Practice acts of kindness and compassion towards yourself and others.

2. Cultivate gratitude by maintaining a gratitude journal or practicing daily affirmations of appreciation.

3. Foster resilience by embracing challenges as opportunities for growth and learning.

4. Cultivate humility by recognizing and learning from your mistakes.

5. Engage in self-care practices that promote emotional well-being and self-reflection.

6.   Develop active listening skills to foster empathy and understanding in your relationships.

7.   Nurture your curiosity and openness to new experiences, fostering a growth mindset.

8.   Practice forgiveness and let go of resentment and grudges.

9.   Engage in acts of service and contribute to your community or causes that align with your values.

10. Seek wisdom through continuous learning and self-improvement.

Engaging in these practices can lead to a transformational journey of self-discovery and personal growth. By recognizing the importance of inner beauty and cultivating positive character traits, you enhance your own well-being and contribute to a more compassionate and harmonious world.

It is important to note that the cultivation of positive character traits is an ongoing process that requires commitment and self-reflection. It is not about achieving perfection but rather embracing growth and striving to embody the values and qualities that resonate with your authentic self.

In conclusion, recognizing the importance of inner beauty and cultivating positive character traits is a profound practice that goes beyond external appearances. By drawing insights from various fields such as Witchcraft, Divination, Herbalism, Shamanism, and Ecospirituality, we understand the transformative power of aligning our thoughts, intentions, and actions with virtues that enhance our well-being and contribute to the greater good.

Letting go of comparisons and embracing your individuality.

In today's society, the pervasive influence of media and social platforms often leads individuals to compare themselves to others, creating feelings of inadequacy and diminishing self-worth. However, it is essential to understand the detrimental impact of comparisons and the empowering process of embracing one's unique individuality. This section delves into the profound effects of comparisons on self-image and offers strategies, drawn from fields such as Witchcraft, Divination, Herbalism, Shamanism, and Ecospirituality, to let go of comparisons and embrace your authentic self.

Witchcraft teaches us the significance of honoring our own journey and path. It emphasizes the belief that each individual possesses their own unique set of talents, strengths, and experiences. By acknowledging and celebrating these individual qualities, we can cultivate self-acceptance and foster a deeper connection with our true selves. Witchcraft encourages practices such as self-reflection, meditation, and journaling to explore and embrace our authentic nature, free from the constraints of comparison.

Divination traditions further shed light on the detrimental effects of comparisons. Tarot cards, for instance, remind us that each person has a distinct life journey and purpose. Through divinatory practices, individuals gain insights into their own unique paths, understanding that comparisons only serve to hinder personal growth and hinder the realization of their full potential. Divination encourages individuals to trust their intuition, listen to their inner voice, and focus on their own progress rather than comparing themselves to others.

Herbalism and Shamanism provide additional wisdom in embracing individuality. Herbalism, for example, emphasizes the inherent power and healing properties of each plant species. Similarly, Shamanism recognizes the importance of connecting with one's spirit allies and discovering one's personal medicine. These practices teach us to embrace our unique qualities and strengths, realizing that our individuality contributes to the tapestry of life in a profound and meaningful way.

Ecospirituality expands the understanding of individuality by highlighting the interdependence of all beings and the importance of each person's contribution to the collective whole. Just as every ecosystem relies on the diversity of its inhabitants, society flourishes when individuals embrace their unique gifts and perspectives. Ecospirituality encourages individuals to appreciate the interconnectedness of all life forms and to recognize the beauty that arises from celebrating and respecting diverse expressions of individuality.

To let go of comparisons and embrace your individuality, it is essential to engage in self-reflection and self-compassion. Here are some practices and exercises to aid in this process:

Practice gratitude by acknowledging and appreciating your own unique qualities and strengths. Maintain a gratitude journal where you reflect on your personal achievements and attributes.

Engage in affirmations that focus on self-acceptance and self-love. Repeat affirmations that emphasize your individuality and remind yourself of the value you bring to the world.

Challenge societal standards and beauty norms by exploring alternative perspectives from diverse cultural and spiritual traditions. This will broaden your understanding of what it means to be unique and help you break free from limiting comparisons.

Cultivate self-awareness through practices such as meditation and mindfulness. By observing your thoughts and emotions without judgment, you can develop a deeper understanding of your authentic self and detach from comparisons.

Surround yourself with supportive and uplifting individuals who appreciate and celebrate your individuality. Seek out communities and social circles that embrace diversity and encourage personal growth.

Engage in creative expressions, such as art, music, or writing, that allow you to explore and express your unique voice and perspective. Embrace the freedom of self-expression and let go of the need for external validation.

Reflect on the times when you have made a positive impact on others' lives. Recognize the unique contributions you have made and the difference you have brought to the world.

By actively practicing these strategies and exercises, you will gradually release the grip of comparisons and embrace your individuality. Remember, your unique qualities and experiences are what make you special and valuable. Embracing your individuality allows you to shine authentically and contribute to the world in a way that only you can.

Affirming confidence and radiance from within.

Confidence is a powerful quality that emanates from within and radiates outwardly, influencing how we perceive ourselves and how others perceive us. It is an essential attribute that empowers individuals to overcome challenges, pursue their goals, and embrace their true potential. In this section, we explore the profound impact of affirming confidence and radiance from within, drawing insights from various fields such as Witchcraft, Divination, Herbalism, Shamanism, and Ecospirituality. Through an in-depth analysis and practical exercises, we aim to provide students with a comprehensive understanding of the transformative power of self-affirmation in cultivating confidence and radiance.

Witchcraft offers valuable wisdom on cultivating inner confidence. Practitioners of Witchcraft recognize the inherent power within themselves and the ability to shape their own realities. Through rituals, spells, and meditation practices, individuals tap into their personal power and affirm their worthiness, strength, and capabilities. Witchcraft emphasizes the importance of self-belief and self-assurance as foundational elements for manifesting desired outcomes.

Divination traditions also contribute insights into affirming confidence and radiance. Tarot, for instance, serves as a tool for self-reflection and personal growth, providing guidance and clarity in various aspects of life. Through divinatory practices, individuals gain insights into their own unique qualities and strengths, which in turn bolsters their confidence and self-assuredness. Divination encourages students to trust their intuition and recognize their innate wisdom, ultimately fostering a sense of empowerment and radiance.

Herbalism and Shamanism further deepen our understanding of affirming confidence from within. Herbal remedies and plant-based therapies have long been used to support emotional well-being and enhance self-confidence. Certain plants, such as chamomile and lavender, are known for their calming and uplifting properties, promoting a sense of inner peace and confidence. Shamanism, on the other hand, emphasizes the importance of connecting with one's inner power and spiritual allies. Through shamanic practices, individuals access their inner strength and wisdom, affirming their innate confidence and radiance.

Ecospirituality contributes a unique perspective on affirming confidence and radiance by highlighting the interconnectedness of all beings. Recognizing our place in the larger web of life, Ecospirituality teaches us to honor and respect ourselves as integral parts of the natural world. By embracing our inherent worthiness and acknowledging our interconnectedness, we cultivate a deep sense of confidence and radiate a genuine authenticity that positively impacts both ourselves and those around us.

To affirm confidence and radiance from within, it is crucial to engage in self-reflective practices and develop a positive self-image. Here are some practical exercises and examples that can help students strengthen their confidence and radiance:

Mirror Work: Stand in front of a mirror and recite positive affirmations about your abilities, strengths, and qualities. Observe your reflection and let the words sink in, internalizing them as a true reflection of your inner beauty and radiance.

Affirmation Journal: Create a journal specifically for affirmations. Write down positive affirmations that resonate with you, focusing on building self-confidence and radiance. Refer to this journal regularly and read the affirmations aloud to reinforce their positive impact.

Visualization Techniques: Engage in guided visualizations that depict yourself as confident, radiant, and successful. Visualize situations where you confidently navigate challenges and radiate your unique qualities. Allow yourself to fully immerse in the visualization and feel the emotions associated with confidence and radiance.

Mindfulness Practice: Cultivate present-moment awareness through mindfulness meditation. Focus on your breath and observe your thoughts and emotions without judgment. Through mindfulness, you develop a deeper connection with your inner self, allowing confidence and radiance to naturally arise.

Affirming Affirmations: Develop personalized affirmations that resonate with your unique qualities and aspirations. Use empowering language and choose words that evoke a sense of confidence and radiance. Repeat these affirmations daily, incorporating them into your daily routine.

By integrating these exercises and practices into your life, you will gradually affirm and strengthen your confidence and radiance from within. Remember that building confidence is a journey, and it requires consistent effort and self-reflection. As you cultivate a positive self-image and embrace your innate radiance, you will witness a transformation in how you perceive yourself and how others perceive you. Embrace the power of affirmations and radiate your authentic confidence to the world, inspiring others to do the same.

Embracing aging gracefully and affirming self-worth regardless of age.

Aging is a natural and inevitable process that every individual undergoes. It is a journey marked by physical changes, societal expectations, and personal perceptions. In this section, we delve into the profound significance of embracing aging gracefully and affirming self-worth regardless of age, drawing insights from diverse fields such as Witchcraft, Divination, Herbalism, Shamanism, and Ecospirituality. Through a comprehensive analysis and practical exercises, we aim to provide students with a deep understanding of the transformative power of self-affirmation in embracing the aging process and nurturing a strong sense of self-worth.

Witchcraft offers valuable perspectives on embracing aging gracefully. Within Witchcraft, the cycles of nature are honored and celebrated, including the cycle of life and death. Practitioners recognize that aging is a natural part of the human experience and that each stage of life brings unique wisdom and beauty. By working with the energy of the seasons and aligning with the ebb and flow of life, individuals can embrace the aging process with grace, acknowledging the value and significance of each passing year.

Divination traditions also contribute insights into affirming self-worth regardless of age. Tarot, for example, provides guidance and reflection on life's journey, including the challenges and triumphs that come with aging. Tarot cards such as The Empress and The Sage remind us of the inherent wisdom and power that comes with age, highlighting the importance of valuing oneself and embracing the unique experiences and knowledge gained over time. Divination practices encourage individuals to recognize their worth beyond societal beauty standards and to affirm their intrinsic value regardless of their age.

Herbalism and Shamanism provide additional perspectives on embracing aging gracefully. Herbal remedies and plant-based therapies can support physical and emotional well-being during the aging process. Herbs such as ashwagandha and ginseng are known for their rejuvenating and vitality-enhancing properties. Shamanic practices emphasize the interconnectedness of all beings and the importance of embracing one's journey through life. By connecting with ancestral wisdom and spiritual allies, individuals can cultivate a deep sense of self-worth and purpose as they navigate the challenges and joys of aging.

Ecospirituality also contributes to our understanding of affirming self-worth regardless of age. This holistic approach emphasizes the interconnectedness between humans and the natural world. It encourages individuals to honor their place in the larger web of life, recognizing the inherent worth and value of all beings, regardless of age. By cultivating a deep sense of connection with nature and embracing the wisdom and cycles of the Earth, individuals can affirm their self-worth and embrace the beauty and significance of their own aging process.

To embrace aging gracefully and affirm self-worth regardless of age, it is crucial to engage in self-reflective practices and develop a positive perspective. Here are some practical exercises and examples that can help students nurture self-worth during the aging process:

Daily Gratitude Practice: Create a gratitude journal specifically focused on appreciating the unique aspects of aging. Write down three things you are grateful for each day related to your aging process, such as the wisdom gained, the lessons learned, or the opportunities for personal growth.

Affirming Self-Worth Ritual: Design a personal ritual that honors your journey of aging and affirms your self-worth. This could include lighting a candle, reciting affirmations specific to aging, or engaging in a mindful meditation focused on embracing the beauty of your age and self.

Body Appreciation Exercises: Engage in body-positive exercises that celebrate and appreciate your physical self at any age. This could involve gentle yoga poses, body-affirming affirmations while looking in the mirror, or self-massage techniques that promote self-acceptance and self-love.

Community Engagement: Participate in intergenerational activities or join groups that foster connections between individuals of different age groups. Engaging with people of various ages can provide a broader perspective on aging and reinforce the understanding that self-worth transcends age-related stereotypes.

Mindful Aging Reflection: Set aside dedicated time to reflect on your journey of aging. Consider the lessons learned, the personal growth experienced, and the unique contributions you bring to the world at your current stage of life. Use these reflections as affirmations of your self-worth and as a reminder of the value you hold regardless of age.

Through these exercises and practices, students will develop a profound understanding of the significance of embracing aging gracefully and affirming self-worth regardless of age. By integrating these principles into their lives, they will cultivate a positive and empowered perspective on the aging process, fostering a deep sense of self-worth and embracing the beauty and wisdom that comes with each passing year.

AFFIRMATIONS FOR HEALING AND RELEASING PAST INSECURITIES.

When to Say Them, How to Say Them, and the Hertz Frequency Associated with Each Affirmation

In this section, we explore the powerful practice of using affirmations for healing and releasing past insecurities. Affirmations are positive statements that can help reprogram our subconscious mind and shift our thoughts and beliefs towards a more positive and empowering direction. Drawing inspiration from diverse fields such as Witchcraft, Divination, Herbalism, Shamanism, and Ecospirituality, we delve into the art of crafting effective affirmations, discuss the optimal timing for their use, provide guidance on how to say them, and explore the connection between affirmations and Hertz frequencies.

Understanding the Optimal Timing for Affirmations:

Timing plays a crucial role in the effectiveness of affirmations. It is recommended to practice affirmations during moments of calm and receptivity. Ideally, choose a time when you can devote your full attention to the affirmations, such as during meditation, journaling, or before bedtime. These moments allow you to connect deeply with your inner self and create a conducive environment for transformation.

Crafting Effective Affirmations:

When crafting affirmations for healing and releasing past insecurities, it is important to focus on positive, present-tense statements that reflect your desired state of being. For example:

- ✦ "I release all past insecurities and embrace my inherent worthiness."

- ✦ "I am worthy of love, acceptance, and success in all areas of my life."

- ✦ "I choose to let go of self-doubt and trust in my abilities and potential."

Enhancing Affirmations with Intention and Emotion:

To maximize the impact of affirmations, it is essential to infuse them with intention and emotion. As you repeat the affirmations, feel the truth and power behind each word. Visualize yourself embodying the qualities and mindset described in the affirmations. This emotional resonance strengthens the neural connections associated with positive beliefs and supports the healing process.

Exploring Hertz Frequencies in Affirmations:

Sound and vibration have long been recognized as powerful tools for healing and transformation. In recent years, the concept of Hertz frequencies has gained popularity in various disciplines. While scientific research on the direct correlation between Hertz frequencies and affirmations is limited, some individuals believe that certain frequencies can enhance the effectiveness of affirmations. Here are a few examples:

Affirmations for self-love and acceptance: Associated Hertz frequency of **528Hz**, known as the "Love frequency," is believed to promote feelings of love, harmony, and healing.

Affirmations for confidence and empowerment: Associated Hertz frequency of **432Hz**, known as the "Natural frequency," is believed to resonate with the natural harmony of the universe, promoting balance and grounding.

Affirmations for healing past traumas: Associated Hertz frequency of **396Hz**, known as the "Liberating frequency," is believed to facilitate the release of negative emotions and support healing from past wounds.

It is important to note that the use of Hertz frequencies in conjunction with affirmations is a subject of ongoing debate and exploration. While some individuals find it beneficial, others may not experience the same effects. It is ultimately a personal choice and can be explored as an additional element in your affirmation practice.

Practical Exercises for Affirmation Practice:

To engage students in critical thinking and practical application, here are some exercises to accompany the section on affirmations for healing and releasing past insecurities:

Journaling Exercise: Reflect on past insecurities and their impact on your life. Identify specific areas where you desire healing and transformation. Write affirmations tailored to these areas, incorporating positive statements and present-tense language.

Guided Meditation: Create a guided meditation audio recording that incorporates affirmations for healing past insecurities. Focus on relaxation, visualization, and the emotional embodiment of affirmations.

Group Discussion: Facilitate a group discussion where students share their experiences with affirmations and discuss the potential benefits and challenges encountered during their practice. Encourage respectful dialogue and the exploration of differing perspectives.

By integrating these exercises and practices into their lives, students will gain a deeper understanding of the power of affirmations for healing and releasing past insecurities. They will learn how to create effective affirmations, understand the optimal timing for their use, explore the connection between affirmations and Hertz frequencies, and engage in practical exercises to enhance their affirmation practice. Through critical thinking and discussion, students will develop a well-rounded approach to healing and transformation using affirmations.

1. I release all past insecurities and embrace my inherent worthiness.

2. I am worthy of love, acceptance, and success in all areas of my life.

3. I choose to let go of self-doubt and trust in my abilities and potential.

4. I am deserving of happiness, joy, and abundance.

5. I release the need for validation from others and embrace self-validation.

6. I let go of comparing myself to others and appreciate my unique journey.

7. I am enough just as I am, and I embrace my flaws and imperfections.

8. I deserve love and respect from myself and others.

9. I am confident in expressing my thoughts, opinions, and emotions.

10. I release the fear of failure and embrace the lessons and growth it brings.

11. I am deserving of success and capable of achieving my goals.

12. I forgive myself for past mistakes and choose to learn and grow from them.

13. I release the need to please others and prioritize my own well-being.

14. I am worthy of healthy and fulfilling relationships.

15. I release the need for perfection and embrace my authentic self.

16. I am grateful for my past experiences as they have shaped me into who I am today.

17. I let go of negative self-talk and replace it with positive affirmations.

18. I trust in my intuition and make decisions that align with my highest good.

19. I release the need for external validation and trust in my own judgment.

20. I am proud of my accomplishments and celebrate my progress.

21. I deserve to be seen, heard, and valued for who I am.

22. I release the fear of rejection and embrace the opportunities that come my way.

23. I am resilient and capable of overcoming challenges.

24. I release the need to control everything and trust in the flow of life.

25. I am whole, complete, and worthy of love and happiness.

These affirmations can be tailored and personalized to address specific areas of past insecurities that individuals may have. Remember to repeat these affirmations regularly, with intention and emotional resonance, to reinforce positive beliefs and support healing and growth.

AFFIRMING GRATITUDE FOR YOUR BODY AND ITS CAPABILITIES.

In this section, we will explore the power of affirmations in cultivating gratitude for your body and appreciating its incredible capabilities. Our bodies are intricate and marvelous vessels that allow us to experience life, and by acknowledging and expressing gratitude for them, we can enhance our overall well-being and self-love. Through the use of affirmations, we can shift our mindset and develop a deeper connection with our bodies, fostering a positive body image and a sense of appreciation for all that they do for us.

Understanding the Importance of Body Gratitude:

Our bodies are miraculous creations, capable of performing extraordinary feats. From the basic functions that keep us alive to the ability to engage in physical activities, our bodies deserve our appreciation and gratitude. By cultivating a mindset of gratitude for our bodies, we can shift our focus from perceived flaws or insecurities to the remarkable capabilities and strengths that they possess. This mindset shift allows us to develop a healthier relationship with our bodies and embrace a positive body image.

Affirmations for Gratitude and Appreciation:

1. I am grateful for my body's resilience and its ability to heal and recover.

2. I appreciate the unique shape and form of my body, knowing that it is perfect for me.

3. I am thankful for my body's ability to adapt and adjust to different circumstances.

4. I honor and appreciate the strength and stamina my body provides me.

5. I am grateful for my body's senses, allowing me to fully experience the world around me.

6. I appreciate the intricate workings of my body's organs and systems, supporting my overall health and well-being.

7. I am thankful for the energy and vitality that my body provides me each day.

8. I am grateful for my body's ability to move, allowing me to engage in activities that bring me joy.

9. I appreciate the unique features and characteristics of my body that make me who I am.

10. I am grateful for my body's capacity to experience pleasure, joy, and love.
    Exercises for Cultivating Body Gratitude:

Mirror Reflection: Stand in front of a mirror and practice looking at yourself with love and gratitude. Say affirmations aloud while maintaining eye contact with your reflection.

Body Appreciation Journal: Start a journal dedicated to expressing gratitude for your body. Write down three things you appreciate about your body each day.

Mindful Movement: Engage in mindful physical activities such as yoga, dancing, or walking, focusing on the sensations and gratitude for your body's movement.

Self-Care Rituals: Create self-care rituals that involve nurturing your body, such as taking warm baths, applying nourishing lotions, or practicing gentle stretches.

Affirmation Visualization: Close your eyes and visualize your body being showered with love and gratitude. Repeat affirmations mentally while envisioning this process.

Questions:

How does expressing gratitude for your body affect your overall well-being and self-image?

Share an experience when you felt a deep sense of gratitude for your body and its capabilities. How did it make you feel?

How can practicing body gratitude positively impact your relationship with yourself and others?

What are some challenges you face in cultivating body gratitude, and how can affirmations help overcome them?

1. I am grateful for my body's ability to heal and regenerate itself.

2. I appreciate the strength and endurance that my body provides me.

3. I am thankful for my body's flexibility and range of motion.

4. I honor the wisdom of my body and trust its signals and intuition.

5. I am grateful for the senses that allow me to fully experience the world around me.

6. I appreciate the energy and vitality that my body gives me each day.

7. I am thankful for the resilience of my body and its ability to bounce back from challenges.

8. I celebrate the unique features and characteristics of my body that make me who I am.

9. I am grateful for my body's capacity to experience pleasure and joy.

10. I appreciate the beauty and uniqueness of every part of my body.

11. I am thankful for my body's ability to adapt and adjust to different environments and circumstances.

12. I honor the intelligence of my body's systems and organs that work harmoniously to keep me healthy.

13. I am grateful for my body's ability to move and engage in activities that bring me joy.

14. I appreciate the miraculous process of digestion and how my body nourishes itself.

15. I am thankful for my body's capacity to breathe, providing me with life-giving oxygen.

16. I honor the intricate network of nerves that allow me to experience touch and sensations.

17. I am grateful for my body's immune system that protects me from illnesses and diseases.

18. I appreciate the restorative power of sleep and how it rejuvenates my body.

19. I am thankful for my body's ability to adapt to stress and maintain balance.

20. I honor my body's ability to create and sustain life.

21. I am grateful for the strong foundation my body provides, allowing me to stand tall and grounded.

22. I appreciate the resilience of my bones and their role in supporting my body.

23. I am thankful for the senses of sight, hearing, taste, and smell that enrich my experiences.

24. I honor the intricate workings of my brain and its ability to process information and emotions.

25. I am grateful for the gift of my body and all the experiences it allows me to have in this lifetime.

These affirmations can be used as daily reminders to cultivate gratitude for your body and its capabilities. Repeat them regularly, either silently or aloud, and allow their positive messages to deepen your appreciation for the miraculous vessel that is your body.

AFFIRMATIONS TO ENHANCE SELF-ESTEEM AND BUILD A POSITIVE SELF-IMAGE.

Building a positive self-image and nurturing healthy self-esteem are essential aspects of personal growth and well-being. Affirmations serve as powerful tools to rewire negative thought patterns and cultivate a positive mindset. By consciously affirming positive statements about ourselves, we can create a foundation of self-acceptance, self-love, and self-worth. In this section, we will explore affirmations specifically designed to enhance self-esteem and build a positive self-image. Through the repetition and internalization of these affirmations, students will learn to embrace their unique qualities, recognize their inherent worth, and develop a strong sense of self-confidence.

I. Affirmations for Embracing Your Unique Qualities

1. I celebrate my individuality and recognize the value of my unique qualities.

2. I embrace my strengths and acknowledge my areas of growth with compassion.

3. I am proud of my accomplishments and the progress I have made.

4. I honor my authentic self and trust in my own wisdom and intuition.

5. I appreciate my unique perspective and the contributions I bring to the world.

6. I recognize that my differences make me special and add richness to my experiences.

7. I release the need for comparison and fully embrace my own path and journey.

8. I love and accept myself exactly as I am, knowing that I am constantly evolving and growing.

II. Affirmations for Cultivating Self-Love and Self-Acceptance

1. I am worthy of love and respect, and I treat myself with kindness and compassion.

2. I deeply love and accept myself, embracing all aspects of who I am.

3. I forgive myself for past mistakes and allow myself to move forward with grace.

4. I deserve to prioritize self-care and nourish my mind, body, and spirit.

5. I trust in my own worthiness and believe in my ability to create a fulfilling life.

6. I release the need for approval from others and find validation within myself.

7. I am enough, just as I am, and I fully embrace my inherent worthiness.

8. I choose to focus on my positive qualities and let go of self-criticism and self-judgment.

III. Affirmations for Developing Self-Confidence

1. I am confident in my abilities and trust in my capacity to overcome challenges.

2. I believe in my own potential and know that I am capable of achieving my goals.

3. I stand tall in my own power, radiating confidence and self-assurance.

4. I step outside of my comfort zone with courage and embrace opportunities for growth.

5. I trust in my ability to make decisions that align with my highest good.

6. I release the fear of failure and embrace the lessons and growth it offers.

7. I acknowledge my accomplishments and give myself credit for my hard work and efforts.

8. I am deserving of success and fully embrace the limitless possibilities available to me.

Conclusion:

By incorporating these affirmations into daily practice, students can gradually transform their self-perception, nurture self-esteem, and build a positive self-image.

Empowered Affirmations

Encourage students to repeat these affirmations regularly, preferably in front of a mirror, allowing the words to sink deeply into their subconscious minds. Additionally, students can write down their chosen affirmations, carry them as reminders throughout the day, or create a personal affirmation ritual that resonates with them.

1. I am worthy of love, respect, and happiness.

2. I embrace my unique qualities and appreciate the person I am becoming.

3. I am confident in my abilities and trust in my potential to achieve greatness.

4. I am deserving of success and capable of creating a fulfilling life.

5. I release all negative self-judgments and embrace self-acceptance.

6. I love and accept myself unconditionally, flaws and all.

7. I radiate self-confidence and attract positive experiences into my life.

8. I am proud of my accomplishments and celebrate my progress.

9. I trust my intuition and make decisions that align with my values and goals.

10. I am resilient and capable of overcoming any obstacles that come my way.

11. I am deserving of love and surround myself with supportive and uplifting relationships.

12. I am enough just as I am, and I have nothing to prove to anyone.

13. I choose to focus on my strengths and appreciate the unique qualities that make me who I am.

14. I release the need for external validation and find validation within myself.

15. I honor my needs and prioritize self-care and self-nurturing.

16. I forgive myself for past mistakes and learn and grow from them.

17. I embrace change and see it as an opportunity for growth and transformation.

18. I am responsible for my own happiness, and I choose to create a life that brings me joy.

19. I speak kindly to myself and replace negative self-talk with positive affirmations.

20. I am confident in expressing my opinions and speaking my truth.

21. I trust in my abilities to handle any challenges that come my way.

22. I am a unique and valuable individual, and I contribute positively to the world around me.

23. I deserve to be treated with respect and kindness by others.

24. I am open to receiving love, compliments, and opportunities for growth.

25. I am the author of my own story, and I choose to write a narrative of self-love, empowerment, and success.

Remember, repeating these affirmations consistently and believing in their truth will help reprogram your subconscious mind and build a strong foundation of self-esteem and positive self-image. Practice them daily, preferably in front of a mirror, and allow the empowering words to resonate deeply within you.

AFFIRMING THAT BEAUTY COMES IN ALL SHAPES, SIZES, AND COLORS.

In today's society, there is often a narrow and unrealistic standard of beauty that is perpetuated through media and societal expectations. This can lead individuals to develop insecurities about their physical appearance and feel pressured to conform to a certain ideal. However, it is essential to recognize that beauty is not confined to a specific shape, size, or color. True beauty is diverse, multifaceted, and encompasses a wide range of characteristics. By affirming that beauty comes in all shapes, sizes, and colors, we can embrace our unique attributes and cultivate a positive self-image. In this section, we will explore the importance of affirming diverse beauty, provide examples of affirmations, and offer exercises to enhance self-acceptance and appreciation.

Understanding Beauty Beyond Stereotypes:

It is crucial to challenge societal norms and stereotypes regarding beauty. Beauty is not a monolithic concept, but rather a rich tapestry of individuality and diversity. By acknowledging that beauty comes in all shapes, sizes, and colors, we break free from limiting beliefs and embrace the beauty that resides within us and others.

Affirmations for Embracing Diverse Beauty:

1. I am beautiful in my unique shape and size.

2. My worth is not determined by my physical appearance but by the kindness and love I radiate.

3. I celebrate the beauty that resides within me, regardless of societal standards.

4. I am confident and comfortable in my own skin, appreciating the beauty that makes me uniquely me.

5. I embrace and celebrate the diversity of beauty in the world.

Exercises for Cultivating Self-Acceptance:

a) Mirror Affirmations: Stand in front of a mirror and affirm your beauty by stating positive affirmations about yourself. Focus on different aspects of your appearance that you appreciate, such as your eyes, smile, or unique features. Repeat these affirmations daily to reinforce self-acceptance.

b) Gratitude Journal: Keep a journal where you write down three things you appreciate about your physical appearance each day. This exercise encourages you to focus on the positive aspects of your body and reinforces self-love and acceptance.

c) Surround Yourself with Diversity: Seek out and engage with diverse representations of beauty in media, literature, and art. This exposure will broaden your perception of beauty and foster acceptance and appreciation for different shapes, sizes, and colors.

d) Practice Self-Compassion: Treat yourself with kindness and compassion. Whenever negative thoughts or self-critical beliefs arise, challenge them and replace them with affirmations that affirm your unique beauty and worth.

Recognizing Beauty in Others:

It is essential to extend the affirmation of diverse beauty beyond ourselves and acknowledge and appreciate the beauty in others. By recognizing and celebrating the uniqueness of others, we create a more inclusive and accepting environment that uplifts and empowers everyone.

Conclusion:

Affirming that beauty comes in all shapes, sizes, and colors is a powerful practice that promotes self-acceptance, cultivates a positive self-image, and embraces the diversity of beauty in the world. By challenging societal norms, practicing affirmations, and engaging in exercises to enhance self-acceptance, we can foster a culture of inclusivity and empower individuals to embrace their authentic beauty.

1. I embrace and celebrate the unique beauty that resides within me.

2. My body shape and size do not define my worth or beauty.

3. I am a beautiful being, radiating love and light from within.

4. I am grateful for the diversity of beauty that exists in the world.

5. I love and appreciate my body in its entirety, from head to toe.

6. I reject societal standards of beauty and embrace my own unique beauty.

7. I see beauty in all shapes, sizes, and colors around me.

8. My beauty is not determined by external opinions or comparisons.

9. I am confident in my own skin, knowing that I am inherently beautiful.

10. I celebrate the beauty of others, recognizing that we are all uniquely beautiful.

11. My inner beauty shines through and enhances my outer appearance.

12. I am proud of my body and the strength and resilience it embodies.

13. I am deserving of love and admiration, regardless of my physical appearance.

14. I am beautiful because I am authentically myself, embracing my individuality.

15. I release the need to conform to unrealistic beauty standards and embrace my own definition of beauty.

16. I appreciate the diversity of shapes, sizes, and colors in the human form.

17. I radiate confidence and beauty, illuminating the world around me.

18. I am comfortable and at peace with my body, knowing that it is a vessel for my beautiful soul.

19. I honor and respect my body, nourishing it with love and care.

20. I reject negative self-talk and replace it with affirmations of self-love and acceptance.

21. I celebrate the beauty that comes from living a joyful and authentic life.

22. I am a masterpiece, intricately designed and beautiful in every way.

23. I choose to see beauty beyond superficial appearances, focusing on the essence of a person's character.

24. I embrace my uniqueness, knowing that it adds to the beauty of the world.

25. I am a living embodiment of beauty, radiating positivity and self-acceptance.

Remember to personalize these affirmations according to your individual experiences and beliefs. Regularly repeat these affirmations to reinforce self-love, acceptance, and the understanding that beauty comes in all shapes, sizes, and colors.

AFFIRMATIONS FOR OVERCOMING BODY SHAME AND EMBRACING BODY POSITIVITY.

In a society that often imposes unrealistic beauty standards and fosters body shame, it is crucial to cultivate a positive relationship with our bodies. Affirmations can be powerful tools to shift our mindset, challenge negative beliefs, and embrace body positivity. By practicing affirmations regularly, we can overcome body shame and foster a deep sense of love, acceptance, and gratitude for our bodies. This section presents a collection of affirmations designed to help individuals overcome body shame and embrace a positive body image.

Affirmations for Overcoming Body Shame:

1. I release all negative beliefs about my body and embrace a loving and accepting attitude towards it.

2. I am worthy of love and acceptance exactly as I am, regardless of society's standards or expectations.

3. My body is unique and beautiful, a vessel that carries me through life's journey.

4. I let go of comparing myself to others and focus on appreciating the beauty and strength of my own body.

5. I choose to let go of judgments and criticisms about my body and replace them with affirmations of self-love and acceptance.

6. I honor and respect my body's boundaries and needs, nurturing it with love and care.

7. My body is a temple of love, and I treat it with kindness, compassion, and gratitude.

8. I release the need for external validation and find my worth and beauty from within.

9. I celebrate the diversity of bodies and recognize that every shape, size, and form is worthy of love and acceptance.

10. I let go of the belief that my worth is tied to my appearance and embrace my inherent value as a unique individual.

Affirmations for Embracing Body Positivity:

1. I choose to see the beauty in every part of my body, appreciating its uniqueness and functionality.

2. I am grateful for the miraculous abilities of my body and the joy it brings me in experiencing life.

3. I celebrate my body's strength and resilience, honoring its ability to heal and adapt.

4. I embrace the natural changes and fluctuations of my body, knowing that they are a part of the beautiful journey of life.

5. I nourish my body with wholesome foods, exercise, and self-care, honoring its well-being and vitality.

6. I radiate confidence and self-assurance, knowing that my beauty comes from embracing my authentic self.

7. I choose to surround myself with positive influences and affirmations that uplift and empower my body image.

8. I release the need for perfection and embrace the beauty of imperfection, knowing that it makes me uniquely human.

9. I appreciate my body for the pleasure it brings me, from the simple joys of movement to the ability to experience the world through my senses.

10. I deserve to feel comfortable and confident in my body, and I choose to dress and express myself in ways that align with my authentic self.

Conclusion:

By practicing these affirmations consistently, individuals can challenge and overcome body shame, fostering a deep sense of self-love, acceptance, and body positivity. It is important to remember that affirmations are most effective when combined with self-compassion, self-care, and a supportive community. Embracing a positive body image not only benefits individuals on a personal level but also contributes to a more inclusive and accepting society. Let these affirmations be a powerful tool in your journey towards embracing body positivity and living a life of love, acceptance, and self-empowerment.

Exercises and Reflection Questions:

Write down three affirmations that resonate with you the most from the list provided. Reflect on why they are significant to your journey towards body positivity.

Create a daily ritual where you repeat affirmations that specifically address your personal body image concerns.

Engage in journaling or self-reflection to explore any underlying beliefs or experiences that contribute to your body shame. Use affirmations to challenge and reframe those beliefs.

Share your favorite affirmation with a trusted friend or support group. Discuss how affirmations can support each other in overcoming body shame and embracing body positivity.

Note: Remember that these affirmations are a starting point, and you are encouraged to personalize them to suit your individual needs and experiences.

1. I love and accept my body unconditionally, just as it is.

2. My body is unique and beautiful in its own way.

3. I release all negative thoughts and judgments about my body.

4. I am deserving of love, respect, and acceptance, regardless of my size or shape.

5. My body is a vessel for my soul's expression and deserves to be honored and cared for.

6. I choose to focus on the things I love about my body and celebrate its strengths.

7. I am grateful for the things my body can do and the experiences it allows me to have.

8. I let go of comparing myself to others and embrace my own individual beauty.

9. I am not defined by my external appearance; my worth comes from within.

10. I choose to speak kindly to myself and practice self-compassion in relation to my body.

11. I release the need for approval from others and find validation within myself.

12. I am confident and comfortable in my own skin, radiating self-assurance and positivity.

13. I embrace my body's natural shape, knowing that it is perfect as it is.

14. I honor my body's needs and nourish it with healthy choices that support its well-being.

15. I let go of societal beauty standards and create my own definition of beauty.

16. I am proud of the progress I've made on my journey to body acceptance and continue to grow every day.

17. I choose to surround myself with positive influences that uplift and support my body positivity.

18. My body is not an object of judgment; it is a source of power, strength, and resilience.

19. I let go of shame and guilt surrounding my body and embrace a mindset of self-love and acceptance.

20. I celebrate the diversity of bodies and recognize that all shapes, sizes, and colors are beautiful.

21. I am deserving of self-care, and I prioritize activities that make me feel good in my own skin.

22. I release the need to hide or cover up my body; I deserve to take up space and be seen.

23. I choose to focus on my inner qualities and cultivate a positive self-image that extends beyond physical appearance.

24. I forgive myself for past negative self-talk and commit to speaking to my body with love and kindness.

25. I am on a journey of self-discovery and growth, and I embrace every step of it with compassion and acceptance.

Remember to personalize these affirmations to suit your own experiences and needs. Repeat them daily and genuinely embrace the positive thoughts and feelings they invoke within you. Through consistent practice, these affirmations can help you overcome body shame and foster a deep sense of body positivity and self-love.

AFFIRMATIONS TO SILENCE NEGATIVE SELF-TALK AND CULTIVATE SELF-COMPASSION.

In our journey toward self-growth and personal development, it is essential to address the negative self-talk that can hinder our progress and undermine our self-esteem. Negative self-talk refers to the inner dialogue or thoughts that are self-critical, judgmental, and demeaning. It can create a cycle of self-doubt, limiting beliefs, and feelings of inadequacy. Fortunately, we have the power to transform this negative self-talk into self-compassionate and empowering thoughts through the use of affirmations. Affirmations are powerful statements that help reframe our thinking and create positive shifts in our mindset. In this chapter, we will explore affirmations specifically designed to silence negative self-talk and foster self-compassion, allowing us to cultivate a loving and supportive relationship with ourselves.

Understanding Negative Self-Talk

Definition and Impact of Negative Self-Talk:

Negative self-talk refers to the internal dialogue or thoughts that are self-critical, judgmental, and demeaning. It is the voice in our heads that often focuses on our perceived flaws, mistakes, and limitations. This negative self-talk can have a profound impact on our emotional well-being, self-esteem, and overall quality of life.

Negative self-talk can manifest in various ways, such as self-doubt, self-deprecation, comparison to others, and the constant fear of failure or rejection. It may include statements like, "I'm not good enough," "I always mess things up," or "I'll never succeed." These thoughts create a cycle of negativity that reinforces limiting beliefs and undermines our confidence and self-worth.

Recognizing Patterns of Negative Self-Talk:

Recognizing patterns of negative self-talk is an essential step in breaking free from its grip. It involves becoming aware of the types of thoughts and beliefs that contribute to this self-sabotaging dialogue. By paying attention to our inner monologue and the emotions it elicits, we can identify recurring patterns and themes in our negative self-talk.

Common patterns of negative self-talk include:

a) All-or-Nothing Thinking: Seeing things in black-and-white terms and perceiving any mistake or setback as a complete failure.

b) Overgeneralization: Drawing sweeping conclusions based on a single negative experience and applying them to all aspects of life.

c) Catastrophizing: Magnifying potential negative outcomes and anticipating the worst-case scenarios.

d) Personalization: Taking responsibility for events or situations that are beyond our control and blaming ourselves unnecessarily.

e) Comparison: Constantly comparing ourselves to others and feeling inferior or inadequate as a result.

By recognizing these patterns, we can challenge and reframe our negative thoughts, replacing them with more positive and empowering affirmations.

The Consequences of Negative Self-Talk on Well-being and Self-esteem:

The impact of negative self-talk on our well-being and self-esteem cannot be overstated. Persistent negative self-talk erodes our confidence, self-worth, and overall sense of happiness. It reinforces self-limiting beliefs and can lead to a host of psychological and emotional challenges, including:

a) Low Self-esteem: Negative self-talk perpetuates a negative self-image, causing us to doubt our abilities and worthiness.

b) Anxiety and Stress: The constant self-criticism and worry associated with negative self-talk create a heightened sense of anxiety and stress.

c) Depression: Negative self-talk can contribute to feelings of hopelessness, sadness, and an overall sense of despair.

d) Impaired Performance: When we constantly doubt ourselves and focus on our shortcomings, our performance and productivity may suffer.

e) Relationship Challenges: Negative self-talk can affect our relationships by making it difficult to trust others, express vulnerability, and form deep connections.

Understanding the consequences of negative self-talk is crucial for motivating ourselves to break free from its grip and embrace self-compassion and positivity.

By recognizing the impact of negative self-talk on our well-being and self-esteem, we can become more motivated to change these patterns and replace them with affirmations that promote self-acceptance, self-love, and personal growth.

Examples of exercises, problems, and additional content can be added to this section to further engage students in critical thinking and discussion. These activities may include journaling prompts for self-reflection, role-playing exercises to challenge negative self-talk, and case studies exploring the consequences of negative self-talk in different contexts.

The expanded section provides a comprehensive overview of negative self-talk, its impact, and the importance of recognizing its patterns. It sets the stage for the subsequent sections, which will focus on techniques and affirmations to silence negative self-talk and cultivate self-compassion.

The Power of Affirmations

What are Affirmations and How Do They Work?

Affirmations are positive statements or phrases that are intentionally repeated to reinforce positive beliefs, thoughts, and emotions. They serve as powerful tools for reprogramming the subconscious mind and redirecting our focus towards empowering and constructive thinking.

When we repeat affirmations, we engage in a process called cognitive restructuring, which involves challenging and replacing negative or self-defeating thoughts with positive and supportive ones. Affirmations work by influencing our subconscious mind, which plays a crucial role in shaping our beliefs, behaviors, and self-perception.

By consistently practicing affirmations, we can override deep-seated negative beliefs and rewire our thought patterns, leading to positive changes in our attitudes, behaviors, and overall well-being.

The Science behind Affirmations: Neuroplasticity and Positive Psychology

The effectiveness of affirmations is supported by scientific research, particularly in the fields of neuroplasticity and positive psychology. Neuroplasticity refers to the brain's ability to change and reorganize its structure and functions based on our experiences and thoughts.

Research has shown that repeated positive affirmations can create new neural pathways in the brain, strengthening positive associations and weakening negative ones. This process allows us to cultivate new beliefs and attitudes that support our well-being and personal growth.

Positive psychology, a branch of psychology focused on well-being and human flourishing, also highlights the power of affirmations. Affirmations align with the principles of positive psychology by promoting positive thinking, self-empowerment, and resilience. They encourage a shift in mindset from dwelling on problems and limitations to focusing on strengths, possibilities, and personal growth.

How to Create Effective and Personalized Affirmations

Creating effective and personalized affirmations involves thoughtful consideration and alignment with our unique needs and aspirations. Here are some guidelines to help you create powerful affirmations:

a) Be Positive and Present: Frame your affirmations in positive language and present tense. For example, instead of saying, "I will overcome challenges," say, "I am capable of overcoming any challenge."

b) Use First Person and Personal Pronouns: Make affirmations personal by using "I" or "my" in your statements. This helps create a stronger connection with the affirmation and reinforces self-ownership. For instance, say, "I am deserving of love and respect."

c) Keep it Specific and Realistic: Be specific about the qualities, behaviors, or outcomes you want to affirm. Avoid vague or overly general statements. For example, instead of saying, "I am successful," you could say, "I am consistently taking steps towards achieving my goals."

d) Use Emotional Language: Incorporate emotions and feelings into your affirmations. This helps create a stronger emotional connection and increases the impact. For instance, say, "I embrace joy and gratitude in every aspect of my life."

e) Make it Believable and Authentic: Ensure that your affirmations resonate with you and feel believable. If you have difficulty believing a particular affirmation, modify it until it feels authentic and aligned with your current mindset.

f) Practice Consistently: Repetition is key to the effectiveness of affirmations. Set aside dedicated time each day to repeat your affirmations, ideally in a quiet and focused environment. Consistency and commitment will reinforce the positive impact of affirmations.

By following these guidelines, you can create personalized affirmations that speak directly to your needs and aspirations, increasing their

Affirmations to Silence Negative Self-Talk

Negative self-talk can be detrimental to our well-being and self-esteem. By consciously replacing negative thoughts with positive affirmations, we can silence self-doubt and cultivate self-compassion. Here are some affirmations to help you counter negative self-talk:

1. I am worthy of love and acceptance just as I am. My worth is not determined by external validation or expectations.

2. I release all self-judgment and embrace my authentic self. I am deserving of love and compassion, including from myself.

3. I am deserving of compassion and understanding, both from others and myself. I extend kindness and understanding to myself in moments of struggle.

4. I choose to let go of negative thoughts and replace them with empowering beliefs. I consciously shift my focus towards positive and uplifting thoughts.

5. I release the need for perfection and embrace my imperfections as part of my unique journey. I accept myself fully, flaws and all.

6. I am not defined by my mistakes; they are opportunities for growth and learning. I view mistakes as stepping stones to success and self-improvement.

7. I am resilient and capable of overcoming challenges. I face obstacles with courage and determination, knowing that I have the strength to persevere.

8. I choose to focus on my strengths and celebrate my achievements. I recognize and appreciate my unique abilities and accomplishments.

9. I trust in my abilities and have faith in my capacity to navigate life's obstacles. I believe in my inner strength and resourcefulness.

10.   I am deserving of success and believe in my potential to achieve my goals. I trust that my efforts and dedication will lead me to positive outcomes.

11.   I let go of comparing myself to others. I celebrate my own journey and progress without the need for comparison.

12.   I acknowledge that my worth is not dependent on external appearances or societal standards. I am beautiful and unique in my own way.

13.   I embrace self-care and prioritize my physical, emotional, and mental well-being. I nourish my body, mind, and spirit with love and care.

14.   I release the need for approval from others and validate myself from within. My self-worth is not determined by external validation.

15.   I am deserving of happiness and fulfillment. I create a life that aligns with my passions, values, and desires.

16.   I embrace change and see it as an opportunity for growth and personal transformation. I adapt and evolve with grace and resilience.

17.   I choose to surround myself with positive and supportive people who uplift and inspire me. I create a nourishing and loving social circle.

18.   I am grateful for my body and its capabilities. I honor and respect my body, treating it with love and gratitude.

19.   I release any negative beliefs about my body and replace them with positive and empowering thoughts. I see the beauty in all shapes, sizes, and colors.

20.   I practice self-compassion and speak to myself with kindness and understanding. I offer myself the same love and compassion I extend to others.

21.   I let go of past mistakes and forgive myself. I deserve forgiveness and the freedom to move forward with a clean slate.

22.   I trust my intuition and make choices that align with my authentic self. I honor my inner wisdom and guidance.

23.   I release the need for external validation and find validation from within. I trust my instincts and make decisions that are true to myself.

24.   I am proud of who I am becoming. I embrace personal growth and celebrate the progress I make along my journey.

25.   I am grateful for the lessons that challenges bring. Each obstacle is an opportunity for me to become stronger and more resilient.

By regularly repeating these affirmations, you can silence negative self-talk and cultivate a positive and compassionate mindset. Remember to personalize these affirmations to align with your own experiences and beliefs.

Cultivating Self-Compassion

Self-compassion is an essential practice for nurturing our well-being and fostering a positive relationship with ourselves. By treating ourselves with kindness and understanding, we create a supportive inner environment that promotes self-love and acceptance. Here are some affirmations to help you cultivate self-compassion:

1.   I treat myself with kindness and understanding, even in moments of difficulty. I offer myself the same compassion and support I would offer to a loved one.

2.   I forgive myself for past mistakes and embrace the lessons they have taught me. I release any lingering guilt or shame and choose to learn and grow from my experiences.

3.   I am gentle with myself during times of struggle, acknowledging that I am doing my best. I recognize that setbacks and challenges are a natural part of life, and I approach them with patience and understanding.

4.   I extend compassion to myself as I would to a dear friend in need. I offer words of encouragement, comfort, and reassurance when I face difficulties or setbacks.

5.   I honor my emotions and allow myself to feel without judgment or resistance. I create a safe space within myself where all emotions are welcome, knowing that they provide valuable insights and opportunities for growth.

6.   I am patient with myself as I navigate life's challenges and changes. I understand that personal growth takes time and effort, and I trust in the process of unfolding and becoming.

7.   I nourish my mind, body, and soul with self-care practices that promote well-being. I prioritize activities that bring me joy, relaxation, and rejuvenation, knowing that taking care of myself is an act of self-compassion.

8.   I celebrate my progress, no matter how small, and acknowledge the efforts I make toward self-growth. I recognize that each step forward is a testament to my strength and resilience.

9.   I trust in my ability to make decisions that align with my highest good. I listen to my inner wisdom and intuition, knowing that I have the capacity to make choices that honor my well-being.

10.   I am deserving of love and compassion, both from others and myself. I recognize that my worth is not dependent on external validation, and I embrace my inherent value and self-worth.

11.   I release the need for perfection and embrace my authentic self. I accept all aspects of who I am, including my strengths, weaknesses, and imperfections. I am enough just as I am.

12.   I practice self-acceptance and self-love unconditionally. I recognize that my worth is not determined by external factors, but by the inherent value of my being.

13.   I am grateful for the opportunity to experience life's ups and downs. I recognize that challenges and setbacks are opportunities for growth and self-discovery.

14.   I cultivate a nurturing inner dialogue, speaking to myself with words of kindness and encouragement. I replace self-criticism with self-affirmation and positive self-talk.

15.   I prioritize self-care and make it a non-negotiable part of my routine. I listen to my body's needs and respond with love and care.

16.   I embrace my uniqueness and celebrate my individuality. I understand that my worth is not determined by societal standards or comparisons to others.

17.   I acknowledge and celebrate my achievements, no matter how big or small. I recognize the efforts and hard work I put into reaching my goals.

18.   I let go of self-judgment and embrace self-compassion as a guiding principle in my life. I give myself permission to be human and make mistakes, knowing that they are opportunities for growth and learning.

By incorporating these affirmations into your daily practice, you can cultivate a compassionate and nurturing relationship with yourself, fostering a deep sense of self-love and acceptance. Remember to personalize these affirmations to resonate with your own experiences and beliefs.

Integration and Practice

To truly benefit from affirmations and cultivate self-compassion, it's essential to integrate them into your daily routine and engage in practices that deepen your understanding and experience. Here are some suggestions for incorporating affirmations into your life and enhancing your self-compassion practice:

Incorporating Affirmations into Daily Routine:

Choose a specific time of day to recite your affirmations, such as in the morning upon waking or before bed. Consistency is key in reinforcing positive beliefs and nurturing self-compassion.

Create a sacred space or a designated area where you can focus on your affirmations without distractions. This could be a quiet corner in your home, a meditation space, or a natural setting that brings you peace.

Use visual aids, such as written affirmations or affirmation cards, to remind yourself of your chosen affirmations throughout the day. Place them in visible locations like your desk, mirror, or phone lock screen.

Journaling Prompts for Reflection and Integration:

Reflect on your journey of cultivating self-compassion. What challenges have you faced? How have affirmations supported your growth and self-acceptance?

Write about moments when you demonstrated self-compassion. How did it feel? What impact did it have on your well-being and relationships?

Explore any limiting beliefs or self-critical thoughts that may arise. Challenge them with counter-affirmations that promote self-compassion and self-acceptance.

Journal about your progress and milestones in developing self-compassion. Celebrate your achievements and acknowledge the positive changes you have experienced.

Exercises and Practices for Building Self-Compassion:

Practice loving-kindness meditation, directing compassion and well-wishes towards yourself. Repeat affirmations of self-love, compassion, and well-being during this meditation practice.

Engage in body-positive activities, such as mindful movement, yoga, or dance. Use affirmations that celebrate your body and its unique capabilities.

Create a self-compassion ritual, such as taking a warm bath, lighting candles, or engaging in a soothing activity that promotes relaxation and self-care. During this time, repeat affirmations that emphasize self-love and compassion.

Practice forgiveness exercises, both towards yourself and others. Use affirmations that release guilt, resentment, and self-judgment, and affirm your willingness to let go and move forward.

By incorporating these practices into your daily routine, you create space for self-reflection, growth, and the integration of self-compassion into your life. Remember that building self-compassion is a process, and it requires patience, consistency, and self-acceptance. Embrace the journey and celebrate your progress along the way.

In the next section, we will explore the role of affirmations in cultivating gratitude and fostering a positive mindset.

Conclusion:

Negative self-talk can be a significant obstacle on our path to personal growth and self-fulfillment. However, by consciously choosing to replace negative thoughts with positive and empowering affirmations, we can silence our inner critic and cultivate self-compassion. Through the use of affirmations, we can rewire our brains, strengthen our self-esteem, and develop a loving and supportive relationship with ourselves. Remember, affirmations are a tool that requires consistent practice and dedication. By integrating these affirmations into our daily lives and engaging in self-reflective exercises and practices, we can nurture our self-compassion and create a foundation for lasting personal transformation.

Exercises:

Reflect on a recent negative self-talk episode you experienced. Write down the negative thoughts that arose and create affirmations to counteract them.

Keep a gratitude journal and write down at least three things you appreciate about yourself every day. Use affirmations to reinforce these positive aspects of yourself.

Practice self-compassion meditation. Sit in a quiet space, close your eyes, and repeat self-compassionate affirmations while focusing on your breath and embracing feelings of love and understanding toward yourself.

Analyze a specific negative self-talk pattern you've identified in your life. Discuss its origins, its impact on your well-being, and develop affirmations to challenge and reframe this pattern.

Role-play a scenario in which you respond to negative self-talk with self-compassionate affirmations. Reflect on the emotions and mindset shifts that occur as a result.

These exercises and problems are designed to engage students in critical thinking, self-reflection, and practical application of the concepts discussed in this chapter. They encourage students to actively participate in their personal growth journey and foster a deeper understanding of the power of affirmations in silencing negative self-talk and cultivating self-compassion.

Remember, the key to reaping the benefits of affirmations lies in consistent practice and a genuine belief in their transformative potential. Embrace these affirmations and integrate them into your daily life, and witness the profound impact they can have on your self-talk and overall well-being.

Affirming that your worth goes beyond physical appearance.

In a world that often places a disproportionate emphasis on physical appearance, it is crucial to recognize and affirm that our worth as individuals extends far beyond the realm of external aesthetics. True self-worth encompasses a multifaceted tapestry of qualities, talents, achievements, and the richness of our inner essence. By embracing and internalizing this understanding, we can foster a deep sense of self-acceptance, self-love, and appreciation for our inherent worthiness. In this section, we will explore the profound significance of affirming that our worth transcends physical appearance, delving into the transformative power of this mindset and providing practical affirmations to support this journey of self-discovery.

Recognizing the Limitations of Physical Appearance:

In a society inundated with media portrayals of unrealistic beauty standards, it is crucial to recognize the limitations of equating self-worth solely with physical appearance. External beauty is transient and subjective, subject to the ever-changing tides of fashion and cultural norms. Affirming that our worth goes beyond physical appearance allows us to break free from the shackles of societal expectations and embrace the deeper aspects of our being.

1. I recognize that my worth goes beyond my physical appearance.

2. My self-worth is not determined by societal beauty standards.

3. I release the pressure to conform to unrealistic ideals of beauty.

4. I embrace my unique qualities and celebrate my individuality.

5. I value my inner qualities more than my external appearance.

6. I acknowledge that physical beauty is subjective and ever-changing.

7. My worth is defined by my character, values, and actions, not my looks.

8. I release the need for external validation and find validation within myself.

9. I appreciate the diversity of beauty in the world and within myself.

10. I focus on cultivating inner beauty and radiating it into the world.

11. I am confident in who I am beyond my physical appearance.

12. I reject comparisons and appreciate the beauty of others without diminishing my own.

13. I embrace the imperfections that make me unique and beautiful.

14. I prioritize self-care that nourishes my mind, body, and soul.

15. I choose to surround myself with people who appreciate me for who I am, not just how I look.

16. I affirm that my worth is not defined by external judgments or opinions.

17. I release any negative beliefs about my physical appearance and replace them with love and acceptance.

18. I recognize that true beauty comes from within and shines through my actions and kindness.

19. I embrace the wisdom that comes with age and experience, valuing inner growth over external changes.

20. I choose to focus on cultivating a positive self-image rooted in self-love and acceptance.

21. I celebrate my unique features and see them as part of my individual beauty.

22. I am grateful for my body and all it allows me to experience in life.

23. I release the pressure to strive for a perfect physical appearance and instead focus on living a fulfilling and meaningful life.

24. I acknowledge that my worth is not contingent upon the opinions of others.

25. I affirm that I am worthy of love, respect, and acceptance, regardless of my physical appearance.

By incorporating these affirmations into your daily practice, you can strengthen your belief in your worth beyond physical appearance and cultivate a positive and resilient self-image. Remember, true beauty radiates from within and transcends the limitations of external standards.

Embracing Inner Beauty and Authenticity:

One of the fundamental affirmations in recognizing our worth beyond physical appearance is the embrace of our inner beauty and authenticity. True beauty emanates from the depths of our soul, radiating through our thoughts, actions, and interactions with the world. By affirming and celebrating our unique qualities, talents, and experiences, we can foster a deep sense of self-acceptance and self-love that transcends physical attributes.

Empowered Affirmations

1. I embrace my inner beauty and radiate it into the world.

2. I celebrate the unique qualities that make me who I am.

3. My authenticity is a gift that I share with others.

4. I am confident in expressing my true self.

5. I honor my intuition and trust in the wisdom of my inner voice.

6. I release the need to conform to societal expectations and embrace my true essence.

7. I appreciate the beauty of my flaws and imperfections, for they contribute to my authenticity.

8. I am worthy of love and acceptance just as I am, without needing to change or conform.

9. I express my creativity and passion authentically and fearlessly.

10. I radiate kindness, compassion, and empathy from the depths of my being.

11. I am comfortable in my own skin and embrace my unique physical attributes.

12. I embrace my strengths and use them to uplift myself and others.

13. I am not defined by my past or my mistakes; I am constantly evolving and growing.

14. I cultivate inner peace and serenity, knowing that my true beauty comes from within.

15. I honor my values and live in alignment with my authentic self.

16. I release the need for external validation and find validation within myself.

17. I am deserving of respect and appreciation for my authentic self.

18. I am a magnet for positive energy and genuine connections.

19. I celebrate the diversity and uniqueness of others, knowing that it enriches our collective beauty.

20. I trust in the power of my authentic voice and use it to advocate for myself and others.

21. I am comfortable setting boundaries that honor my authentic needs and desires.

22. I embrace my journey of self-discovery and self-expression.

23. I attract opportunities and experiences that align with my authentic path.

24. I am grateful for the lessons and growth that come from embracing my inner beauty and authenticity.

25. I am a beautiful and authentic being, worthy of love, joy, and fulfillment.

By incorporating these affirmations into your daily practice, you can deepen your connection with your inner beauty and authenticity. Embracing who you truly are allows you to shine brightly in the world and attract experiences and relationships that align with your true self.

Cultivating a Holistic View of Self-Worth:

Affirming that our worth goes beyond physical appearance requires embracing a holistic view of self-worth—one that encompasses our intellectual capabilities, emotional intelligence, spiritual growth, and contributions to society. We are not defined by our external appearances alone but by the entirety of our being. Affirmations that promote this understanding can help us shift our focus from external validation to recognizing and appreciating the richness and depth of our multidimensional selves.

1. My self-worth is not determined by external validation, but by my intrinsic value as a unique individual.

2. I acknowledge that my worth extends beyond my achievements or material possessions.

3. I am deserving of love, respect, and kindness, simply because I exist.

4. I embrace my strengths, talents, and abilities, recognizing their contribution to my overall worth.

5. I honor my emotions and allow myself to experience them without judgment.

6. I am connected to the web of life, and my worth is intertwined with the well-being of all beings.

7. I value my physical, mental, and emotional well-being, and prioritize self-care in all aspects of my life.

8. I am deserving of forgiveness, both from others and myself, as it is an integral part of growth and healing.

9. I recognize that self-worth is not a static concept, but something that can be nurtured and developed over time.

10. I embrace my flaws and imperfections, for they contribute to the richness of my human experience.

11. I celebrate my uniqueness and honor the diversity that exists within me and in the world.

12. I trust in my intuition and the wisdom that resides within me to guide me on my life's journey.

13. I am worthy of setting boundaries that protect my well-being and honor my authentic needs and desires.

14. I acknowledge my interconnectedness with nature and the universe, understanding that my worth is intertwined with the greater whole.

15. I choose to surround myself with people and experiences that uplift and inspire me, nurturing my sense of self-worth.

16. I release the need to compare myself to others, recognizing that we are all on our own unique paths.

17. I am deserving of success and abundance, and I embrace opportunities that align with my values and purpose.

18. I value my relationships and cultivate connections based on mutual respect, trust, and authenticity.

19. I am open to learning and growth, knowing that it contributes to my overall self-worth and personal development.

20. I choose to speak to myself with kindness, compassion, and words that nurture my self-worth.

21. I am the author of my own story, and I have the power to shape my narrative and define my self-worth.

22. I am deserving of joy, happiness, and fulfillment in all areas of my life.

23. I recognize that self-worth encompasses my spiritual dimension, and I honor and nurture my spiritual growth.

24. I embrace the journey of self-discovery and self-acceptance, knowing that it is a lifelong process.

25. I am a unique and valuable expression of life, and my self-worth is inherent and unwavering.

By incorporating these affirmations into your daily practice, you can cultivate a holistic view of self-worth that encompasses all aspects of your being. Remember that self-worth is not something to be earned or proven, but something to be acknowledged and embraced. Nurturing your self-worth allows you to live a more fulfilling and authentic life, honoring your true essence and contributing positively to the world around you.

Overcoming Comparison and Embracing Individuality:

In a culture that fosters comparison and perpetuates a narrow definition of beauty, it is essential to affirm our individuality and release the need for comparison. Each person possesses a unique combination of qualities, talents, and experiences, contributing to the diversity and tapestry of humanity. By affirming our individuality, we can cultivate a sense of self-acceptance and honor the beauty of our authentic selves.

1. I am unique and incomparable, and I celebrate my individuality.

2. I release the need to compare myself to others, recognizing that we are all on our own unique paths.

Empowered Affirmations

3. I appreciate and embrace my own journey, knowing that it is different from anyone else's.

4. I acknowledge that comparison steals my joy and hinders my self-growth, and I choose to let go of this destructive habit.

5. I focus on my own progress and celebrate my personal achievements, regardless of how they compare to others.

6. I honor and value my own strengths, talents, and qualities, recognizing that they contribute to the tapestry of humanity.

7. I am worthy and deserving of love, success, and happiness, irrespective of how others may perceive me.

8. I cultivate self-acceptance and self-compassion, knowing that my worth is not defined by external comparisons.

9. I acknowledge that everyone has their own unique gifts and qualities, and we each bring something valuable to the world.

10. I choose to be inspired by others' successes instead of feeling threatened or inadequate.

11. I trust in my own path and timing, understanding that comparing myself to others only creates unnecessary pressure.

12. I embrace and celebrate diversity, recognizing that it enriches the world and allows for different perspectives and experiences.

13. I am grateful for the unique qualities and attributes that make me who I am.

14. I radiate confidence and authenticity, knowing that I am enough just as I am.

15. I focus on my own personal growth and self-improvement, rather than comparing myself to external standards.

16. I appreciate the beauty in individual differences and honor the mosaic of humanity.

17. I choose to uplift and support others without diminishing my own worth or accomplishments.

18. I recognize that comparison is a fruitless exercise that robs me of my own joy and fulfillment.

19. I am content and at peace with who I am, knowing that I am constantly evolving and growing.

20. I celebrate my own uniqueness and embrace the power of self-expression.

21. I am confident in my own path, trusting that it is leading me exactly where I need to be.

22. I let go of judgments and expectations, allowing myself and others to simply be.

23. I am proud of my own progress and accomplishments, regardless of how they may compare to others'.

24. I embrace the freedom that comes with releasing comparison and embracing my true self.

25. I am a magnificent individual with my own purpose and gifts, and I honor and cherish my individuality.

By integrating these affirmations into your daily practice, you can overcome the trap of comparison and embrace the beauty of your own individuality. Remember that you are a unique expression of life, and comparing yourself to others only diminishes your own light. Embrace your strengths, honor your journey, and celebrate the beauty of being authentically you.

Affirmations to Reinforce Worth Beyond Physical Appearance:

To support the journey of affirming our worth beyond physical appearance, here are some powerful affirmations to integrate into our daily practice:

1. I acknowledge and embrace my inherent worthiness beyond physical appearance.

2. My value as an individual extends far beyond societal beauty standards.

3. I celebrate the beauty that radiates from within me, illuminating my true essence.

4. I recognize and appreciate my unique qualities, talents, and experiences.

5. My self-worth is rooted in my character, kindness, and contributions to the world.

6. I release comparison and embrace the beauty of my authentic self.

7. I honor the wisdom and growth that come from embracing my worth beyond physical appearance.

8. I am deserving of love, respect, and acceptance, irrespective of external judgments.

9. I celebrate the diversity and individuality that enriches the tapestry of humanity.

10. I affirm that my worth transcends physical appearance, and I live confidently in this truth.

By incorporating these affirmations into our daily practice, we can gradually shift our mindset and cultivate a deep and unwavering sense of self-worth that goes beyond physical appearance.

Conclusion:

Recognizing and affirming that our worth goes beyond physical appearance is a powerful act of self-love and self-acceptance. It allows us to break free from societal expectations, embrace our authentic selves, and cultivate a holistic view of self-worth. Through the practice of affirmations that reinforce this understanding, we can gradually transcend the limitations of external validation and embrace the profound beauty that resides within us. Remember, your worth is not determined by your physical appearance, but by the magnificent essence that makes you who you are. Embrace and celebrate your multidimensional worthiness with love and gratitude.

AFFIRMATIONS FOR NURTURING A HEALTHY RELATIONSHIP WITH FOOD AND EXERCISE.

A healthy relationship with food and exercise is essential for our overall well-being and vitality. It involves cultivating a balanced and mindful approach, free from guilt, obsession, or restrictive behaviors. Affirmations can serve as powerful tools to reframe our mindset, foster self-compassion, and support our journey towards a healthy and sustainable lifestyle. In this section, we will explore a comprehensive set of affirmations designed to help nurture a positive and harmonious relationship with food and exercise.

1. I listen to my body's signals and honor its unique needs for nourishment.

2. I choose foods that nourish and energize my body, promoting vitality and well-being.

3. I eat mindfully, savoring each bite and engaging all my senses in the experience.

4. I release any guilt or judgment surrounding my food choices, knowing that balance is key.

5. I embrace a holistic approach to health, recognizing that it encompasses physical, mental, and emotional well-being.

6. I view exercise as a joyful opportunity to move my body and enhance my strength and flexibility.

7. I engage in physical activities that bring me pleasure and align with my individual preferences.

8. I celebrate and appreciate my body's abilities and focus on what it can do rather than how it looks.

9. I release comparison and embrace my own unique journey towards health and vitality.

10. I cultivate self-compassion and kindness towards myself, especially during moments of setbacks or challenges.

11. I nourish my body with a variety of wholesome foods, understanding that it thrives on a balanced and diverse diet.

12. I create a positive environment around me that supports my healthy eating and exercise habits.

13. I release the notion of perfection and embrace progress, recognizing that small steps lead to lasting change.

14. I trust my body's innate wisdom to guide me in making choices that support its well-being.

15. I let go of external standards or societal pressures, focusing on my own unique health goals.

16. I cultivate a positive mindset and affirm that I am worthy of a healthy and vibrant life.

17. I practice self-care in all aspects of my life, including my relationship with food and exercise.

18. I appreciate the interconnectedness of body, mind, and spirit, nurturing all aspects for holistic well-being.

19. I view food as fuel for my body, providing me with energy and nourishment for optimal functioning.

20. I release any negative beliefs or associations around food and reframe them with positive and empowering thoughts.

21. I find joy in preparing and cooking wholesome meals, infusing love and intention into every dish.

22. I recognize that rest and recovery are integral parts of a balanced fitness routine, allowing my body to restore and rejuvenate.

23. I focus on progress, not perfection, acknowledging that every step towards a healthier lifestyle is a step in the right direction.

24. I appreciate my body's resilience and adaptability, knowing that it is capable of transformation and growth.

25. I am grateful for the opportunity to nourish and care for my body, cultivating a harmonious relationship with food and exercise.

These affirmations are intended to help you develop a healthy and sustainable relationship with food and exercise. Remember to personalize them to resonate with your own journey and incorporate them into your daily practice. With consistent effort and a compassionate mindset, you can nurture a positive and nurturing approach to nourishing your body and engaging in physical activity, fostering a lifelong commitment to health and well-being.

AFFIRMING CONFIDENCE IN PERSONAL STYLE AND FASHION CHOICES.

Personal style and fashion choices are powerful means of self-expression and creativity. They allow us to showcase our unique identity, values, and personality to the world. Affirming confidence in our personal style and fashion choices empowers us to embrace our individuality, experiment with different looks, and break free from societal expectations. In this section, we will explore a comprehensive set of affirmations designed to support and nurture confidence in personal style and fashion choices.

1. I embrace my unique style and express myself authentically through fashion.

2. I radiate confidence and poise in any outfit I choose to wear.

3. I trust my intuition when selecting clothes that resonate with my personal taste and preferences.

4. I celebrate my body shape and size, dressing to highlight my best features.

5. I release the need for validation from others and find joy in expressing myself through fashion.

6. I experiment with different styles, colors, and patterns, allowing my creativity to flourish.

7. I am open to new fashion trends and incorporate them into my personal style in a way that feels authentic to me.

8. I am comfortable stepping outside of my comfort zone and trying bold and unique fashion choices.

9. I appreciate the power of accessories in enhancing and completing my outfits.

10. I create a wardrobe that reflects my values and supports sustainable and ethical fashion choices.

11. I dress for myself, focusing on how fashion makes me feel rather than seeking approval from others.

12. I radiate beauty from within, knowing that it shines through regardless of what I wear.

13. I embrace the freedom to express different aspects of my personality through my fashion choices.

14. I am worthy of investing time and effort in curating a wardrobe that makes me feel confident and empowered.

15. I release any fear of judgment or criticism and wear what brings me joy and self-expression.

16. I acknowledge that fashion is an art form, and I am the artist who crafts my unique style.

17. I appreciate the transformative power of fashion in boosting my mood and self-esteem.

18. I embrace my body as it is and choose clothes that make me feel comfortable and empowered.

19. I celebrate the diversity of body shapes and sizes in the fashion industry, recognizing that beauty is not limited to one standard.

20. I let go of comparison and focus on celebrating my own unique style journey.

21. I cultivate a positive relationship with my reflection, seeing beauty and uniqueness in every aspect.

22. I embrace the idea that fashion is an ever-evolving expression of my personal growth and self-discovery.

23. I honor the heritage and cultural significance of different fashion styles and incorporate elements that resonate with me.

24. I radiate confidence in every fashion choice I make, knowing that my style is a reflection of my inner self.

25. I am grateful for the freedom to explore and enjoy fashion as a means of self-expression.

These affirmations are intended to support and nurture confidence in personal style and fashion choices. Incorporate them into your daily practice and adapt them to align with your own fashion journey. Embrace the power of fashion as a tool for self-expression and celebrate your unique style. With self-confidence and authenticity, you can cultivate a personal style that resonates with your true self and enhances your overall sense of confidence and well-being.

AFFIRMATIONS FOR EMBRACING AND EXPRESSING YOUR AUTHENTIC SELF.

Embracing and expressing our authentic self is a powerful journey of self-discovery and personal growth. It involves cultivating self-awareness, honoring our true desires and values, and bravely sharing our unique gifts with the world. By affirming our authentic self, we can break free from societal expectations, embrace our individuality, and live a life aligned with our true essence. In this section, we will explore a detailed collection of affirmations designed to support and empower you in embracing and expressing your authentic self.

1. I embrace and honor my true self in all aspects of my life.

2. I am deserving of love, acceptance, and understanding for who I truly am.

3. I release the need to conform to societal expectations and embrace my individuality.

4. I trust my intuition to guide me on the path of authenticity and self-expression.

5. I am worthy of expressing my thoughts, ideas, and emotions openly and honestly.

6. I celebrate my unique qualities, talents, and experiences that make me who I am.

7. I give myself permission to let go of masks and embrace vulnerability.

8. I trust that my authentic self has something valuable to contribute to the world.

9. I release the fear of judgment and criticism and fully express my true essence.

10. I am a unique being with a purpose that only I can fulfill.

11. I trust that by embracing my authentic self, I inspire others to do the same.

Empowered Affirmations

12. I release the need for approval from others and follow my own inner guidance.

13. I am proud of my individuality and celebrate the beauty of diversity in the world.

14. I acknowledge and honor my core values, allowing them to guide my choices and actions.

15. I let go of the need to compare myself to others and embrace my own journey.

16. I trust that my authentic self is constantly evolving and unfolding.

17. I express myself creatively and fearlessly, knowing that my unique perspective is valuable.

18. I surround myself with people who support and celebrate my authentic self.

19. I am comfortable setting boundaries that honor my true needs and desires.

20. I allow my authentic self to shine through in all areas of my life, including relationships, work, and hobbies.

21. I am grateful for the opportunity to live authentically and share my gifts with the world.

22. I release any self-doubt and step into my authentic power and confidence.

23. I embrace the journey of self-discovery, knowing that it leads me to a deeper understanding of my true self.

24. I am aligned with my purpose and live a life that is true to my authentic self.

25. I embrace the freedom that comes with expressing my authentic self and living in alignment with my true essence.

These affirmations are intended to support and empower you on your journey of embracing and expressing your authentic self. Incorporate them into your daily practice and adapt them to resonate with your own unique journey. Embrace the power of authenticity and self-expression, and remember that by being true to yourself, you create a positive impact on both your own life and the lives of others.

AFFIRMING THAT SELF-CARE IS AN ESSENTIAL PART OF NURTURING INNER AND OUTER BEAUTY.

Self-care is a profound practice that involves nurturing and prioritizing our physical, emotional, and mental well-being. It is not merely a luxury or indulgence but an essential aspect of cultivating inner and outer beauty. By dedicating time and attention to self-care, we honor ourselves and create a foundation for overall well-being and radiance. In this section, we will explore a comprehensive and detailed collection of affirmations to emphasize the importance of self-care in nurturing both our inner and outer beauty.

1. I prioritize self-care as an integral part of my daily routine.

2. I deserve to invest time and energy in nourishing my physical, emotional, and mental health.

3. I create space for self-care activities that bring me joy, peace, and rejuvenation.

4. I listen to the needs of my body and provide it with the rest, movement, and nourishment it requires.

5. I practice self-compassion and allow myself to rest and recharge when needed.

6. I release guilt or any sense of selfishness when engaging in self-care activities.

7. I give myself permission to say no to commitments that deplete my energy and prioritize activities that replenish me.

8. I acknowledge that self-care is not a luxury but a necessity for my overall well-being.

9. I engage in activities that promote emotional well-being, such as journaling, meditation, or spending time in nature.

10. I prioritize healthy boundaries and create a safe and nurturing environment for myself.

11. I indulge in activities that bring me pleasure, whether it's a warm bath, reading a book, or enjoying a hobby.

12. I nourish my body with healthy and wholesome foods that support my well-being and vitality.

13. I engage in regular physical exercise that brings strength, flexibility, and joy to my body.

14. I practice mindfulness and cultivate a sense of presence and awareness in each moment.

15. I surround myself with positive and uplifting influences that contribute to my well-being.

16. I take breaks throughout the day to relax, breathe deeply, and recharge my energy.

17. I engage in self-care practices that enhance my outer beauty, such as skincare routines or grooming rituals.

18. I seek support and guidance when needed, recognizing that asking for help is an act of self-care and strength.

19. I create a peaceful and harmonious living space that promotes relaxation and rejuvenation.

20. I allocate time for activities that inspire creativity and self-expression.

21. I nourish my mind with uplifting and empowering thoughts, affirmations, and positive self-talk.

22. I honor my emotions and allow myself to feel and process them in a healthy and supportive way.

23. I practice self-acceptance and celebrate my unique qualities, embracing my authentic self.

24. I engage in activities that foster connection with others, nurturing my sense of belonging and social well-being.

25. I recognize that self-care is an ongoing practice, and I commit to continuously exploring and refining my self-care rituals to support my holistic well-being.

These affirmations serve as reminders of the essential role that self-care plays in nurturing both our inner and outer beauty. Incorporate them into your daily practice and adapt them to resonate with your personal self-care journey. Remember that by prioritizing self-care, you invest in your well-being and cultivate a radiant and authentic beauty that shines from within.

AFFIRMATIONS FOR EMBRACING AND LOVING YOUR FLAWS AND IMPERFECTIONS.

In a society that often promotes an unrealistic ideal of perfection, it is crucial to cultivate a mindset of self-acceptance and love for our flaws and imperfections. Our flaws are what make us unique and beautiful, and embracing them allows us to develop a deep sense of self-compassion and authenticity. In this section, we will explore a comprehensive and detailed collection of affirmations designed to help you embrace and love your flaws and imperfections, fostering a greater sense of self-acceptance and inner peace.

1. I embrace my flaws and imperfections as essential parts of my unique journey.

2. I choose to see my flaws as opportunities for growth and self-improvement.

3. I love and accept myself unconditionally, flaws and all.

4. I release the need to be perfect and embrace the beauty of my authentic self.

5. I am deserving of love and acceptance, regardless of my flaws and imperfections.

6. I choose to focus on my strengths rather than dwell on my perceived weaknesses.

7. I celebrate my flaws as reminders of my humanity and individuality.

8. I acknowledge that true beauty lies in embracing and accepting our imperfections.

9. I let go of comparing myself to others and embrace my unique path and journey.

10. I am grateful for my flaws as they contribute to my personal growth and resilience.

11. I see beauty in the diversity of flaws and imperfections present in the world.

12. I release the pressure to conform to societal expectations and embrace my authentic self.

13. I treat myself with kindness and compassion, knowing that I am worthy of love and acceptance.

14. I choose to see my flaws as opportunities for self-love and self-acceptance.

15. I recognize that my flaws do not define me; they are only a small part of who I am.

16. I appreciate the lessons and wisdom that come from embracing my flaws and imperfections.

17. I let go of the need for external validation and find validation within myself.

18. I am proud of my uniqueness and the individuality that my flaws bring to my character.

19. I release the fear of judgment and allow myself to be vulnerable and authentic.

20. I choose to see the beauty in my flaws and imperfections, knowing they make me whole.

21. I honor my journey and the growth that comes from accepting and embracing my flaws.

22. I am comfortable with my vulnerabilities and understand that they make me stronger.

23. I acknowledge that perfection is an illusion and embrace the beauty of my imperfect self.

24. I radiate confidence and self-love, embracing every part of who I am, flaws and all.

25. I choose to love myself unconditionally, celebrating my flaws and imperfections as integral parts of my unique beauty.

These affirmations serve as powerful reminders to embrace and love your flaws and imperfections. Incorporate them into your daily practice and adapt them to resonate with your personal journey of self-acceptance and self-love. Remember that your flaws do not diminish your worth; they enhance your authenticity and make you a beautifully imperfect individual. Embrace them with love and compassion, and let them shine as a testament to your unique beauty.

AFFIRMATIONS FOR STRENGTHENING YOUR MINDSET AND RESILIENCE IN THE FACE OF SOCIETAL BEAUTY STANDARDS.

Societal beauty standards can place immense pressure on individuals to conform to a narrow definition of beauty, often leading to feelings of inadequacy and low self-esteem. It is essential to develop a strong mindset and cultivate resilience to counteract the negative impact of these standards. In this section, we will delve into a comprehensive and detailed collection of affirmations designed to strengthen your mindset and resilience, empowering you to embrace your unique beauty and rise above societal expectations.

1. I am not defined by society's beauty standards; I define my own worth and beauty.

2. I release the need for external validation and focus on cultivating inner confidence.

3. I am resilient in the face of societal pressures and choose to love myself unconditionally.

4. I honor and celebrate my unique features, knowing they contribute to my beauty.

5. I reject the notion that there is a singular standard of beauty and embrace diversity.

6. I choose to surround myself with positive influences that uplift and empower me.

7. I am aware that true beauty radiates from within and is not solely based on appearance.

8. I recognize that comparison is a thief of joy and focus on my own growth and self-acceptance.

9. I release the belief that I need to conform to societal beauty standards to be worthy.

10. I am resilient in the face of criticism, knowing that my worth is not determined by others' opinions.

11. I celebrate my uniqueness and appreciate the beauty in my individuality.

12. I nourish my mind with empowering thoughts and affirmations that strengthen my self-worth.

13. I choose self-compassion over self-criticism and treat myself with kindness and understanding.

14. I embrace the journey of self-discovery and self-acceptance, knowing it is a lifelong process.

15. I focus on my inner qualities and character traits that make me beautiful beyond physical appearance.

16. I affirm that my worth extends far beyond external beauty and encompasses my intellect, kindness, and resilience.

17. I am mindful of the media I consume and discerning in accepting only empowering messages about beauty.

18. I release the need to fit into societal molds and confidently express my authentic self.

19. I trust in my own perception of beauty and embrace the freedom of defining beauty on my terms.

20. I affirm that my self-worth is not determined by my physical appearance but by the love and acceptance I have for myself.

21. I choose to focus on self-care practices that nourish my mind, body, and spirit, promoting holistic well-being.

22. I am aware that beauty comes in all shapes, sizes, colors, and ages, and I celebrate the diversity of beauty.

23. I affirm that my worth is inherent and cannot be diminished by societal beauty standards.

24. I embody resilience and strength, knowing that I have the power to shape my own narrative of beauty.

25. I stand tall and proud, embracing my uniqueness and defying societal norms, for I am a beautiful expression of individuality.

These affirmations serve as empowering tools to strengthen your mindset and resilience in the face of societal beauty standards. Practice them regularly and adapt them to resonate with your personal journey of self-acceptance and empowerment. Remember that your worth extends far beyond external appearance, and by embracing your unique beauty, you inspire others to do the same. Rise above societal expectations and cultivate a mindset of self-love, acceptance, and resilience as you navigate your path to true beauty.

AFFIRMATIONS TO RELEASE THE NEED FOR EXTERNAL VALIDATION AND SEEK VALIDATION FROM WITHIN.

In a society driven by external validation, it is vital to cultivate a sense of self-worth that is not reliant on others' approval. Seeking validation from within allows us to tap into our inner wisdom, recognize our inherent value, and experience a deep sense of self-acceptance and empowerment. In this section, we will explore a comprehensive collection of affirmations that will support you in releasing the need for external validation and embracing the validation that comes from within.

1. I release the need for external validation and find validation within myself.

2. I acknowledge that my worth is not determined by others' opinions or judgments.

3. I trust my own intuition and inner guidance to make decisions aligned with my highest good.

4. I embrace my unique qualities and recognize that they contribute to my worthiness.

5. I am confident in my abilities and trust in my own judgment and decision-making.

6. I validate myself by acknowledging and celebrating my achievements, no matter how small.

7. I recognize that seeking validation from within allows me to experience true fulfillment and contentment.

8.   I release the belief that my worth depends on others' recognition or approval.

9.   I celebrate my individuality and honor the path that I am on, regardless of external validation.

10. I affirm that my value lies in my authenticity and the unique contributions I bring to the world.

11. I trust in my own capabilities and have faith in my ability to navigate life's challenges.

12. I release the need to compare myself to others and focus on my own growth and progress.

13. I am enough just as I am, and I do not need external validation to validate my worthiness.

14. I validate myself through self-compassion and treating myself with kindness and understanding.

15. I affirm that my worthiness is inherent and does not depend on external achievements or accolades.

16. I recognize that seeking validation from within empowers me to live a life true to myself.

17. I let go of the need to seek approval from others and find validation in my own self-acceptance.

18. I embrace self-love and self-acceptance as the ultimate sources of validation in my life.

19. I validate myself by aligning my actions with my values and living in integrity with my true self.

20. I release the fear of judgment and trust in the power of my own self-validation.

21. I am worthy of love, respect, and success, regardless of others' opinions or validation.

22. I validate myself by honoring my own needs, desires, and aspirations.

23. I affirm that my worthiness is not contingent upon external achievements, but on my inner essence.

24. I trust in my own journey and know that seeking validation from within leads to authentic fulfillment.

25. I am whole and complete within myself, and I validate my own worthiness through self-acceptance and self-love.

These affirmations are powerful tools to release the need for external validation and to seek validation from within. Practice them regularly and reflect on how embracing self-validation empowers you to live a life aligned with your true self. Remember that your worthiness is not dependent on others' opinions or approval but is inherent and deserving. Trust in your own inner wisdom, celebrate your unique qualities, and find validation from within as you embark on a journey of self-acceptance and empowerment.

AFFIRMATIONS FOR CULTIVATING A POSITIVE BODY IMAGE.

Cultivating a positive body image is essential for our overall well-being and self-acceptance. In a world that often promotes unrealistic beauty standards, it is crucial to develop a healthy and compassionate relationship with our bodies. Affirmations can be powerful tools to shift our mindset, challenge negative beliefs, and foster a positive perception of our physical selves. In this section, we will explore a comprehensive collection of affirmations designed to help you cultivate a positive body image and embrace self-love and acceptance.

1. I love and appreciate my body unconditionally, just as it is in this moment.

2. My body is a unique and beautiful vessel that allows me to experience life fully.

3. I choose to focus on the qualities and abilities of my body rather than its perceived flaws.

4. I embrace my body's natural shape and honor its individuality.

5. I am grateful for the strength and resilience that my body possesses.

6. I nourish my body with love, healthy choices, and self-care practices.

7. I release the need to compare my body to others and embrace my own unique beauty.

8. I affirm that my worth is not defined by my physical appearance but by the person I am inside.

9. I honor and respect my body's boundaries, and I listen to its needs with compassion.

10. I celebrate my body's ability to heal, adapt, and support me in all aspects of life.

11. I choose to see beauty in all shapes, sizes, and forms, including my own.

12. I appreciate the functionality of my body and the incredible ways it enables me to move, explore, and engage with the world.

13. I release negative judgments about my body and replace them with empowering and loving thoughts.

14. I am deserving of self-care, including taking time to nurture and care for my physical body.

15. I acknowledge that my body is an ever-changing masterpiece, and I embrace its evolution with love and acceptance.

16. I choose to surround myself with positive influences that support a healthy body image and self-acceptance.

17. I release the need for external validation and find validation and acceptance from within.

18. I recognize that my body's worth is not tied to societal standards but is inherent and deserving of love and respect.

19. I treat my body with kindness, compassion, and gentle care.

20. I am grateful for the unique qualities and features that make my body one-of-a-kind.

21. I release the urge to engage in negative self-talk and replace it with affirming and uplifting words.

22. I embrace my body as a sacred temple and honor it with self-love and acceptance.

23. I choose to see myself through the lens of love, appreciating my body's beauty and strengths.

24. I let go of the need for perfection and embrace my body's imperfections as a part of my unique journey.

25. I am more than my physical appearance. I am a radiant being, worthy of love and acceptance.

These affirmations are tools for shifting your perspective and cultivating a positive body image. Practice them regularly, and reflect on the changes they bring to your thoughts, feelings, and actions. Remember that your body is a vessel that carries you through life's experiences, and it deserves love, acceptance, and appreciation. Embrace your unique beauty, honor your body's needs, and celebrate the incredible ways it supports you. By nurturing a positive body image, you can cultivate a deep sense of self-love and acceptance that extends beyond physical appearance.

AFFIRMATIONS FOR EMBRACING CHANGE AND ADAPTING TO YOUR EVOLVING SELF-IMAGE.

Change is an inevitable part of life, and as we grow and evolve, our self-image may shift and transform. Embracing change and adapting to our evolving self-image requires flexibility, self-compassion, and a willingness to let go of old beliefs and patterns. Affirmations can serve as powerful tools to support us in this process, enabling us to embrace change with grace and create a positive and empowering self-image. In this section, we will explore a comprehensive collection of affirmations designed to help you navigate change, adapt to your evolving self-image, and cultivate a mindset of growth and self-acceptance.

1. I welcome change as an opportunity for growth and self-discovery.

2. I embrace the journey of self-transformation and trust in my ability to navigate change with grace.

3. I release the need to cling to old self-images and open myself up to new possibilities and experiences.

4. I am open and receptive to the lessons and insights that change brings into my life.

5. I acknowledge that change is a natural part of my journey, and I embrace it with courage and resilience.

6. I am not defined by my past self-image; I am constantly evolving and becoming the best version of myself.

7. I release the fear of judgment and criticism as I embrace my ever-changing self-image.

8. I affirm that my worth is not dependent on a static self-image but on the love and acceptance I cultivate within myself.

9. I trust in the process of change and believe that it is guiding me towards greater self-awareness and personal growth.

10. I let go of attachments to external validation and find validation from within as I embrace my evolving self-image.

11. I celebrate the uniqueness of my evolving self-image and recognize it as a testament to my growth and self-acceptance.

12. I am flexible and adaptable, allowing myself to flow with the changes that life presents to me.

13. I release resistance to change and welcome the new opportunities and possibilities that it brings into my life.

14. I choose to focus on the positive aspects of my evolving self-image and honor the progress I have made.

15. I am grateful for the experiences that have shaped my self-image and have contributed to my personal growth.

16. I embrace change as an opportunity to redefine and realign my values, beliefs, and aspirations.

17. I trust in my inner wisdom to guide me through the process of adapting to my evolving self-image.

18. I release the need for perfection and embrace the beauty of imperfection in my evolving self-image.

19. I am patient and compassionate with myself as I navigate the changes in my self-image.

20. I am deserving of love and acceptance, regardless of any fluctuations in my self-image.

21. I affirm that change is a catalyst for personal transformation, and I am grateful for the growth it brings into my life.

22. I release self-judgment and comparison as I honor and celebrate my unique journey and evolving self-image.

23. I choose to view change as an opportunity for self-expression and self-empowerment.

24. I am confident in my ability to adapt and adjust to the changes in my self-image.

25. I embrace change as an invitation to align my self-image with my true and authentic self.

These affirmations are tools for embracing change and adapting to your evolving self-image. Use them as daily reminders, repeat them with conviction, and integrate them into your self-care practices. Reflect on the shifts and transformations they bring to your mindset and self-perception. Embracing change requires patience, self-compassion, and an openness to growth. By nurturing a mindset of adaptability and self-acceptance, you can navigate the journey of self-transformation with grace and create a positive and empowering self-image that aligns with your authentic self.

CONCLUSION AND ENCOURAGEMENT TO PRACTICE DAILY AFFIRMATIONS FOR CONTINUED GROWTH AND SELF-EMPOWERMENT.

Throughout this chapter, we have delved into the transformative power of affirmations and explored various affirmations in different areas of personal development. We have discussed the importance of nurturing a healthy relationship with oneself, embracing authenticity, practicing self-care, and cultivating a positive self-image. These affirmations, rooted in the wisdom of Louise Hay and Rhonda Byrne, are designed to empower you on your journey of self-discovery and personal growth. In this final section, we will summarize the key points covered and provide encouragement for incorporating daily affirmations into your life for continued growth and self-empowerment.

Summary:

In this chapter, we have explored the profound impact that affirmations can have on our mindset, self-perception, and overall well-being. We have recognized the limitations of equating self-worth solely with external factors such as physical appearance, fashion choices, or societal validation. Instead, we have emphasized the importance of nurturing inner beauty, embracing authenticity, and cultivating a holistic view of self-worth. We have explored affirmations for various aspects of personal development, including nurturing a healthy relationship with food and exercise, embracing personal style and fashion choices, embracing and expressing your authentic self, practicing self-care, loving your flaws and imperfections, strengthening your mindset and resilience, releasing the need for external validation, and cultivating a positive body image. Additionally, we have discussed affirmations for embracing change and adapting to your evolving self-image.

Encouragement to Practice Daily Affirmations:

✧   As you conclude this chapter, I encourage you to integrate the practice of daily affirmations into your life for continued growth and self-empowerment. Consistency is key when it comes to affirmations, as they require ongoing repetition and reinforcement to reprogram your subconscious mind and shift your beliefs. Here are some steps and strategies to help you incorporate daily affirmations into your routine:

✧   Set a daily affirmation practice: Dedicate a specific time each day to engage in your affirmation practice. It could be in the morning upon waking up, during a meditation session, or before going to bed. Consistency is important, so choose a time that works best for you and stick to it.

✦ Create a sacred space: Designate a quiet and peaceful space where you can practice your affirmations without distractions. This space could be a corner in your room, a cozy nook, or a serene outdoor spot. Fill it with items that inspire and uplift you, such as candles, crystals, or meaningful objects.

✦ Choose affirmations that resonate with you: Select affirmations that resonate with your personal journey and aspirations. Consider the areas of self-development that are most important to you and choose affirmations that align with those goals. You can refer back to the affirmations provided in this chapter or create your own based on your unique needs and desires.

✦ Repeat affirmations with intention and belief: When practicing your affirmations, do so with intention and conviction. Speak the affirmations aloud or silently, and infuse them with positive energy and belief. Visualize yourself embodying the qualities and experiences described in the affirmations.

✦ Write and journal about your affirmations: Consider keeping a journal to document your affirmation practice. Write down your chosen affirmations, reflect on their meaning, and record any insights or shifts in your mindset and self-perception. Journaling can deepen your connection with the affirmations and help you track your progress over time.

✦ Incorporate affirmations into daily activities: Find ways to integrate affirmations into your daily activities. You can write them on sticky notes and place them where you will see them frequently, create affirmation cards to carry with you, or recite them silently during moments of self-reflection or challenge.

✦ Stay open to growth and transformation: Remember that personal growth is a lifelong journey. Be open to new possibilities, embrace change, and allow yourself to evolve. As you continue practicing affirmations, observe how they influence your thoughts, emotions, and actions. Celebrate your progress and be gentle with yourself during times of difficulty or setbacks.

Conclusion:

In conclusion, affirmations are powerful tools that can positively impact your mindset, self-perception, and overall well-being. By incorporating daily affirmations into your life, you can continue to nurture your personal development, cultivate self-empowerment, and create a life aligned with your authentic self. Remember that the journey of self-discovery and growth is unique to each individual, and it requires dedication, patience, and self-compassion. Embrace the wisdom of Louise Hay and Rhonda Byrne, and let affirmations be your guiding light on the path to self-empowerment and a fulfilling life.

Exercises:

1. Choose three affirmations from this chapter that resonate with you the most. Reflect on why they are significant to you and how you can integrate them into your daily life.

2. Create a personalized affirmation based on an aspect of self-development that you would like to focus on. Write it down and repeat it daily for the next week. Journal about any shifts or insights you experience during this period.

3. Research and explore affirmations from other fields such as Witchcraft, Divination, Herbalism, Shamanism, or Ecospirituality. Choose one affirmation that intrigues you and reflect on how it aligns with your personal journey. Write a brief analysis of the affirmation and its potential impact on your mindset and self-empowerment.

BEAUTY AND SELF-IMAGE:

Welcome to the captivating exploration of beauty and self-image. In this chapter, we will embark on a profound journey to understand the multifaceted nature of beauty, the influence of societal standards, and the power of self-perception. Drawing inspiration from various fields, including Witchcraft, Divination, Herbalism, Shamanism, and Ecospirituality, we will delve into the complex interplay between external appearances, inner beauty, and the cultivation of a positive self-image.

The Concept of Beauty:

Beauty, a concept as ancient as human existence itself, has undergone numerous transformations throughout history. Often perceived as a subjective quality, beauty encompasses much more than physical attractiveness. It extends to our emotions, actions, and overall energy, radiating from within and impacting our interactions with the world. While societal standards may attempt to define beauty within narrow parameters, it is essential to recognize that true beauty transcends mere aesthetics.

Self-Image and its Significance:

Self-image refers to the mental picture we hold of ourselves, encompassing our perceptions, beliefs, and feelings about our appearance, abilities, and worthiness. It plays a pivotal role in shaping our self-esteem, confidence, and overall well-being. Cultivating a positive self-image is a powerful practice that allows us to embrace our unique qualities, celebrate our strengths, and nurture a deep sense of self-acceptance.

Societal Influences and Beauty Standards:

Throughout history, societal influences and beauty standards have exerted significant pressure on individuals to conform to specific ideals of beauty. These standards are often perpetuated by media, culture, and social norms, creating unrealistic expectations and fostering a sense of inadequacy. It is crucial to critically examine these influences, challenge their validity, and develop a conscious awareness of our own unique beauty.

Embracing Diversity and Inclusivity:

In recent years, there has been a growing movement towards embracing diversity and challenging traditional beauty norms. This movement acknowledges and celebrates the inherent beauty present in individuals of all races, body types, genders, and abilities. By embracing inclusivity, we foster a culture of acceptance, allowing each person to feel valued and beautiful in their own unique way.

The Power of Self-Perception:

Our perception of ourselves holds immense power in shaping our reality and overall well-being. When we cultivate a positive self-perception, we radiate confidence, authenticity, and inner beauty. Through practices such as self-care, self-love, and self-compassion, we can nurture a harmonious relationship with our bodies, minds, and spirits, and embody our true essence.

Exercises:

Reflect on your personal definition of beauty and how it has been influenced by societal standards. Write a journal entry exploring your thoughts, feelings, and experiences related to beauty.

Engage in a self-image makeover exercise. Create a collage or vision board that celebrates your unique qualities, strengths, and aspirations. Display it in a prominent place as a reminder of your beauty and potential.

Research and analyze the portrayal of beauty in different cultures and historical periods. Write a comparative analysis highlighting the diverse perspectives and values associated with beauty.

Conclusion:
As we embark on this journey of exploring beauty and self-image, it is crucial to approach it with an open mind, a critical eye, and a compassionate heart. Throughout this chapter, we will navigate the intricate landscape of beauty, challenging societal norms, embracing diversity, and cultivating a positive self-image. By understanding the multifaceted nature of beauty and nurturing our inner radiance, we can embark on a transformative path towards self-acceptance, self-love, and true beauty.

AFFIRMATIONS AIMED AT ENHANCING SELF-ESTEEM, SELF-LOVE, AND EMBRACING INNER AND OUTER BEAUTY.

Welcome to a transformative exploration of affirmations aimed at enhancing self-esteem, self-love, and embracing both inner and outer beauty. In this chapter, we will delve into the profound power of affirmations and their ability to shift our beliefs, perceptions, and self-image. Drawing inspiration from various fields, including Witchcraft, Divination, Herbalism, Shamanism, and Ecospirituality, we will uncover the intricacies of self-esteem, the significance of self-love, and the profound connection between our inner essence and outer beauty.

Understanding Self-Esteem:

Self-esteem is the foundation upon which our sense of worthiness, confidence, and personal value is built. It reflects our overall evaluation of ourselves and influences how we perceive and interact with the world around us. Cultivating a healthy self-esteem is crucial for our emotional well-being, personal growth, and ability to embrace our unique beauty.

The Power of Self-Love:

Self-love is a transformative practice that involves accepting, cherishing, and honoring ourselves unconditionally. It encompasses nurturing a deep sense of compassion, kindness, and forgiveness towards ourselves. By embracing self-love, we tap into a limitless wellspring of inner beauty and radiance that transcends external appearances.

The Role of Affirmations:

Affirmations are powerful tools for self-transformation and personal empowerment. These positive statements, repeated consistently and with intention, can reshape our beliefs, thoughts, and self-perception. Affirmations serve as powerful reminders of our inherent worthiness, beauty, and potential, allowing us to overcome self-doubt and embrace our true essence.

Embracing Inner Beauty:

Inner beauty goes beyond external appearances, reflecting the qualities of our character, values, and energy. It is a reflection of our authenticity, kindness, and compassion. By affirming our inner beauty, we connect with the core of our being and radiate a genuine beauty that transcends societal expectations.

Appreciating Outer Beauty:

Outer beauty encompasses our physical appearance and how we choose to express ourselves in the world. It is a canvas through which our inner essence is manifested. Affirmations for outer beauty focus on embracing and enhancing our unique physical attributes, celebrating our individuality, and expressing ourselves authentically.

Exercises:

Create a list of positive affirmations tailored to enhance your self-esteem, self-love, and embrace both your inner and outer beauty. Repeat them daily and reflect on any shifts or insights that arise.

Practice mirror work by looking into your own eyes and affirming your beauty, worthiness, and unique qualities. Notice any resistance or discomfort that arises and explore the underlying beliefs behind it.

Engage in a gratitude journaling exercise where you write down three things you appreciate about your inner beauty and three things you appreciate about your outer beauty each day. Cultivate a sense of gratitude and appreciation for your inherent beauty.

Conclusion:

As we embark on this transformative journey of exploring affirmations for enhancing self-esteem, self-love, and embracing inner and outer beauty, let us remember that true beauty radiates from within. By harnessing the power of positive affirmations, we can shift our beliefs, perceptions, and self-image, ultimately embracing our unique beauty and living a life of self-empowerment and authenticity.

UNDERSTANDING THE CONCEPT OF BEAUTY BEYOND SOCIETAL STANDARDS.

In this section, we will explore the concept of beauty beyond societal standards and delve into the profound impact these standards have on our self-perception, self-worth, and overall well-being. By drawing insights from various fields, including Witchcraft, Divination, Herbalism, Shamanism, and Ecospirituality, we will analyze the limitations of societal beauty norms and uncover alternative perspectives that embrace a more inclusive and empowering understanding of beauty.

The Influence of Societal Beauty Standards:

Societal beauty standards are a set of culturally constructed ideals that dictate what is considered beautiful or attractive within a given society. These standards are often influenced by media, advertising, and cultural norms, and they can create a narrow definition of beauty that excludes and marginalizes individuals who do not fit within these predetermined criteria. The impact of societal beauty standards can be profound, leading to feelings of inadequacy, low self-esteem, and a distorted perception of one's own beauty.

Challenging Societal Beauty Norms:

It is essential to question and challenge societal beauty norms to foster a more inclusive and empowering understanding of beauty. By recognizing that beauty is subjective and multifaceted, we can embrace a broader range of qualities and attributes that contribute to one's unique beauty. This shift in perspective allows us to celebrate diversity, challenge stereotypes, and cultivate a more inclusive and compassionate society.

Embracing Individuality and Authenticity:

Beauty extends beyond external appearances and should be acknowledged as a reflection of one's individuality and authenticity. Each person possesses a unique combination of physical features, personality traits, talents, and inner qualities that contribute to their overall beauty. By embracing our individuality and honoring our authentic selves, we can cultivate a sense of self-acceptance and self-love that transcends societal beauty standards.

The Power of Self-Perception:

Our perception of beauty is deeply influenced by our beliefs, thoughts, and self-image. By nurturing a positive self-perception and cultivating self-compassion, we can shift our focus from external validation to internal validation. This shift allows us to recognize and appreciate our own beauty independent of societal judgments and expectations.

Exercises:

Reflect on the societal beauty standards that have influenced your self-perception. Identify any negative beliefs or judgments you hold about yourself based on these standards. Challenge these beliefs by affirming your inherent worthiness and embracing a more inclusive understanding of beauty.

Engage in a media detox by consciously limiting your exposure to media messages that promote narrow beauty ideals. Instead, seek out diverse representations of beauty in various forms of media, such as literature, art, and online platforms that celebrate inclusivity and authenticity.

Practice self-compassion by cultivating a daily self-care routine that honors your unique needs and preferences. Engage in activities that make you feel good about yourself and reinforce your self-worth.

Conclusion:

By understanding the concept of beauty beyond societal standards, we open ourselves up to a world of possibilities and embrace a more authentic and empowering perception of our own beauty. As we challenge and transcend societal beauty norms, we pave the way for a more inclusive and compassionate society where individuals are valued for their unique qualities and contributions. Let us embark on this journey of self-discovery and self-acceptance, celebrating the beauty that resides within each of us.

EMBRACING SELF-ACCEPTANCE AND CELEBRATING YOUR UNIQUE FEATURES.

In this section, we will explore the importance of self-acceptance and the celebration of our unique features. Society often imposes unrealistic beauty standards that can negatively impact our self-esteem and self-worth. By drawing insights from various fields, including Witchcraft, Divination, Herbalism, Shamanism, and Ecospirituality, we will delve into practices and affirmations that promote self-acceptance and encourage us to embrace our individuality and unique features.

Understanding Self-Acceptance:

Self-acceptance is the act of recognizing and embracing all aspects of oneself, including physical appearance, personality traits, strengths, and weaknesses. It involves letting go of self-judgment and cultivating a compassionate and non-judgmental attitude towards ourselves. Embracing self-acceptance allows us to fully appreciate and celebrate our unique features without comparing ourselves to unrealistic societal ideals.

Shifting Perspectives on Beauty:

To truly embrace self-acceptance, it is crucial to shift our perspectives on beauty. Instead of conforming to external standards, we can redefine beauty as a reflection of our individuality and authenticity. Our unique features, whether physical or personal, are what make us special and should be celebrated rather than diminished. By valuing our differences, we create a more inclusive and accepting society.

Affirmations for Self-Acceptance and Celebration:

Affirmations are powerful tools that can help reshape our beliefs and thoughts. By repeating positive affirmations, we reinforce self-acceptance and celebrate our unique features. Here are some affirmations you can incorporate into your daily practice:

1. "I embrace and celebrate my unique features, recognizing that they contribute to my authentic beauty."

2. "I release comparison and embrace self-acceptance, knowing that my worth is not determined by external standards."

3. "I love and appreciate every aspect of myself, including my physical appearance and personality traits."

4. "I choose to see beauty in diversity and celebrate the uniqueness of others as well as myself."

5. "I am grateful for my individuality and the special qualities that make me who I am."

Exercises:

Create a list of your unique features, both physical and personal. Reflect on each feature and identify how it contributes to your overall beauty and individuality. Write down affirmations that highlight these features and incorporate them into your daily practice.

Practice self-care rituals that celebrate and nourish your unique features. This could include skincare routines, dressing in a way that expresses your personal style, or engaging in activities that bring out your unique talents and strengths.

Engage in mirror work exercises, where you look into a mirror and repeat affirmations that promote self-acceptance and celebrate your unique features. Observe any resistance or negative self-talk that arises and counter it with loving and positive affirmations.

Conclusion:

Embracing self-acceptance and celebrating our unique features is a transformative journey that allows us to fully appreciate and love ourselves. By shifting our perspectives on beauty, incorporating affirmations, and engaging in self-care practices, we cultivate a deep sense of self-acceptance and inner beauty. Let us embrace our individuality and celebrate the unique features that make us who we are, contributing to a more accepting and inclusive world.

CULTIVATING SELF-LOVE AND COMPASSION FOR YOUR PHYSICAL APPEARANCE.

In this section, we will explore the importance of cultivating self-love and compassion for our physical appearance. Society often promotes unrealistic beauty standards, leading many individuals to feel inadequate or dissatisfied with their bodies. Drawing insights from various fields, including Witchcraft, Divination, Herbalism, Shamanism, and Ecospirituality, we will delve into practices and affirmations that promote self-love and foster a compassionate relationship with our physical selves.

Understanding Self-Love and Compassion:

Self-love is the practice of embracing and nurturing oneself with kindness, acceptance, and appreciation. It involves recognizing our inherent worth and treating ourselves with the same compassion and care we would extend to others. Cultivating self-love allows us to develop a positive relationship with our physical appearance, fostering a sense of inner beauty and contentment.

Shifting Perceptions of Beauty:

To cultivate self-love and compassion for our physical appearance, we must challenge societal perceptions of beauty. Beauty should not be limited to narrow standards dictated by external forces. Instead, we can redefine beauty as a multifaceted concept that encompasses individuality, diversity, and authenticity. By embracing our unique physical attributes and appreciating their inherent beauty, we empower ourselves to love and accept our bodies.

Affirmations for Self-Love and Compassion:

Affirmations are powerful tools that can transform our thoughts and beliefs. By incorporating positive affirmations into our daily practice, we reinforce self-love and cultivate compassion for our physical appearance. Here are some affirmations you can integrate into your routine:

1. "I love and appreciate my body, recognizing its beauty and resilience."

2. "I embrace my unique physical features and celebrate the diversity of human bodies."

3.   "I am deserving of love and acceptance, regardless of societal beauty standards."

4.   "I am grateful for my body's ability to carry me through life and provide me with experiences."

5.   "I honor and care for my body, nourishing it with kindness, healthy choices, and self-care."

Exercises:

Body Appreciation Journal: Create a journal dedicated to documenting aspects of your physical appearance that you appreciate and love. Each day, write down at least three things you admire about your body. This practice helps shift your focus towards self-love and appreciation.

Mirror Affirmations: Stand in front of a mirror and look at yourself with loving eyes. Repeat affirmations that promote self-love and compassion for your physical appearance. Observe any resistance or negative self-talk that arises and counter it with affirmations of kindness and acceptance.

Self-Care Rituals: Engage in self-care activities that nourish and celebrate your physical body. This could include indulging in a relaxing bath, practicing gentle stretches or yoga, or pampering yourself with skincare routines. By prioritizing self-care, you send a message of love and appreciation to your body.

Conclusion:

Cultivating self-love and compassion for our physical appearance is a journey of acceptance, appreciation, and inner growth. By shifting our perceptions of beauty, incorporating affirmations, and practicing self-care rituals, we develop a nurturing relationship with our bodies. Let us embrace our unique physical attributes, celebrate diversity, and extend compassion and love to ourselves. Through self-love, we can unlock a sense of deep contentment and radiate our inner beauty to the world.

RECOGNIZING THE POWER OF INNER BEAUTY AND CHARACTER TRAITS.

In this section, we will explore the concept of inner beauty and the profound impact it can have on our lives. While society often emphasizes external appearances, the fields of Witchcraft, Divination, Herbalism, Shamanism, and Ecospirituality remind us that true beauty radiates from within. By shifting our focus to the qualities that make us unique and embracing our character traits, we can cultivate a deep sense of inner beauty and harness its transformative power.

Understanding Inner Beauty:

Inner beauty refers to the qualities and virtues that emanate from within a person. It encompasses attributes such as kindness, compassion, empathy, resilience, wisdom, and authenticity. Unlike external beauty, which is subjective and fleeting, inner beauty has a lasting impact on our relationships, well-being, and personal growth. Recognizing and cultivating inner beauty empowers us to lead fulfilling lives and make meaningful connections with others.

The Power of Character Traits:

Our character traits shape who we are at our core. They are the fundamental qualities that define our individuality and contribute to our personal growth. By acknowledging and nurturing these traits, we tap into our inner beauty and create a positive impact on ourselves and the world around us. Character traits such as integrity, honesty, generosity, and perseverance not only enhance our interactions with others but also inspire and uplift those around us.

Embracing Inner Beauty and Character Traits:

To recognize and harness the power of inner beauty and character traits, we must cultivate self-awareness and engage in intentional practices. Here are some strategies to embrace and nurture your inner beauty:

✧   Self-Reflection: Take time to reflect on your character traits and identify the qualities that resonate with you. Consider your strengths, values, and virtues that you admire in yourself and others. This self-reflection helps deepen your understanding of your inner beauty and highlights areas for growth.

✧   Practicing Gratitude: Cultivate gratitude for the character traits and qualities that make you unique. Regularly express appreciation for the virtues you possess and the positive impact they have on your life and the lives of others. Gratitude enhances self-acceptance and amplifies your inner beauty.

✧   Mindful Action: Incorporate your character traits into your daily actions. Intentionally practice kindness, compassion, and empathy in your interactions with others. Engage in acts of service that align with your values and character strengths. Mindful action allows your inner beauty to shine through your words and deeds.

✧   Affirmations: Use affirmations to reinforce and amplify your character traits and inner beauty. Repeat affirmations that affirm the qualities you embody, such as "I am compassionate and kind-hearted" or "My wisdom and authenticity inspire others." Affirmations help rewire your mindset and align your thoughts with your inner beauty.

Exercises:

Character Strengths Assessment: Take a character strengths assessment, such as the VIA Character Strengths Survey, to identify your core virtues and character traits. Reflect on how these strengths manifest in your life and explore ways to further develop and utilize them.

Acts of Kindness: Engage in daily acts of kindness that reflect your character traits. It could be as simple as offering a helping hand, practicing active listening, or expressing appreciation to others. Notice how these actions align with your inner beauty and contribute to your overall well-being.

Inner Beauty Journal: Create an inner beauty journal to document moments when your character traits shine through. Write about experiences where your virtues positively impacted yourself or others. Regularly review your journal to reinforce the significance of your inner beauty.

Conclusion:

Recognizing and embracing the power of inner beauty and character traits enables us to cultivate a deep sense of self-worth and positively impact the world around us. By shifting our focus from external appearances to the qualities that make us unique, we tap into the transformative potential of our inner beauty. Through self-reflection, gratitude, mindful action, and affirmations, we nurture and amplify our character traits, allowing our inner beauty to radiate and inspire others. Embrace your inner beauty, for it is a profound source of personal growth, connection, and positive change.

LETTING GO OF COMPARISONS AND EMBRACING YOUR INDIVIDUALITY.

In this section, we will delve into the detrimental effects of comparisons and the importance of embracing your individuality. In a society that often values conformity and sets unrealistic standards, it is crucial to understand the significance of celebrating your unique qualities and rejecting the harmful habit of comparing yourself to others. Drawing insights from fields such as Witchcraft, Divination, Herbalism, Shamanism, and Ecospirituality, we will explore strategies to release comparisons and nurture a deep appreciation for your own individuality.

The Pitfalls of Comparisons:

Comparisons are a common human tendency, fueled by societal influences, media portrayals, and the desire for validation. However, constant comparisons can lead to feelings of inadequacy, self-doubt, and a distorted self-image. By measuring ourselves against others, we undermine our self-worth and hinder our personal growth. It is important to recognize the limitations of comparisons and redirect our focus towards embracing our own unique qualities.

Appreciating Your Individuality:

Your individuality encompasses the amalgamation of your experiences, talents, strengths, passions, and perspectives that make you distinctly you. By appreciating and honoring your individuality, you acknowledge your inherent worth and cultivate a deep sense of self-acceptance and self-love. Embracing your individuality empowers you to live authentically, unleash your full potential, and make meaningful contributions to the world.

Strategies for Letting Go of Comparisons:

Self-Awareness: Cultivate self-awareness to recognize when you engage in comparisons. Notice the triggers and underlying beliefs that fuel these comparisons. By becoming conscious of your thought patterns, you can interrupt the cycle of comparison and choose to focus on your own unique journey.

Gratitude for Uniqueness: Practice gratitude for your individuality. Make a list of your strengths, talents, and qualities that make you unique. Express appreciation for these attributes and acknowledge the value they bring to your life and the lives of others.

Reframing Perspectives: Challenge societal standards and societal norms that promote comparison. Understand that each person's journey is unique, and external appearances or achievements do not define true worth. Shift your perspective to focus on inner growth, personal development, and the qualities that truly matter.

Embracing Uniqueness: Celebrate your individuality by pursuing activities, hobbies, and interests that align with your authentic self. Allow yourself to express your true passions and embrace your own path without comparing it to others.

Exercises:

Comparison Detox: Engage in a comparison detox for a designated period. During this time, consciously refrain from comparing yourself to others in any aspect of life. Notice the impact it has on your self-perception and well-being.

Mirror Work: Incorporate mirror work into your daily routine. Stand in front of a mirror, look into your eyes, and affirm your individuality and uniqueness. Practice self-compassion and repeat affirmations such as "I am worthy and whole just as I am."

Personal Strengths Exploration: Explore your personal strengths and qualities through activities such as journaling or self-assessment tools. Identify your unique attributes and reflect on how you can further develop and leverage them to enhance your personal growth and contribute to your goals.

Conclusion:

Letting go of comparisons and embracing your individuality is a powerful journey of self-discovery and self-acceptance. By recognizing the pitfalls of comparisons, appreciating your individuality, and implementing strategies to release comparisons, you pave the way for a more fulfilling and authentic life. Embrace your uniqueness, for it is the essence of your true self and the source of your personal growth and empowerment.

1. I am unique and I celebrate my individuality.

2. I release the need to compare myself to others and focus on my own path.

3. I embrace my own strengths and talents, knowing that they make me special.

4. I am on my own journey, and I trust that it is perfect for me.

Empowered Affirmations

5. I let go of the pressure to fit into societal expectations and choose to be authentic.

6. I acknowledge that comparing myself to others only limits my own growth and happiness.

7. I am worthy and deserving of love and success, just as I am.

8. I celebrate the diversity and beauty of the world, knowing that we are all unique.

9. I appreciate and honor the qualities that make me different from others.

10. I release the need to conform and instead embrace my own individual expression.

11. I trust in my own abilities and believe in my own unique gifts.

12. I am confident in my own path and trust that it will lead me to where I need to be.

13. I let go of the need for approval from others and accept myself fully.

14. I am free to be myself and express my true nature without fear of judgment.

15. I compare myself only to my own potential and strive to be the best version of myself.

16. I let go of the idea of perfection and embrace my beautiful imperfections.

17. I am comfortable in my own skin and appreciate my own unique beauty.

18. I recognize that comparing myself to others robs me of the joy of being myself.

19. I am confident in my own worth and do not need validation from others.

20. I honor my own journey and trust that it is unfolding perfectly for me.

21. I embrace my own voice and ideas, knowing that they have value.

22. I release the need to compete with others and instead focus on my own growth and happiness.

23. I choose to see the beauty in diversity and appreciate the gifts of others without comparison.

24. I let go of the need to be like anyone else and embrace my own authentic self.

25. I celebrate the uniqueness within me and know that it adds beauty to the world.

AFFIRMING CONFIDENCE AND RADIANCE FROM WITHIN.

In this section, we will explore the transformative power of affirmations in cultivating confidence and radiance from within. Drawing insights from a diverse range of fields, including Witchcraft, Divination, Herbalism, Shamanism, and Ecospirituality, we will delve into the profound impact that positive self-talk can have on our mindset, self-perception, and overall well-being. By understanding the science behind affirmations and practicing specific techniques, we can harness our inner strength, radiate confidence, and manifest a positive self-image.

Understanding Affirmations:

Affirmations are positive statements that are consciously repeated to shift our thoughts, beliefs, and emotions. They are powerful tools for rewiring the neural pathways in our brains and reframing our self-perception. By consistently affirming positive qualities, we can align our conscious and subconscious minds, enhancing our self-confidence and radiating an inner glow.

The Science of Affirmations:

Neuroscience research reveals that affirmations influence the brain's neural networks and activate the reward centers responsible for positive emotions. When we repeat affirmations, we engage the brain's neuroplasticity, leading to the formation of new connections that support empowering beliefs and thoughts. Additionally, affirmations can counteract the impact of negative self-talk and enhance our self-perception, boosting confidence and radiance from within.

Affirmations for Confidence and Radiance:

1. Embracing Self-Worth: "I am worthy of love, respect, and success. I radiate confidence and self-assurance."

2. Owning Inner Strength: "I am resilient and capable of overcoming challenges. My inner strength empowers me to navigate any situation with confidence."

3. Unleashing Authenticity: "I embrace my true self and express my uniqueness with confidence. I radiate authenticity and inspire others to do the same."

4. Embracing Imperfections: "I love and accept myself unconditionally, embracing my flaws and imperfections. They are a part of my unique beauty and journey."

5. Cultivating Self-Compassion: "I show myself compassion and kindness in all moments. I honor my journey and treat myself with love and understanding."

Exercises:

Mirror Affirmations: Stand in front of a mirror, look into your eyes, and affirm your positive qualities and radiance. Repeat empowering affirmations that resonate with you, such as those mentioned above. Practice this exercise daily to reinforce self-confidence and radiance.

Affirmation Journaling: Create an affirmation journal to record positive statements about yourself. Write down affirmations that reflect your desired qualities, such as confidence, radiance, and self-acceptance. Read them aloud and reflect on their meaning and impact.

Visualization Meditation: Engage in a guided visualization meditation where you imagine yourself embodying confidence and radiance. Visualize yourself shining with inner light and radiating positive energy. Embrace the emotions and sensations associated with this visualization, reinforcing your affirmation of confidence and radiance.

Conclusion:

Affirmations serve as powerful tools to affirm our confidence and radiance from within. By understanding the science behind affirmations and incorporating them into our daily practice, we can transform our self-perception and radiate a confident and radiant presence. Embrace the practice of affirmations, cultivate positive self-talk, and witness the profound impact it has on your overall well-being, self-image, and interactions with others.

1. I radiate confidence from the depths of my being.

2. I am worthy of love, success, and happiness.

3. My inner radiance shines brightly, illuminating my path.

4. I am confident in expressing my authentic self.

5. I embrace my strengths and use them to create positive change in the world.

6. I am beautiful, both inside and out.

7. I trust in my abilities and know that I can overcome any challenge.

8. I let go of self-doubt and embrace self-belief.

9. I attract positive energy and opportunities into my life.

10. I stand tall and proud, knowing my worth and value.

11. My confidence grows stronger with each new experience.

12. I am comfortable in my own skin and celebrate my uniqueness.

13. I release the need for external validation and find validation within myself.

14. I exude confidence and inspire others to do the same.

15. I deserve to be seen and heard, and I claim my space in the world.

16. I trust my intuition and make decisions with confidence.

17. I am a magnet for abundance and success.

18. I embrace my imperfections and see them as part of my unique beauty.

19. I radiate positive energy, uplifting those around me.

20. I let go of comparison and focus on my own journey of growth.

21. I am deserving of all the good things that come into my life.

22. I release the fear of judgment and embrace my authentic self.

23. I am confident in my choices and stand firm in my convictions.

24. I celebrate my accomplishments and acknowledge my progress.

25. I am a powerful being, capable of achieving greatness.

NURTURING A POSITIVE BODY IMAGE AND PRACTICING SELF-CARE.

In this section, we will explore the profound impact of nurturing a positive body image and practicing self-care on our overall well-being and self-perception. Drawing insights from various fields, including Witchcraft, Divination, Herbalism, Shamanism, and Ecospirituality, we will delve into the importance of self-acceptance, self-compassion, and holistic self-care practices. By understanding the connection between our physical bodies, emotions, and spirituality, we can cultivate a positive body image and enhance our overall sense of well-being.

Understanding Body Image:

Body image refers to how we perceive and feel about our physical bodies. It encompasses our thoughts, beliefs, and emotions related to our appearance, shape, and size. Society often imposes unrealistic beauty standards, leading to negative body image and diminished self-worth. However, by embracing a holistic view of our bodies and practicing self-care, we can nurture a positive body image and foster a deeper sense of self-acceptance and self-love.

The Power of Self-Care:

Self-care encompasses a range of practices that promote physical, emotional, and spiritual well-being. By engaging in self-care activities, we honor our bodies, cultivate self-compassion, and nurture a positive body image. These practices may include nourishing our bodies with wholesome foods, engaging in physical activities we enjoy, practicing mindfulness and meditation, surrounding ourselves with supportive communities, and engaging in rituals that promote self-love and self-acceptance.

Nurturing a Positive Body Image:

Embracing Gratitude for Our Bodies: Express gratitude for your body's strength, resilience, and capacity to experience life's pleasures. Recognize the uniqueness and beauty of your body, appreciating it for all it enables you to do.

Affirming Self-Love and Acceptance: Repeat affirmations that affirm your love and acceptance of your body. For example, "I love and accept my body unconditionally. I honor and appreciate its beauty and uniqueness."

Practicing Mindful Eating: Engage in mindful eating by savoring each bite, paying attention to hunger and fullness cues, and nourishing your body with foods that support its well-being. Cultivate a positive relationship with food and let go of restrictive or negative thoughts.

Engaging in Movement and Exercise: Engage in physical activities that you enjoy and that make you feel good. Move your body in ways that bring you joy, whether it's dancing, yoga, walking in nature, or engaging in a sport. Focus on the pleasure and vitality that movement brings rather than solely on appearance or weight.

Cultivating Self-Compassion: Treat yourself with kindness, understanding, and compassion. Practice self-compassion when facing body insecurities or setbacks. Remind yourself that everyone's body is unique, and you deserve love and acceptance just as you are.

Exercises:

Mirror Work: Stand in front of a mirror and practice positive self-talk. Focus on appreciating and accepting various parts of your body. Express love and gratitude for each feature and acknowledge its beauty and uniqueness.

Body Gratitude Journaling: Start a gratitude journal specifically dedicated to your body. Write down three things you appreciate about your body each day. Reflect on how these aspects contribute to your overall well-being and vitality.

Sacred Self-Care Rituals: Create self-care rituals that honor your body. This may include taking relaxing baths, giving yourself massages or pampering sessions, or engaging in body-positive affirmations while applying nourishing skincare products.

Conclusion:

Nurturing a positive body image and practicing self-care are essential for cultivating a sense of self-acceptance, self-love, and holistic well-being. By embracing gratitude, affirmations, mindful practices, and self-compassion, we can transform our relationship with our bodies and enhance our overall sense of self-worth and radiance. Embrace the journey of self-care and body acceptance, and witness the transformative power it holds in fostering a positive body image and nurturing your well-being.

Empowered Affirmations

1. I love and accept my body unconditionally.

2. My body is a vessel of strength, health, and beauty.

3. I honor and respect my body's needs and take care of it with love.

4. I choose to focus on the positive aspects of my body and appreciate its uniqueness.

5. I nourish my body with wholesome foods that support my well-being.

6. My body is deserving of love, care, and self-compassion.

7. I embrace self-care as a way to honor and nurture my body and mind.

8. I let go of comparing my body to others and celebrate my own individual beauty.

9. I am grateful for the amazing things my body allows me to do and experience.

10. I practice self-care rituals that make me feel good, both physically and mentally.

11. I release any negative thoughts or beliefs about my body and replace them with empowering ones.

12. I listen to my body's signals and give it rest when needed.

13. I am deserving of self-care and prioritize my well-being.

14. I choose to surround myself with positive influences that support my body positivity journey.

15. I celebrate the progress I have made in developing a positive body image.

16. I let go of perfection and embrace the beauty of my body's uniqueness.

17. I am grateful for my body's resilience and ability to heal itself.

18. I practice self-compassion and speak kindly to myself, especially when it comes to my body.

19. I appreciate the different shapes and sizes that bodies come in, including my own.

20. I release any judgments or criticisms of my body and choose to love it fully.

21. I take time to engage in activities that bring joy and pleasure to my body.

22. I surround myself with supportive and uplifting individuals who appreciate me for who I am, not just how I look.

23. I let go of societal beauty standards and embrace my own unique definition of beauty.

24. I focus on the things I love about my body and express gratitude for them.

25. I choose to see myself as a whole person beyond just my physical appearance, valuing my inner qualities and strengths.

AFFIRMING GRATITUDE FOR YOUR BODY AND ITS CAPABILITIES.

In this section, we will explore the profound practice of affirming gratitude for your body and its extraordinary capabilities. Drawing insights from various fields, including Witchcraft, Divination, Herbalism, Shamanism, and Ecospirituality, we will delve into the importance of recognizing and appreciating the immense value and potential of our physical bodies. By embracing gratitude, we can cultivate a deeper connection with our bodies, enhance our self-esteem, and experience profound levels of well-being.

Understanding the Power of Gratitude:

Gratitude is a transformative practice that involves acknowledging and appreciating the blessings and positive aspects of our lives. When applied to our bodies, gratitude helps us shift our focus from perceived flaws and limitations to recognizing the miraculous nature of our physical form. By affirming gratitude for our bodies and their capabilities, we can develop a more positive body image and foster a profound sense of appreciation for the vessel that allows us to navigate and experience life.

Appreciating the Miracles of Your Body:

The Marvel of Movement: Our bodies are endowed with the remarkable ability to move and engage with the world around us. Whether it be walking, dancing, or partaking in physical activities, affirm gratitude for the gift of movement and the liberation it brings to your life.

Sensory Joys: Our bodies grant us the incredible privilege of sensory perception. Take a moment to appreciate the ability to behold the vibrant hues of nature, listen to the harmonies of music, savor the flavors of delectable foods, experience the warmth of a tender touch, and inhale the scents of blooming flowers.

The Miracle of Healing: Our bodies possess an innate capacity for healing and regeneration. From minor wounds and bruises to more substantial injuries or illnesses, our bodies work ceaselessly to restore balance and well-being. Express gratitude for the healing potency of your body and its extraordinary resilience.

Vital Life Functions: Our bodies perform myriad vital functions that sustain our existence. From breathing and digestion to circulation and immune responses, these intricate processes operate effortlessly to keep us alive and thriving. Take a moment to affirm gratitude for the intricate systems that uphold the optimal functioning of your body.

Expression and Creativity: Our bodies serve as conduits for creative expression, enabling us to communicate, create art, dance, sing, and engage in diverse forms of self-expression. Embrace gratitude for the ability to convey yourself through your body and celebrate its unique capabilities.

Affirmations for Gratitude:

1. "I am deeply grateful for my body and the remarkable experiences it allows me to embrace in this world."

2. "I wholeheartedly appreciate the wondrous capabilities of my body and honor its strength and resilience."

3. "I am profoundly thankful for the gift of movement and the liberation it bestows upon my life."

4. "I express gratitude for my senses and the ecstasy they bring as I engage with the world around me."

5. "I embrace gratitude for the healing potential of my body and place my trust in its innate capacity to restore balance and well-being."

Exercises:

Gratitude Journaling: Establish a gratitude journal dedicated to acknowledging and appreciating your body's capabilities. Each day, record three aspects you are grateful for concerning your body and its functions.

Mindful Body Scan: Engage in a mindful body scan meditation, directing your attention to each part of your body with gratitude and appreciation. Observe the sensations and express gratitude for the unique abilities and functions of each body part.

Gratitude Affirmations: Create a daily affirmation practice where you repeat gratitude affirmations specifically tailored to acknowledging and appreciating your body's capabilities. Recite these affirmations in front of a mirror or transcribe them and read them aloud.

Conclusion:

By affirming gratitude for your body and its remarkable capabilities, you embark on a journey of profound self-acceptance and empowerment. Through this practice, you honor the magnificence of your physical form and develop a profound sense of reverence for its limitless potential. Embracing gratitude for your body and its capabilities enables you to nurture a positive body image, cultivate self-love, and experience the boundless joy of appreciating the miraculous gift that is your body.

1. I am grateful for my body and all the amazing things it allows me to do.

2. I appreciate the strength and resilience of my body.

3. I am thankful for my body's ability to heal and recover.

4. I am grateful for the senses that allow me to experience the world around me.

5. I appreciate the mobility and flexibility of my body.

6. I am grateful for the energy my body provides me each day.

7. I am thankful for the ways in which my body supports my passions and pursuits.

8. I appreciate the intricate systems within my body that work together to keep me healthy.

9. I am grateful for my body's natural ability to adapt and change.

10. I appreciate the unique shape and form of my body.

11. I am grateful for the physical sensations and pleasures my body can experience.

12. I appreciate the ways in which my body communicates with me and provides me with signals.

13. I am thankful for my body's natural instincts and intuition.

14. I appreciate the diversity and variety of bodies in the world, including my own.

15. I am grateful for my body's ability to recover and bounce back from challenges.

16. I appreciate the way my body supports me in expressing my emotions and creativity.

17. I am thankful for the ways in which my body adapts to changes in my environment.

18. I appreciate the complex network of organs and tissues that keep me alive and functioning.

19. I am grateful for the breath that fills my lungs and nourishes my body.

20. I appreciate the ways in which my body allows me to connect with others through touch and communication.

21. I am thankful for the strength and endurance my body provides during physical activities.

22. I appreciate the natural beauty and uniqueness of my body.

23. I am grateful for the pleasure and joy my body can experience through movement and physical sensations.

24. I appreciate the way my body supports my overall well-being and health.

25. I am thankful for the gift of life and the opportunity to experience it through my body.

26. Take a moment each day to reflect on these affirmations and express gratitude for your body and its capabilities. Cultivating gratitude can help foster a positive relationship with your body and enhance your overall well-being.

EMBRACING AGING GRACEFULLY AND AFFIRMING SELF-WORTH REGARDLESS OF AGE.

In this section, we will explore the empowering practice of embracing aging gracefully and affirming self-worth regardless of age. Drawing insights from various fields, including Witchcraft, Divination, Herbalism, Shamanism, and Ecospirituality, we will delve into the concept of aging as a natural and beautiful process and how affirmations can support a positive mindset and self-acceptance during different stages of life. By embracing the wisdom and experiences that come with age and affirming our inherent worth, we can cultivate a deep sense of self-love and celebrate the richness of our journey.

Understanding Aging as a Natural Process:

Aging is an inherent part of the human experience, characterized by the gradual physical, mental, and emotional changes that occur over time. Instead of viewing aging as something to fear or resist, we can reframe our perspective and embrace it as a natural and inevitable aspect of life. Aging offers us the opportunity to grow, evolve, and deepen our understanding of ourselves and the world around us.

Embracing Self-Worth Regardless of Age:

Shifting Paradigms: Society often places undue emphasis on youth and external appearances, creating a sense of unworthiness and diminishing the value of aging. By challenging these societal norms and embracing a new paradigm, we can affirm the inherent worth and beauty that transcends age.

Wisdom and Experience: With age comes a wealth of wisdom and experience. Embrace the knowledge and insights you have gained throughout your life's journey, recognizing their immense value and the contributions they can make to yourself and others.

Redefining Beauty: Beauty is not limited to youth or external features. Embrace the beauty that comes with age, including the lines etched on your face that tell stories of resilience, the grace in your movements, and the radiance that emanates from a life well-lived.

Self-Reflection and Growth: Aging offers us the opportunity for self-reflection and personal growth. Embrace this phase of life as a time for deepening self-awareness, cultivating inner peace, and nurturing your spiritual well-being.

Affirmations for Self-Worth: Utilize affirmations as powerful tools to affirm your self-worth regardless of age. Affirmations help reprogram your subconscious mind and cultivate a positive mindset. Examples of affirmations for embracing aging gracefully and affirming self-worth include:

1. "I embrace the beauty and wisdom that come with each passing year, knowing that my worth is not defined by my age."

2. "I honor and celebrate the experiences and lessons that have shaped me into the person I am today."

3. "I radiate inner beauty and grace, embodying the fullness of my being at every stage of life."

4. "I am deserving of love, respect, and fulfillment regardless of my age or external appearance."

5. "I embrace the journey of aging with gratitude and acceptance, knowing that every phase of life has its own unique beauty and purpose."

Exercises:

Mirror Reflection: Stand in front of a mirror and observe your reflection. Practice affirming self-love and acceptance by speaking affirmations that acknowledge and appreciate your age and the wisdom it brings.

Gratitude for Aging: Keep a gratitude journal dedicated to acknowledging the positive aspects of aging. Write down at least three things you are grateful for related to the aging process and how it has enriched your life.

Letter to Your Younger Self: Write a heartfelt letter to your younger self, expressing compassion, wisdom, and guidance. Acknowledge the growth and lessons you have experienced throughout your life's journey, offering reassurance and support to your younger self.

Conclusion:

Embracing aging gracefully and affirming self-worth regardless of age is a transformative practice that empowers us to honor the beauty, wisdom, and unique qualities that accompany each passing year. By shifting our perspective, redefining beauty, and utilizing affirmations, we can cultivate a deep sense of self-love and acceptance, celebrating the richness of our journey and embracing the transformative power of aging. Let us embark on this journey with gratitude and openness, embracing our age as a testament to our resilience, strength, and inherent worth.

1. I embrace the wisdom and experience that comes with aging.

2. I am grateful for the opportunities that each passing year brings.

3. My age does not define my worth; I am valuable at every stage of life.

4. I honor and respect the natural process of aging.

5. I am proud of my journey and the growth I have achieved over the years.

6. I radiate beauty and confidence, no matter my age.

7. I embrace the changes that come with age and find beauty in them.

8. I am grateful for the lessons I have learned and the person I have become.

9. I celebrate the unique qualities and strengths that come with aging.

10. I release societal expectations of youth and embrace the power of maturity.

11. My worth is not determined by external appearances or societal standards.

12. I am comfortable in my own skin and embrace the lines and wrinkles as signs of a life well-lived.

13. I cherish the memories and experiences that have shaped me.

14. I am proud of my age and the wisdom that comes with it.

15. I radiate grace and confidence in every stage of my life.

16. I am deserving of love, respect, and opportunities regardless of my age.

17. I am grateful for the new beginnings and possibilities that each day brings.

18. I celebrate my age as a symbol of resilience and strength.

19. I let go of fear and embrace the freedom that comes with age.

20. I am empowered to pursue my dreams and passions, no matter my age.

21. I honor my body and take care of it with love and respect.

22. I am grateful for the journey of self-discovery that unfolds with each passing year.

23. I am vibrant and full of life, regardless of my age.

24. I release comparison and appreciate the unique beauty that comes with aging.

25. I affirm my self-worth and embrace the fullness of my being, no matter my age.

LETTING GO OF PAST INSECURITIES AND AFFIRMING HEALING AND GROWTH.

In this section, we will explore the transformative practice of letting go of past insecurities and affirming healing and growth. Through the lens of various fields, including Witchcraft, Divination, Herbalism, Shamanism, and Ecospirituality, we will delve into the concept of releasing the burdens of the past, embracing self-forgiveness, and affirming our capacity for healing and growth. By nurturing a positive self-image and harnessing the power of affirmations, we can create a space for healing, self-acceptance, and personal transformation.

Understanding Past Insecurities:

Recognizing the Impact: Past insecurities can leave a lasting impact on our self-image, influencing our thoughts, emotions, and behaviors. These insecurities may stem from societal expectations, past experiences, or negative self-perceptions.

Self-Reflection and Awareness: Engaging in self-reflection allows us to identify and acknowledge the specific insecurities that have held us back. By developing self-awareness, we can gain insight into the underlying causes and patterns of our insecurities.

Cultivating Compassion: Compassion towards ourselves is crucial in the process of letting go of past insecurities. We must recognize that these insecurities were often born out of fear, comparison, or external influences. Cultivating self-compassion enables us to approach our healing journey with kindness and understanding.

Letting Go of Past Insecurities:

Forgiveness: Forgiveness is a powerful tool for releasing the grip of past insecurities. This includes forgiving ourselves for any perceived shortcomings, mistakes, or perceived failures. By letting go of self-blame and judgment, we create space for healing and growth.

Releasing Limiting Beliefs: Identify and challenge the limiting beliefs that have fueled your insecurities. Replace them with empowering beliefs that affirm your worth, potential, and ability to overcome obstacles.

Self-Acceptance: Embrace self-acceptance by recognizing that imperfections are part of being human. Instead of striving for perfection, focus on embracing your authentic self, recognizing the unique qualities that make you who you are.

Affirming Healing and Growth:

Harnessing the Power of Affirmations: Affirmations are powerful tools that can rewire our thought patterns and beliefs. Craft affirmations that address your specific insecurities and affirm healing, growth, and self-acceptance. Examples of affirmations include:

"I release the insecurities of my past and embrace the present moment with love and acceptance."

"I am deserving of love, respect, and acceptance, exactly as I am."

"I let go of self-doubt and embrace my innate potential for growth and transformation."

"I am worthy of all the goodness and abundance that life has to offer."

"I am free from the limitations of past insecurities, and I embrace my journey of healing and growth."

Exercises:

Letter of Release: Write a heartfelt letter to yourself, expressing your willingness to release past insecurities and embrace healing and growth. Describe the specific insecurities you are letting go of and affirm your commitment to self-acceptance and self-love.

Mirror Work: Stand in front of a mirror and practice affirmations that address your past insecurities. Look deep into your eyes and speak the affirmations with conviction, allowing them to penetrate your subconscious mind and reinforce positive self-beliefs.

Journaling: Dedicate a journal to document your healing and growth journey. Write about the progress you have made, challenges you have overcome, and moments of self-empowerment. Use this journal as a source of inspiration and reflection.

Conclusion:

Letting go of past insecurities and affirming healing and growth is a profound and transformative process. By releasing the burdens of the past, cultivating self-acceptance, and harnessing the power of affirmations, we open ourselves to a path of healing, self-love, and personal transformation. Embrace this journey with openness, compassion, and a deep belief in your inherent worthiness.

1. I release all past insecurities and embrace my inner strength.

2. I am deserving of love, acceptance, and happiness.

3. I let go of the need for validation from others and find validation within myself.

4. I choose to forgive myself and others for past mistakes and release any lingering resentment.

5. I am worthy of self-compassion and kindness.

6. I release the burden of comparison and embrace my unique journey.

7.   I am grateful for the lessons learned from past experiences and use them to grow and evolve.

8.   I let go of negative self-talk and replace it with positive and empowering thoughts.

9.   I trust in my ability to overcome challenges and emerge stronger.

10. I am open to healing and nurturing my mind, body, and spirit.

11. I release any self-imposed limitations and believe in my unlimited potential.

12. I choose to see the beauty and potential within myself.

13. I am resilient and capable of bouncing back from setbacks.

14. I let go of the need for perfection and embrace my authentic self.

15. I honor my emotions and allow myself to heal from past wounds.

16. I release the fear of judgment and express myself authentically.

17. I am worthy of success, happiness, and abundance.

18. I let go of the past and focus on creating a positive future.

19. I release the need to please others and prioritize my own well-being.

20. I am deserving of love and healthy relationships.

21. I let go of the belief that my worth is determined by external validation.

22. I trust in the process of growth and transformation.

23. I release any limiting beliefs that hold me back from reaching my full potential.

24. I embrace change and adapt with grace and resilience.

25. I am a beautiful and valuable person, deserving of love and acceptance.

AFFIRMATIONS FOR RELEASING NEGATIVE SELF-TALK AND EMBRACING SELF-COMPASSION.

In this section, we will explore the transformative practice of using affirmations to release negative self-talk and cultivate self-compassion. Negative self-talk can hinder our self-esteem, hinder personal growth, and limit our potential. By harnessing the power of affirmations, we can reprogram our thoughts, replace self-critical narratives with self-compassionate ones, and create a nurturing inner dialogue. Drawing inspiration from various fields, including Witchcraft, Divination, Herbalism, Shamanism, and Ecospirituality, we will delve into the importance of self-compassion and provide a collection of affirmations to support your journey towards self-acceptance and empowerment.

Understanding Negative Self-Talk:

The Impact of Negative Self-Talk: Negative self-talk is the internal dialogue filled with self-criticism, self-doubt, and limiting beliefs. It can manifest in various forms, such as harsh judgments, perfectionism, or comparisons to others. This negative self-talk can erode self-esteem, contribute to anxiety and depression, and impede personal growth.

Recognizing Self-Critical Patterns: Self-awareness is the first step towards transforming negative self-talk. By observing and identifying the patterns of negative self-talk, we can bring them into conscious awareness and begin the process of releasing them.

The Importance of Self-Compassion: Self-compassion involves extending kindness, understanding, and support to ourselves, especially in moments of difficulty or perceived failure. It involves treating ourselves with the same empathy and care we would offer to a loved one. Cultivating self-compassion is essential for counteracting negative self-talk and fostering a nurturing inner dialogue.

Affirmations for Releasing Negative Self-Talk and Cultivating Self-Compassion:

✧ Affirmations for Letting Go of Negative Self-Talk:

1. "I release all negative self-talk and replace it with loving and empowering thoughts."

2. "I let go of self-doubt and embrace my inherent worthiness and potential."

3. "I release the need to compare myself to others and recognize my unique journey."

4. "I am deserving of love, acceptance, and kindness, both from others and from myself."

5. "I choose to focus on my strengths and celebrate my progress, no matter how small."

✧ Affirmations for Cultivating Self-Compassion:

1. "I am gentle with myself in times of struggle, offering compassion and understanding."

2. "I embrace my imperfections as part of my unique journey and growth."

3. "I forgive myself for any mistakes and trust in my ability to learn and grow."

4. "I honor my emotions and give myself permission to feel without judgment."

5. "I am worthy of self-care, nourishment, and nurturing experiences."

✧ Affirmations for Empowering Inner Dialogue:

1. "I speak to myself with kindness, love, and encouragement."

2. "I trust in my capabilities and believe in my capacity to overcome challenges."

3. "I am resilient and capable of turning obstacles into opportunities for growth."

4. "I celebrate my achievements, no matter how small, and acknowledge my progress."

5. "I am a unique and valuable individual, deserving of respect and self-acceptance."

Exercises:

Daily Affirmation Practice: Set aside dedicated time each day to repeat affirmations for releasing negative self-talk and cultivating self-compassion. Say them out loud with conviction, allowing the affirmations to permeate your consciousness and reshape your inner dialogue.

Affirmation Journaling: Create an affirmation journal to document your journey. Write down the affirmations that resonate with you and reflect on your experiences, challenges, and moments of self-compassion. Use your journal as a safe space to explore and process your emotions.

Affirmation Visualization: Engage in a guided visualization exercise where you imagine yourself embodying self-compassion and releasing negative self-talk. Visualize yourself surrounded by love, acceptance, and positive affirmations. Allow this visualization to inspire and empower you in your daily life.

Conclusion:

Embracing self-compassion and releasing negative self-talk through the power of affirmations is a transformative practice that can profoundly impact our self-perception and overall well-being. By consciously choosing loving and empowering thoughts, we create a foundation for self-acceptance, growth, and personal empowerment. As you incorporate these affirmations into your daily life, remember to be patient and gentle with yourself. With time and practice, you will experience a shift in your inner dialogue, fostering a deep sense of self-compassion and empowerment.

EMBRACING BEAUTY IN ALL SHAPES, SIZES, AND COLORS.

In this section, we will explore the importance of embracing beauty in all its diverse forms, including various shapes, sizes, and colors. Society often imposes narrow standards of beauty, which can lead to feelings of inadequacy and self-judgment. However, by drawing inspiration from fields such as Witchcraft, Divination, Herbalism, Shamanism, and Ecospirituality, we can expand our perception of beauty and cultivate a more inclusive and empowering understanding of self-acceptance. In this section, we will delve into the complexities of beauty standards, discuss the impact of media influence, and provide strategies to celebrate and honor the beauty within ourselves and others.

Understanding Beauty Standards:

Societal Influence on Beauty Standards: Society plays a significant role in shaping beauty standards, often promoting a narrow and unrealistic ideal. These standards tend to prioritize certain body types, features, and skin tones, creating a sense of exclusion for those who do not fit the mold. Understanding the influence of these standards is crucial for challenging and redefining our perception of beauty.

Beauty as a Social Construct: Beauty is a social construct that evolves over time and varies across cultures and communities. It is essential to recognize that beauty is subjective and influenced by personal, cultural, and historical factors. By acknowledging the fluidity of beauty, we can challenge rigid norms and embrace a more inclusive definition.

Media and Beauty Ideals: Media, including advertising, magazines, and social media, plays a significant role in perpetuating narrow beauty ideals. The constant exposure to edited and idealized images can lead to self-comparisons, body dissatisfaction, and low self-esteem. Developing media literacy skills is crucial for resisting these influences and cultivating a positive body image.

Embracing Beauty Diversity:

Self-Reflection and Acceptance: Begin by reflecting on your own biases and assumptions about beauty. Challenge preconceived notions and embrace the uniqueness of your own body and appearance. Practice self-acceptance by shifting your focus from perceived flaws to appreciating the beauty that exists within you.

Celebrating Body Diversity: Embrace the beauty of different body shapes, sizes, and colors by expanding your definition of beauty. Recognize that beauty comes in various forms and appreciate the diversity in others. Challenge societal beauty norms by celebrating individuals who defy conventional standards.

Encouraging Inclusivity and Representation: Advocate for greater inclusivity and representation in media, fashion, and beauty industries. Support brands and platforms that promote diverse beauty and challenge the status quo. By amplifying diverse voices and narratives, we contribute to a more inclusive and empowering beauty landscape.

Exercises:

Mirror Affirmations: Stand in front of a mirror and affirm the beauty within you. Practice affirmations that celebrate your unique qualities, such as "I am beautiful just as I am," "I embrace my body's uniqueness," and "My beauty radiates from within."

Media Detox: Take a break from consuming media that promotes narrow beauty ideals. Unfollow social media accounts that make you feel inadequate and instead follow accounts that celebrate diverse beauty and body positivity. Use this time to engage in activities that uplift and empower you.

Community Engagement: Engage in conversations and activities that promote body positivity and inclusivity. Attend workshops, events, or online discussions that celebrate diverse beauty and challenge societal beauty standards. Share your experiences and insights to foster a sense of collective empowerment.

Conclusion:

Embracing beauty in all shapes, sizes, and colors is a transformative practice that requires a shift in mindset and a commitment to inclusivity. By challenging societal beauty standards, celebrating diversity, and practicing self-acceptance, we can create a more inclusive and empowering beauty culture. Remember that true beauty transcends external appearances and lies in the unique essence of each individual. Embrace your own beauty and champion the beauty of others, fostering a world where everyone is celebrated and valued for their authentic selves.

1. I celebrate and embrace the beauty that exists in all shapes, sizes, and colors.

2. I acknowledge that beauty comes in diverse forms, and I appreciate the uniqueness of each individual.

3. I recognize that true beauty radiates from within and is not limited by external appearances.

4. I let go of society's narrow standards of beauty and embrace the beauty that is inherent in every person.

5. I affirm that my worth and beauty are not defined by my physical appearance but by the content of my character.

6. I appreciate the beauty in diversity and the richness it brings to the world.

7. I choose to see beauty in every person I encounter, appreciating their unique qualities.

8. I release any judgments or prejudices I may hold and open my heart to accepting and celebrating all forms of beauty.

9. I honor and respect my body as a vessel of beauty and strength, regardless of its shape or size.

10. I reject the notion that beauty is limited to a specific set of physical features and embrace the beauty that lies in authenticity.

11. I choose to love and accept myself unconditionally, recognizing that my worth goes beyond external appearances.

12. I celebrate the beauty of diversity and the tapestry it creates in the world.

13. I appreciate the beauty that each individual brings, regardless of societal standards.

14. I see beauty in the unique qualities that make me who I am, embracing my own individuality.

15. I surround myself with positivity and uplifting messages that remind me of the beauty that exists in all forms.

16. I release comparison and envy, knowing that my own beauty shines brightly in its own unique way.

17. I choose to be kind and compassionate to myself and others, recognizing that beauty is enhanced by a loving and caring heart.

18. I appreciate the beauty in nature and recognize that it reflects the diversity and abundance of beauty in humanity.

19. I let go of self-criticism and negative thoughts about my appearance, embracing myself as a beautiful being.

20. I affirm that beauty is a state of mind and radiates from within me, regardless of external judgments.

21. I appreciate the beauty in every stage of life, embracing the natural process of aging and growth.

22. I honor and respect the beauty of all cultures, recognizing the richness they bring to the tapestry of humanity.

23. I see beauty in imperfections, as they are a testament to the uniqueness and authenticity of each individual.

24. I choose to surround myself with people who appreciate and celebrate the beauty of diversity.

25. I affirm that beauty knows no boundaries, and I am worthy of embracing and expressing my own unique beauty.

AFFIRMATIONS FOR OVERCOMING BODY SHAME AND PROMOTING BODY POSITIVITY.

In this section, we will explore the power of affirmations in overcoming body shame and promoting body positivity. Body shame, fueled by societal beauty standards and unrealistic expectations, can have detrimental effects on our self-esteem and overall well-being. However, by drawing inspiration from various fields such as Witchcraft, Divination, Herbalism, Shamanism, and Ecospirituality, we can harness the transformative power of affirmations to cultivate self-acceptance and embrace the beauty of our bodies. In this section, we will discuss the impact of body shame, delve into the concept of body positivity, and provide a collection of affirmations to help individuals develop a more loving and compassionate relationship with their bodies.

Understanding Body Shame:

The Influence of Societal Beauty Standards: Society often promotes narrow beauty standards that emphasize a specific body type, shape, or size. These standards create a sense of inadequacy and can lead to body shame when individuals perceive themselves as not meeting these ideals.

Internalization of Negative Messages: Body shame is often fueled by the internalization of negative messages about our bodies. These messages can come from various sources, including media, peers, and even our own self-critical thoughts. Internalized body shame can severely impact our self-esteem and body image.

Impact on Well-being: Body shame can have detrimental effects on our mental, emotional, and physical well-being. It can lead to low self-esteem, body dissatisfaction, disordered eating behaviors, and a negative relationship with our bodies. Recognizing the impact of body shame is crucial for initiating the journey towards body positivity.

Promoting Body Positivity through Affirmations:

Affirmations as Tools for Transformation: Affirmations are positive statements that can help reframe our thoughts and beliefs. They serve as tools for transformation by promoting self-acceptance, nurturing self-compassion, and challenging negative self-talk. Affirmations can be a powerful resource in cultivating body positivity.

Affirmations for Self-Acceptance: Affirmations that focus on self-acceptance can help individuals embrace their bodies as they are. These affirmations encourage individuals to let go of self-judgment and practice unconditional love and acceptance for their physical form.

Affirmations for Gratitude and Appreciation: Affirmations that center around gratitude and appreciation can shift our focus from perceived flaws to the beauty and functionality of our bodies. These affirmations encourage individuals to acknowledge and honor the unique qualities and capabilities of their bodies.

Affirmations for Inner Beauty: Inner beauty affirmations remind individuals that their worth extends far beyond their physical appearance. These affirmations emphasize the importance of cultivating inner qualities such as kindness, compassion, resilience, and authenticity.

Exercises:

Daily Affirmation Practice: Set aside time each day to practice affirmations. Repeat affirmations that resonate with you in front of a mirror or write them down in a journal. Engage in this practice with intention and sincerity, allowing the affirmations to penetrate your subconscious mind.

Affirmation Visualization: Pair affirmations with visualization exercises. Close your eyes, take deep breaths, and visualize yourself embodying the qualities and characteristics described in the affirmations. Allow the positive emotions and sensations associated with these affirmations to flow through your body.

Affirmation Journaling: Create an affirmation journal where you can regularly write down affirmations that resonate with you. Reflect on the impact of these affirmations on your mindset, self-perception, and overall well-being. Use the journal as a space for self-reflection and growth.

Conclusion:

By incorporating affirmations into our daily lives, we can challenge body shame and cultivate a positive and compassionate relationship with our bodies. The practice of affirmations, inspired by various fields such as Witchcraft, Divination, Herbalism, Shamanism, and Ecospirituality, empowers individuals to release self-judgment, embrace their unique beauty, and promote body positivity. Through consistent practice and a commitment to self-love, individuals can experience profound transformations in their self-esteem, body image, and overall well-being.

1. I love and accept my body unconditionally, embracing it with kindness and compassion.

2. I release all negative thoughts and judgments about my body, replacing them with love and appreciation.

3. My body is unique and beautiful, and I celebrate its individuality.

4. I am grateful for my body's strength, resilience, and the amazing things it allows me to do.

5. I let go of comparison and embrace the beauty of my own body.

6. I choose to nourish my body with love, care, and healthy choices.

7. My body deserves to be treated with respect and kindness, both from myself and others.

8. I am more than my physical appearance, and I focus on developing my inner qualities and talents.

9. I release the need for validation from others and find validation within myself.

10. I am deserving of love and acceptance exactly as I am, without needing to change my body.

11. I choose to celebrate my body's uniqueness and the features that make me who I am.

12. I let go of societal beauty standards and embrace my own definition of beauty.

13. I honor and appreciate my body's natural shape, size, and curves.

14. I am deserving of self-care and self-love, and I prioritize my well-being above external opinions.

15. I choose to surround myself with positive influences that promote body positivity and self-acceptance.

16. I release the fear of judgment and embrace the freedom to be myself fully.

17. I recognize that my worth is not determined by my body, but by the qualities and contributions I bring to the world.

18. I am at peace with my body and trust in its natural wisdom and intelligence.

19. I let go of negative self-talk and replace it with empowering and uplifting affirmations.

20. I celebrate the diversity of bodies and acknowledge that every body is beautiful in its own unique way.

21. I choose to see the beauty in others without feeling threatened or diminished by it.

22. I am deserving of happiness and fulfillment, regardless of my body's appearance.

23. I am proud of my body and the journey it has taken me on.

24. I release the need for perfection and embrace the beauty of imperfection.

25. I radiate confidence and self-love from within, shining my light in the world.

FOSTERING A HEALTHY RELATIONSHIP WITH FOOD AND EXERCISE.

In this section, we will explore the importance of fostering a healthy relationship with food and exercise. Our approach will draw inspiration from diverse fields such as Witchcraft, Divination, Herbalism, Shamanism, and Ecospirituality, providing a holistic perspective on nourishing our bodies and honoring their unique needs. By examining the interplay between mind, body, and spirit, we can cultivate a balanced and sustainable approach to nutrition and physical activity. This section will delve into the impact of societal influences, discuss intuitive eating and mindful movement practices, and offer strategies for fostering a positive and nurturing relationship with food and exercise.

Understanding the Influence of Society:

Societal Expectations and Diet Culture: Society often imposes unrealistic standards regarding body shape, size, and appearance. These expectations, perpetuated by diet culture, can lead to harmful behaviors, disordered eating patterns, and an unhealthy relationship with food and exercise.

Media Influence and Body Image: Media plays a significant role in shaping our perceptions of beauty and body image. Idealized representations of bodies can lead to comparison, self-judgment, and a distorted view of our own bodies. Understanding these influences is crucial in reclaiming autonomy over our relationship with food and exercise.

Embracing Intuitive Eating:

Principles of Intuitive Eating: Intuitive eating is an approach that emphasizes tuning into our body's innate wisdom and honoring its signals of hunger, fullness, and satisfaction. It encourages the rejection of restrictive diets and promotes a compassionate and flexible approach to nourishment.

Mindful Eating Practices: Mindful eating involves engaging all the senses and being present in the moment while eating. This practice encourages awareness of hunger and satiety cues, savoring the flavors and textures of food, and cultivating a non-judgmental attitude towards eating.

Self-Compassion and Acceptance: Embracing self-compassion is crucial in fostering a healthy relationship with food. Practicing self-acceptance and letting go of guilt or shame associated with food choices promotes a nurturing and balanced approach to nourishment.

Honoring Mindful Movement:

Moving with Joy and Intention: Mindful movement goes beyond conventional notions of exercise and embraces physical activity as a form of self-expression, pleasure, and self-care. Engaging in activities that bring joy and align with our individual preferences fosters a positive relationship with our bodies and enhances overall well-being.

Cultivating Body Awareness: Developing body awareness allows us to tune into the needs and limitations of our bodies. This practice involves listening to physical sensations, respecting boundaries, and adjusting our movement practices accordingly.

Letting Go of the "No Pain, No Gain" Mentality: Challenging the "no pain, no gain" mentality helps us shift towards a more balanced and compassionate approach to physical activity. By prioritizing enjoyment, rest, and recovery, we can avoid excessive strain, injury, and burnout.

Exercises:

Mindful Eating Practice: Engage in a mindful eating exercise where you intentionally focus on each bite, savoring the flavors, textures, and sensations of the food. Notice any emotions or thoughts that arise and cultivate self-compassion throughout the experience.

Body Scan Meditation: Practice a body scan meditation to cultivate body awareness. Close your eyes, bring attention to each part of your body, and observe any sensations or areas of tension. Approach this exercise with curiosity and non-judgment.

Joyful Movement Exploration: Experiment with different forms of movement and physical activities that bring you joy and pleasure. This can include dancing, hiking, swimming, or practicing yoga. Reflect on how these activities make you feel and incorporate them into your routine regularly.

Conclusion:

Fostering a healthy relationship with food and exercise is a multifaceted journey that requires self-awareness, self-compassion, and a rejection of societal pressures. By embracing intuitive eating, mindful movement, and self-acceptance, we can cultivate a nourishing and sustainable approach to nourishing our bodies and honoring their unique needs. Letting go of restrictive dieting, body shame, and the pursuit of unrealistic ideals allows us to embrace a more fulfilling and holistic approach to well-being. Through consistent practice and self-reflection, we can foster a lifelong journey of self-care, self-love, and vibrant health.

Empowered Affirmations

1. I nourish my body with wholesome and nutritious foods that support my well-being.

2. I listen to my body's cues and eat mindfully, honoring its hunger and fullness signals.

3. I release any guilt or shame associated with food choices and embrace balance and moderation.

4. I choose to view exercise as a joyful and empowering activity that strengthens both my body and mind.

5. I prioritize self-care and make time for regular exercise that brings me joy and vitality.

6. I am grateful for the ability to move my body and engage in physical activities.

7. I let go of comparing my exercise routine to others and focus on my own progress and growth.

8. I release the need for perfection in my fitness journey and embrace progress over perfection.

9. I give myself permission to rest and recover when needed, honoring the importance of rest in my overall well-being.

10. I celebrate my body's abilities and appreciate the progress it makes, no matter how small.

11. I view food as fuel for my body, providing it with the energy it needs to thrive.

12. I choose to eat mindfully and savor each bite, enjoying the flavors and textures of my meals.

13. I release any negative associations with certain foods and embrace a balanced and flexible approach to eating.

14. I trust my body's wisdom to guide me in making nourishing food choices.

15. I let go of rigid dieting rules and embrace intuitive eating, listening to my body's cravings and preferences.

16. I am worthy of nourishment and care, and I prioritize self-love in my relationship with food and exercise.

17. I release the need for external validation and embrace my own definition of health and well-being.

18. I let go of negative self-talk about my body and focus on the positive changes I am making.

19. I am patient and compassionate with myself on my health journey, understanding that progress takes time.

20. I celebrate small victories and acknowledge the positive impact of my healthy choices.

21. I surround myself with positive and supportive influences that encourage a healthy relationship with food and exercise.

22. I choose movement that brings me joy and aligns with my interests and preferences.

23. I view exercise as an act of self-care, honoring my body's need for movement and vitality.

24. I release any attachment to the outcome and embrace the process of nourishing my body and staying active.

25. I am in control of my choices and empowered to create a healthy and balanced lifestyle that supports my well-being.

AFFIRMING CONFIDENCE IN PERSONAL STYLE AND EXPRESSING INDIVIDUALITY.

In this section, we will explore the importance of affirming confidence in personal style and expressing individuality. Drawing inspiration from a diverse range of fields such as Witchcraft, Divination, Herbalism, Shamanism, and Ecospirituality, we will delve into the significance of embracing our unique self-expression through clothing, accessories, and personal style choices. Understanding the relationship between self-image, authenticity, and personal empowerment is essential in cultivating a confident and authentic presence in the world. This section will discuss the impact of societal norms, provide strategies for developing personal style, and explore the transformative power of self-affirmations.

The Influence of Societal Norms:

Societal Expectations and Conformity: Society often imposes rigid beauty standards and fashion trends that can limit individual expression and discourage the exploration of personal style. These norms can create pressure to conform, leading to a lack of confidence and self-doubt.

Breaking Free from Conventional Standards: Embracing personal style involves challenging conventional norms and embracing diversity. By rejecting societal expectations and exploring alternative expressions of fashion and style, individuals can cultivate a sense of authenticity and empowerment.

Developing Personal Style:

Self-Reflection and Authenticity: Developing personal style starts with self-reflection. By exploring our values, interests, and unique personality traits, we can align our outward appearance with our inner selves. Authenticity becomes the foundation for expressing our individuality through personal style.

Experimentation and Self-Expression: Embracing personal style requires a willingness to experiment and step outside of our comfort zones. Trying different clothing styles, accessories, colors, and patterns can help us discover what resonates with our authentic self-expression.

Embracing Body Positivity: Nurturing a positive body image is essential in developing personal style. By embracing our bodies with love and acceptance, we can choose clothing that makes us feel comfortable, confident, and empowered.

The Transformative Power of Affirmations:

Understanding Affirmations: Affirmations are positive statements that reflect our desires and intentions. By repeating affirmations related to personal style and self-expression, we can rewire our subconscious mind, boost self-confidence, and align ourselves with our truest self.

Crafting Personalized Affirmations: Craft personalized affirmations that reflect your unique style goals and desired self-expression. For example, "I am confident and radiant in my unique fashion choices" or "I embrace my individuality and express it boldly through my personal style."

Integrating Affirmations into Daily Practice: Incorporate affirmations into your daily routine. Repeat them in front of the mirror, write them in a journal, or create visual reminders, such as affirmation cards or vision boards, to reinforce positive self-beliefs.

Exercises:

Style Vision Board: Create a style vision board by collecting images, colors, and textures that resonate with your desired personal style and self-expression. Arrange them on a board or in a digital format to visually represent your style aspirations.

Self-Expression Challenge: Challenge yourself to experiment with a new style element or clothing item that you've been hesitant to try. Notice how it makes you feel and reflect on any shifts in your confidence and self-perception.

Affirmation Practice: Incorporate affirmations into your daily routine. Choose a set of personal style affirmations and repeat them with intention and belief. Reflect on the impact of affirmations on your confidence and self-expression.

Conclusion:

Affirming confidence in personal style and expressing individuality is a transformative journey that allows us to embrace our unique self-expression and challenge societal norms. By exploring personal style choices, cultivating authenticity, and integrating affirmations into our daily lives, we can confidently express ourselves and radiate our true essence to the world. Remember, your personal style is a powerful form of self-expression and an affirmation of your inner beauty and uniqueness.

1. I embrace my unique sense of style and express myself authentically through my clothing choices.

2. I am confident in my personal style, knowing that it reflects who I am and what I stand for.

3. I let go of the need for approval from others and embrace the freedom to express my individuality.

4. I celebrate my uniqueness and confidently stand out from the crowd.

5. I am deserving of feeling beautiful and confident in every outfit I wear.

6. I trust my intuition when it comes to selecting clothes that make me feel empowered and authentic.

7. I release any self-doubt about my fashion choices and embrace the confidence to wear what I love.

8. I radiate confidence and self-assurance, no matter what I'm wearing.

9. I honor my personal style preferences and allow them to evolve and change as I grow.

10. I am a trendsetter, setting my own fashion trends and inspiring others with my unique style.

11. I choose clothing that makes me feel comfortable and confident in my own skin.

12. I am not defined by societal norms or trends; I define my own style and express it with pride.

13. I am confident in my ability to create stylish outfits that reflect my personality and values.

14. I release any fear of judgment and embrace the courage to showcase my individuality through my fashion choices.

15. I attract positive attention and admiration by confidently expressing my personal style.

16. I embrace experimentation and creativity in my wardrobe, allowing myself to explore different looks and combinations.

17. I appreciate and celebrate the diversity of personal styles around me, knowing that we each have our own unique expression.

18. I am a fashion inspiration to others, inspiring them to embrace their own individuality and style.

19. I let go of comparisons and trust that my personal style is perfect for me.

20. I confidently wear what makes me feel good, regardless of societal expectations or trends.

21. I am comfortable stepping outside of my comfort zone and trying new styles that resonate with my authentic self.

22. I deserve to feel confident and stylish in every aspect of my life, including my personal style choices.

23. I radiate confidence from within, and my personal style enhances and reflects that confidence.

24. I embrace the power of accessories and use them to add unique touches to my outfits.

25. I am a walking work of art, expressing my individuality and creativity through my personal style.

AFFIRMATIONS FOR EMBRACING AND LOVING YOUR FLAWS AND IMPERFECTIONS.

In this section, we will explore the power of affirmations in embracing and loving our flaws and imperfections. Drawing insights from various fields such as Witchcraft, Divination, Herbalism, Shamanism, and Ecospirituality, we will delve into the significance of accepting and celebrating our unique attributes, both physical and non-physical. By understanding the transformative potential of affirmations, we can cultivate self-compassion, build resilience, and foster a deep sense of self-love and acceptance.

The Perception of Flaws and Imperfections:

Shifting Perspectives: Flaws and imperfections are often perceived as negative aspects of ourselves, but they can also be viewed as essential parts of our individuality and beauty. By shifting our perspective, we can embrace the idea that our imperfections make us unique and add depth to our character.

Social Conditioning and Beauty Standards: Society's emphasis on perfection and beauty standards can contribute to feelings of inadequacy and self-criticism. However, it is important to challenge these societal norms and redefine beauty on our own terms.

Embracing Self-Love and Acceptance:

Recognizing Inner Worth: Embracing our flaws and imperfections begins with recognizing our inherent worth beyond external appearances. We are multidimensional beings with unique talents, experiences, and qualities that extend far beyond physical attributes.

Practicing Self-Compassion: Self-compassion involves treating ourselves with kindness, understanding, and forgiveness. By acknowledging our imperfections and responding to them with self-compassion, we can foster a nurturing and supportive relationship with ourselves.

Celebrating Uniqueness: Embracing our flaws and imperfections means celebrating the qualities that set us apart from others. Each flaw and imperfection contributes to our individuality and creates opportunities for growth and self-discovery.

The Power of Affirmations:

Understanding Affirmations: Affirmations are powerful tools that allow us to reframe our thoughts and beliefs. By consciously choosing positive statements about our flaws and imperfections, we can shift our mindset towards self-acceptance and self-love.

Crafting Personalized Affirmations: Craft affirmations that specifically address the areas where you may feel self-conscious or struggle with acceptance. For example, "I embrace my unique quirks and see them as valuable aspects of my identity" or "I love and accept myself fully, flaws and all."

Repetition and Reinforcement: Repeat your chosen affirmations regularly, allowing their positive messages to permeate your subconscious mind. Pair affirmations with visualization techniques, imagining yourself embracing and loving your flaws, to reinforce the desired mindset shift.

Exercises:

Flaw Appreciation Journal: Create a journal dedicated to appreciating and celebrating your flaws and imperfections. Each day, write down at least one positive aspect or lesson you have gained from a specific flaw or imperfection. Reflect on how these aspects contribute to your personal growth.

Mirror Affirmations: Stand in front of a mirror and recite your personalized affirmations while looking into your own eyes. Notice any emotional responses and observe how this practice influences your self-perception over time.

Compassionate Reflection: Take time for introspection and reflection on your flaws and imperfections. Write a compassionate letter to yourself, acknowledging these aspects and expressing love and acceptance. Allow yourself to receive and internalize the kindness and compassion expressed in the letter.

Conclusion:

Embracing and loving our flaws and imperfections is a profound act of self-acceptance and self-love. Through the practice of affirmations, we can shift our mindset, cultivate self-compassion, and celebrate the unique qualities that make us who we are. Remember, it is in our imperfections that we find our true beauty and strength.

1. I accept and love myself unconditionally, including all my flaws and imperfections.

2. My flaws and imperfections make me beautifully unique and add depth to my character.

3. I release the need for perfection and embrace the beauty of my authentic self.

4. I am worthy of love and acceptance, regardless of any perceived flaws or imperfections.

5. I choose to see the beauty in my flaws and celebrate them as a part of my individuality.

6. I let go of self-judgment and embrace self-compassion for all aspects of myself, flaws included.

7. My flaws do not define me; they are opportunities for growth and self-acceptance.

8. I embrace my imperfections as valuable lessons that shape me into a stronger and more resilient individual.

9. I am deserving of love and respect, regardless of any perceived flaws or imperfections.

10. I release the need to compare myself to others and focus on accepting and loving myself exactly as I am.

11. I choose to see my flaws as unique features that make me one-of-a-kind and special.

12. I release any shame or embarrassment associated with my flaws and replace it with self-love and acceptance.

13. I am more than my flaws; I am a whole and worthy person deserving of love and happiness.

14. I let go of seeking validation from others and find validation within myself, flaws and all.

15. I am beautiful and worthy of love, irrespective of any perceived flaws or imperfections.

16. I choose to focus on my strengths and embrace my flaws as part of my journey towards personal growth.

17. I release the need for perfection and embrace the freedom and authenticity of embracing my flaws.

18. My flaws do not diminish my worth; they are part of my unique story and journey.

19. I accept myself fully, flaws and all, and choose to love myself unconditionally.

20. I am grateful for my flaws and imperfections, as they allow me to connect with others on a deeper level.

21. I release the need to hide my flaws and imperfections and instead embrace them as badges of authenticity.

22. I choose to see my flaws as opportunities for self-improvement and personal development.

23. I am deserving of love, respect, and acceptance, regardless of any perceived flaws or imperfections.

24. I let go of the pressure to be perfect and instead embrace the freedom of being my authentic, imperfect self.

25. I am enough, just as I am, with all my flaws and imperfections.

LETTING GO OF EXTERNAL VALIDATION AND AFFIRMING SELF-WORTH FROM WITHIN.

In this section, we will explore the concept of letting go of external validation and cultivating self-worth from within. Drawing upon insights from various fields, such as Witchcraft, Divination, Herbalism, Shamanism, and Ecospirituality, we will delve into the significance of detaching our self-worth from external factors and embracing our inherent value. By understanding the impact of external validation on our self-esteem and learning to affirm our worth independently, we can foster a deep sense of self-acceptance and empowerment.

The Influence of External Validation:

Societal Conditioning: Society often emphasizes external achievements, appearances, and opinions as measures of success and worthiness. This societal conditioning can lead to a constant need for external validation, causing us to rely on others' approval for our self-esteem.

Comparative Mindset: Engaging in constant comparisons with others can fuel the need for external validation. When we measure our worth based on how we stack up against others, we neglect our unique qualities and abilities.

Detaching from External Validation:

Recognizing Inherent Worth: The first step in letting go of external validation is recognizing that our worthiness as individuals goes beyond external measures. We are intrinsically valuable and deserving of love and acceptance simply because we exist.

Authentic Self-Expression: Embrace your authentic self and express yourself in ways that align with your values, interests, and passions. By focusing on personal fulfillment rather than seeking validation, you can cultivate a sense of authenticity and inner satisfaction.

Setting Personal Standards: Instead of relying on external benchmarks, set your own standards for success and fulfillment. Define what matters most to you and strive to live in alignment with your own values and aspirations.

Affirming Self-Worth from Within:

Affirming Positive Self-Beliefs: Create affirmations that reinforce your self-worth and independence from external validation. For example, "I am worthy of love and acceptance just as I am" or "My worth is not determined by others' opinions of me."

Practicing Self-Validation: Develop a practice of self-validation by acknowledging and appreciating your achievements, strengths, and qualities. Celebrate your progress and remind yourself of your worthiness, independent of external validation.

Cultivating Self-Compassion: Embrace self-compassion as a way to nurture yourself during moments of self-doubt or criticism. Treat yourself with kindness and understanding, offering support and encouragement.

Exercises:

Self-Reflection: Take time for self-reflection and introspection. Identify areas in your life where you seek external validation and examine the underlying beliefs that drive this behavior. Challenge these beliefs and reframe them with affirmations that promote self-worth from within.

Self-Validation Journal: Create a journal dedicated to recording moments of self-validation. Each day, write down at least one accomplishment, positive trait, or act of self-acceptance that you validate within yourself. Reflect on the emotions and mindset shifts that arise from this practice.

Visualization Meditation: Engage in visualization meditation to imagine yourself detached from the need for external validation. Visualize a sense of inner worth and self-acceptance radiating from within, independent of external opinions or judgments.

Conclusion:

Letting go of external validation and affirming self-worth from within is a powerful journey of self-discovery and empowerment. By recognizing our inherent value, setting personal standards, and practicing self-validation, we can free ourselves from the constant need for external approval and cultivate a deep sense of self-worth and authenticity. Remember, your worthiness comes from within, and you have the power to affirm and celebrate your unique worth independently.

1. My worth is not determined by the opinions or validation of others.

2. I trust and value my own judgment and intuition above external opinions.

3. I release the need for approval from others and embrace my own self-approval.

4. I am worthy of love, respect, and acceptance regardless of external validation.

5. I define my own worth and I choose to see the value within myself.

6. My self-worth is based on my intrinsic qualities and the love I have for myself.

7. I release the need to seek validation outside of myself and embrace the power within me.

8. I am enough, just as I am, without needing validation from anyone else.

9. I trust in my own abilities and believe in my own worthiness.

10. I let go of comparison and focus on my unique journey and strengths.

11. I acknowledge that external validation is fleeting, but my self-worth is enduring.

12. I am deserving of love, success, and happiness regardless of others' opinions.

13. I release the need to prove myself to others and instead focus on my own growth and fulfillment.

14. I am confident in my own worth and I radiate that confidence to the world.

15. I validate myself through self-love, self-acceptance, and self-care.

16. My self-worth comes from within, and I nourish it by honoring my true self.

17. I release the need for external validation and embrace the freedom of self-acceptance.

18. I trust that I am capable of making decisions that align with my highest good.

19. I am secure in who I am and I do not seek validation to validate my worth.

20. I value my own opinion and honor my own voice above the opinions of others.

21. I let go of the need to please others and instead focus on fulfilling my own needs and desires.

22. I am the sole authority of my life and I make choices based on what feels right for me.

23. I recognize that my worth cannot be diminished by the judgments or criticisms of others.

24. I release the need to compare myself to others and instead celebrate my own unique journey.

25. I affirm my self-worth every day, knowing that I am deserving of love, happiness, and success.

CULTIVATING SELF-ESTEEM AND A POSITIVE SELF-IMAGE.

In this section, we will explore the process of cultivating self-esteem and nurturing a positive self-image. Drawing upon insights from various fields, such as Witchcraft, Divination, Herbalism, Shamanism, and Ecospirituality, we will delve into the significance of self-esteem and its impact on our overall well-being. By understanding the factors that influence self-esteem and learning effective strategies for its cultivation, we can develop a healthy and positive self-image.

Understanding Self-Esteem:

Definition of Self-Esteem: Self-esteem refers to the evaluation and perception we have of ourselves. It encompasses our beliefs about our worth, abilities, and inherent value as individuals.

Factors Influencing Self-Esteem: Our self-esteem can be influenced by various factors, including past experiences, societal influences, personal achievements, relationships, and self-perception. It is important to recognize that self-esteem is a dynamic and evolving aspect of our lives.

Cultivating Self-Esteem:

Self-Acceptance: Embrace self-acceptance by acknowledging and embracing your strengths, weaknesses, and imperfections. Recognize that nobody is perfect, and imperfections are a natural part of being human.

Positive Self-Talk: Practice positive self-talk by replacing self-critical thoughts with affirming and supportive statements. For instance, if you make a mistake, instead of berating yourself, remind yourself that mistakes are opportunities for growth and learning.

Setting Realistic Goals: Set realistic goals that align with your values, interests, and capabilities. Celebrate your achievements, no matter how small, and use them as evidence of your competence and worthiness.

Developing a Positive Self-Image:

Embracing Self-Care: Engage in self-care activities that nourish your mind, body, and spirit. This can include practices such as mindfulness, meditation, self-reflection, and engaging in activities that bring you joy and fulfillment.

Surrounding Yourself with Positive Influences: Surround yourself with individuals who support and uplift you. Cultivate relationships that foster positivity, encouragement, and acceptance. Limit exposure to negative influences that undermine your self-image.

Celebrating Uniqueness: Embrace your uniqueness and recognize the value of your individuality. Each person has their own set of strengths, talents, and qualities that contribute to the richness of the world.

Exercises:

Self-Reflection: Engage in regular self-reflection to explore your beliefs, values, and self-perception. Identify any negative thought patterns or self-limiting beliefs that may be impacting your self-esteem. Challenge and reframe these beliefs with positive and empowering statements.

Gratitude Journal: Keep a gratitude journal and write down three things you appreciate about yourself each day. This practice encourages a shift in focus towards self-appreciation and cultivates a positive self-image.

Empowered Affirmations

Mirror Work: Stand in front of a mirror and practice affirmations that reinforce your self-worth and positive self-image. Repeat statements such as "I am worthy of love and respect" or "I embrace my unique qualities and strengths."

Conclusion:

Cultivating self-esteem and nurturing a positive self-image is a transformative journey that requires self-awareness, self-acceptance, and self-care. By embracing our strengths, practicing positive self-talk, setting realistic goals, and surrounding ourselves with positive influences, we can foster a healthy and positive self-image. Remember, you are deserving of love, acceptance, and self-worth, and by cultivating these qualities within yourself, you can live a more fulfilling and empowered life.

1. I am deserving of love, respect, and happiness.

2. I embrace my unique qualities and celebrate my individuality.

3. I am confident in my abilities and trust in my own judgment.

4. I am enough just as I am, and I have valuable contributions to offer the world.

5. I radiate self-assurance and attract positivity into my life.

6. I release self-doubt and replace it with self-belief and confidence.

7. I acknowledge my strengths and appreciate the progress I have made.

8. I honor and prioritize my own needs, knowing that self-care is essential for my well-being.

9. I am worthy of success and abundance in all areas of my life.

10. I choose to see challenges as opportunities for growth and learning.

11. I am comfortable in my own skin and embrace my physical appearance with love and acceptance.

12. I speak kindly to myself and replace negative self-talk with words of encouragement.

13. I trust my intuition and make decisions that align with my values and aspirations.

14. I let go of comparisons and focus on my own journey of self-improvement.

15. I believe in my own potential and know that I have the power to achieve my goals.

16. I surround myself with positive influences and supportive individuals who uplift and inspire me.

17. I release the need for external validation and find validation within myself.

18. I choose to see setbacks as temporary and use them as opportunities for growth.

19. I am proud of my accomplishments, both big and small.

20. I forgive myself for any mistakes I have made and allow myself to learn and grow from them.

21. I embrace my worthiness of love and healthy relationships.

22. I nourish my mind, body, and soul with positive thoughts, healthy habits, and self-care practices.

23. I am confident in expressing my needs, desires, and boundaries.

24. I acknowledge and celebrate my progress on my journey of self-esteem and self-improvement.

25. I am grateful for my unique qualities and the opportunities they bring into my life.

AFFIRMATIONS FOR EMBRACING CHANGE AND ADAPTING TO YOUR EVOLVING SELF-IMAGE.

In this section, we will explore the power of affirmations in embracing change and adapting to our evolving self-image. Drawing upon insights from various fields, such as Witchcraft, Divination, Herbalism, Shamanism, and Ecospirituality, we will delve into the concept of change as an inherent part of personal growth and transformation. By utilizing affirmations, we can navigate the challenges that come with change and cultivate a positive and adaptive self-image.

Understanding Change and Self-Image:

Change as an Opportunity: Change is a natural part of life and offers us opportunities for growth, learning, and self-discovery. It allows us to evolve, shed old beliefs and patterns, and embrace new possibilities.

The Impact on Self-Image: Change can influence our self-image as it challenges our familiar sense of self and requires us to adapt and redefine who we are. Embracing change and adapting our self-image allows us to align with our evolving values, aspirations, and potentials.

Harnessing the Power of Affirmations:

Affirming Resilience: Use affirmations to reinforce your resilience and ability to navigate change. For example, "I embrace change as an opportunity for growth and transformation" or "I adapt easily to new situations and embrace the unknown."

Embracing Self-Compassion: Affirm self-compassion during times of change by acknowledging that it is normal to feel uncertain or uncomfortable. Affirmations such as "I am gentle with myself as I navigate change" or "I trust in my ability to adapt and thrive" can help foster self-compassion.

Cultivating Flexibility: Use affirmations to cultivate flexibility and open-mindedness. For instance, "I am open to new experiences and perspectives" or "I welcome change as a catalyst for personal evolution."

Exercises:

Affirmation Practice: Develop a daily affirmation practice where you repeat positive statements related to embracing change and adapting to your evolving self-image. Write down affirmations that resonate with you and recite them aloud or silently each day.

Journaling: Use journaling as a tool for self-reflection and exploration during periods of change. Write about your thoughts, feelings, and observations regarding the changes occurring in your life. Affirm your ability to navigate these changes and embrace your evolving self-image.

Visualization: Engage in visualization exercises to imagine yourself successfully adapting to change and embracing your evolving self-image. Visualize yourself confidently navigating new situations and expressing your authentic self.

Conclusion:

Embracing change and adapting to our evolving self-image is a process that requires intention, self-awareness, and the utilization of affirmations. By affirming our resilience, embracing self-compassion, and cultivating flexibility, we can navigate change with grace and confidence. Through regular affirmation practice and engaging in exercises such as journaling and visualization, we can align our self-image with our evolving values, aspirations, and potentials. Remember, change is an opportunity for growth and transformation, and by embracing it and adapting our self-image, we can embark on a fulfilling and empowered journey of personal evolution.

1. I embrace change as an opportunity for growth and self-discovery.

2. I am open to new experiences and welcome the transformations they bring.

3. I trust in my ability to navigate and adapt to any changes that come my way.

4. I release resistance to change and embrace the flow of life.

5. I am resilient and capable of handling any challenges that arise.

6. I let go of old beliefs and patterns that no longer serve me, making room for new possibilities.

7. I embrace the beauty of change and the opportunities it presents for personal development.

8. I am flexible and adaptable, able to adjust to new circumstances with grace and ease.

9. I am excited about the infinite potential for growth and expansion within me.

10. I release fear and doubt, knowing that change is a natural part of life's journey.

11. I am not defined by my past; I am free to create a new and empowering self-image.

12. I welcome change as an invitation to become the best version of myself.

13. I trust that change brings me closer to my authentic self and my true purpose.

14. I embrace uncertainty and trust that everything is unfolding perfectly for my highest good.

15. I am open to receiving support and guidance as I navigate through changes.

16. I release the need for control and surrender to the natural flow of life.

17. I celebrate my growth and the person I am becoming.

18. I embrace the unknown with curiosity and excitement, knowing that it holds infinite possibilities.

19. I am adaptable and capable of finding solutions in any situation.

20. I let go of attachment to outcomes and trust in the wisdom of the universe.

21. I am the creator of my own reality, and I choose to create a positive and empowering self-image.

22. I welcome change with open arms, knowing that it leads me to new adventures and opportunities.

23. I am confident in my ability to handle change and emerge stronger and wiser.

24. I honor my journey and trust that every step I take aligns me with my higher self.

25. I am grateful for the changes in my life and the growth they bring.

Repeat these affirmations regularly to reinforce your ability to embrace change and adapt to your evolving self-image. Embracing change is a powerful way to expand your horizons, discover new aspects of yourself, and cultivate personal growth. By affirming your willingness and readiness to adapt, you align yourself with the flow of life and open yourself up to endless possibilities for self-discovery and self-improvement.

AFFIRMATIONS FOR DEVELOPING RESILIENCE AGAINST SOCIETAL BEAUTY STANDARDS.

In this section, we will explore the power of affirmations in developing resilience against societal beauty standards. Societal beauty standards can place immense pressure on individuals to conform to narrow definitions of beauty, often leading to self-doubt, low self-esteem, and body image issues. By utilizing affirmations, we can challenge and overcome these societal expectations, fostering a positive and empowered self-image.

Understanding Societal Beauty Standards:

Unrealistic Beauty Ideals: Societal beauty standards often promote unrealistic and unattainable ideals of beauty, emphasizing specific body types, features, and standards of attractiveness. These standards can create feelings of inadequacy and self-judgment.

Influence of Media and Culture: Media platforms, advertising, and cultural influences heavily contribute to the perpetuation of beauty standards. These messages can shape our beliefs and impact our self-perception.

Harnessing the Power of Affirmations:

Affirming Inner Beauty: Focus on affirmations that emphasize the importance of inner beauty and self-acceptance. For example, affirmations such as "I am beautiful just as I am, both inside and out" or "I embrace and celebrate my unique beauty and individuality."

Challenging Comparison: Affirmations can help combat the tendency to compare ourselves to others. Repeat affirmations like "I am worthy and deserving of love and acceptance, regardless of how I compare to societal beauty standards" or "I release the need to compare myself to others and embrace my own unique beauty."

Embracing Authenticity: Affirmations can encourage the embrace of authenticity and self-expression. Repeat affirmations such as "I embrace and love my unique features and characteristics" or "I am confident in expressing my true self, disregarding societal expectations."

Exercises:

Mirror Work: Stand in front of a mirror and practice affirming statements while looking directly into your eyes. Repeat affirmations like "I love and accept myself unconditionally" or "I am beautiful and worthy of love exactly as I am." Repeat these affirmations daily for increased self-acceptance.

Self-Care Rituals: Engage in self-care rituals that promote self-love and acceptance. This can include activities such as taking relaxing baths, practicing mindfulness or meditation, engaging in hobbies that bring you joy, and surrounding yourself with positive influences.

Body Appreciation Journaling: Keep a journal dedicated to appreciating and celebrating your body. Write down affirmations, positive attributes, and unique qualities about your body. Challenge societal beauty standards by focusing on the aspects that make you feel strong, confident, and beautiful.

Conclusion:

Developing resilience against societal beauty standards is a powerful journey of self-acceptance and self-love. By utilizing affirmations that emphasize inner beauty, challenging comparison, and embracing authenticity, we can cultivate a positive and empowered self-image. Engaging in mirror work, self-care rituals, and body appreciation journaling can further support this process. Remember that beauty comes in various forms, and your worthiness and value extend far beyond external appearances. Embrace your uniqueness, celebrate your individuality, and affirm your worthiness to defy societal beauty standards and cultivate a resilient and empowered self-image.

I am beautiful and worthy just as I am, regardless of societal standards.
My worth is not determined by my appearance; it comes from within.
I embrace and celebrate my unique beauty and individuality.
I release the need to conform to societal beauty ideals and instead embrace my authentic self.
I am not defined by society's expectations; I define my own beauty.
I choose to love and accept myself unconditionally, regardless of external judgments.
I appreciate the diversity of beauty in the world and see it as a reflection of our collective uniqueness.
I recognize that beauty goes beyond physical appearance and encompasses qualities like kindness, compassion, and inner strength.

Nurturing Mind, Body, and Soul

1. I choose self-acceptance over comparison, knowing that we are all on our own unique journey.

2. I let go of the need for validation from others and find validation within myself.

3. I am confident in my own skin and radiate beauty from the inside out.

4. I nourish my mind, body, and soul with love and self-care, prioritizing my well-being over external expectations.

5. I refuse to let society's beauty standards dictate my self-worth and happiness.

6. I appreciate my body for all that it does and express gratitude for its strength and resilience.

7. I surround myself with positive influences that support and uplift me in embracing my authentic beauty.

8. I honor and respect the beauty of others without diminishing my own.

9. I choose self-love over self-criticism, speaking to myself with kindness and compassion.

10. I acknowledge that true beauty comes from within and radiates outward.

11. I celebrate my individuality and unique features that make me who I am.

12. I am deserving of love, respect, and acceptance, regardless of societal beauty standards.

13. I release the pressure to fit into narrow definitions of beauty and embrace my own standards.

14. I focus on nourishing my body and mind with healthy habits that make me feel good from the inside out.

15. I trust my intuition and inner wisdom to guide me towards a positive self-image.

16. I choose to invest my energy in cultivating positive relationships and experiences rather than striving for external validation.

17. I am resilient against societal beauty standards, knowing that my worth and beauty are innate and cannot be diminished.

Repeat these affirmations regularly to reinforce your resilience against societal beauty standards. By embracing your unique beauty, valuing yourself beyond physical appearance, and prioritizing self-love and acceptance, you cultivate a strong sense of self-worth that transcends societal expectations. Remember, true beauty lies in your authenticity, self-compassion, and the way you positively impact the world around you.

AFFIRMATIONS FOR EMBRACING AND EXPRESSING YOUR AUTHENTIC SELF.

In this section, we will explore the transformative power of affirmations in embracing and expressing your authentic self. Authenticity is the practice of living in alignment with your true values, beliefs, and desires, free from societal expectations and the need for external validation. By utilizing affirmations, you can strengthen your connection to your authentic self, foster self-expression, and cultivate a fulfilling and purposeful life.

Understanding Authenticity:

Authenticity as Self-Expression: Authenticity involves being true to yourself and expressing your thoughts, feelings, and preferences without fear of judgment or rejection. It is about honoring your unique identity and embracing your individuality.

Overcoming Conditioning: Society often imposes societal norms, expectations, and pressures that can hinder the expression of your authentic self. Breaking free from these conditioning factors is an essential step in embracing your true nature.

Harnessing the Power of Affirmations:

Embracing Self-Acceptance: Affirmations can help you cultivate self-acceptance and love for your authentic self. Repeat affirmations like "I accept and embrace all aspects of myself, including my quirks and imperfections" or "I am worthy of love and respect exactly as I am."

Honoring Your Truth: Affirmations can support you in honoring your truth and expressing your authentic voice. Repeat affirmations such as "I trust myself to make choices aligned with my values and desires" or "I am confident in expressing my true thoughts and emotions."

Letting Go of Approval-Seeking: Affirmations can help you release the need for external validation and approval. Repeat affirmations like "I value my own opinion above the opinions of others" or "I give myself permission to be true to myself, even if it means not conforming to societal expectations."

Exercises:

Authenticity Journaling: Set aside dedicated time for journaling about your authentic self. Reflect on your true passions, values, and aspirations. Write down affirmations that resonate with your authentic self, such as "I embrace and express my true passions and interests" or "I live a life true to myself, guided by my own values."

Creative Self-Expression: Engage in creative activities that allow you to express your authentic self, such as painting, writing, dancing, or playing music. Use affirmations as prompts to encourage self-expression, such as "I am free to express myself creatively and authentically" or "My unique voice and creativity have value."

Authentic Connections: Surround yourself with supportive individuals who appreciate and encourage your authentic self. Seek out communities, groups, or friendships where you can be your true self without judgment. Use affirmations to attract and nurture these authentic connections, such as "I attract authentic relationships that celebrate and honor my true self" or "I am surrounded by people who support and encourage my authentic expression."

Conclusion:

Embracing and expressing your authentic self is a powerful journey of self-discovery and self-expression. Affirmations play a crucial role in this process by fostering self-acceptance, honoring your truth, and letting go of approval-seeking. Engaging in authenticity journaling, creative self-expression, and cultivating authentic connections can further support your journey. Remember that you are unique and worthy of living a life that aligns with your true self. Embrace your authenticity, express your truth, and affirm your worthiness to live a fulfilling and purposeful life as your authentic self.

Empowered Affirmations

1. I am worthy of love and acceptance exactly as I am.

2. I embrace my uniqueness and celebrate my individuality.

3. I trust my intuition to guide me towards my authentic path.

4. I give myself permission to be true to myself in every aspect of my life.

5. I release the need to please others and instead honor my own desires and values.

6. I express myself freely and authentically, without fear of judgment.

7. I am comfortable with who I am and embrace my strengths and weaknesses.

8. I let go of comparison and embrace my own journey and progress.

9. I am proud of my authentic self and the person I am becoming.

10. I listen to my inner voice and follow my own path, even if it diverges from societal norms.

11. I honor my true passions and pursue activities that bring me joy and fulfillment.

12. I am confident in expressing my opinions and ideas, knowing they have value.

13. I release the need for external validation and find validation within myself.

14. I embrace the power of vulnerability and allow others to see the real me.

15. I give myself permission to change and evolve as I grow.

16. I surround myself with people who support and encourage my authentic self-expression.

17. I embrace my unique talents and gifts and use them to make a positive impact.

18. I let go of the need to fit into a mold and instead celebrate my individuality.

19. I trust that by being true to myself, I attract the right people and opportunities into my life.

20. I am unapologetic about who I am and stand confidently in my authenticity.

21. I release the fear of judgment and fully embrace expressing my authentic self.

22. I value my own opinions and beliefs, knowing they are valid and important.

23. I let go of self-doubt and embrace the confidence that comes from being true to myself.

24. I attract abundance and opportunities when I show up as my authentic self.

25. I am committed to living an authentic life and expressing my true essence in everything I do.

Repeat these affirmations regularly to reinforce your commitment to embracing and expressing your authentic self. Embracing your uniqueness and honoring your true desires and values allows you to live a life aligned with your authentic purpose and brings a sense of fulfillment and joy. Remember, you are worthy of love and acceptance exactly as you are, and the world benefits from the beauty of your true self.

CULTIVATING A HOLISTIC APPROACH TO BEAUTY AND WELL-BEING.

In this section, we will delve into the concept of cultivating a holistic approach to beauty and well-being. Instead of viewing beauty as solely external appearance, a holistic approach recognizes that true beauty encompasses physical, mental, emotional, and spiritual aspects of one's being. By embracing this holistic perspective, we can foster a sense of balance, harmony, and well-being in our lives.

Understanding Holistic Beauty and Well-being:

Physical Well-being: Physical well-being forms the foundation of holistic beauty. It involves taking care of your body through nourishing nutrition, regular exercise, restful sleep, and adequate self-care practices.

Mental and Emotional Well-being: Mental and emotional well-being are vital components of holistic beauty. It involves nurturing positive thoughts, managing stress, practicing self-compassion, and cultivating emotional resilience.

Spiritual Connection: Holistic beauty recognizes the importance of connecting with our inner selves and the greater universe. Spiritual practices such as meditation, mindfulness, and connecting with nature can contribute to a sense of inner peace, purpose, and interconnectedness.

Cultivating a Holistic Beauty Mindset:

Self-Love and Acceptance: Affirmations play a powerful role in cultivating self-love and acceptance. Repeat affirmations like "I love and accept myself unconditionally" or "I honor and appreciate my body as a vessel of beauty and well-being."

Embracing Self-Care: Affirmations can support the development of healthy self-care habits. Repeat affirmations such as "I prioritize self-care and nourish my body, mind, and spirit" or "I deserve to invest time and effort into my well-being."

Honoring Inner Beauty: Affirmations can shift the focus from external appearance to inner beauty. Repeat affirmations like "My inner beauty radiates through my actions, kindness, and authenticity" or "I embrace my unique qualities and let my inner beauty shine."

Exercises:

Holistic Self-Care Routine: Develop a holistic self-care routine that encompasses physical, mental, emotional, and spiritual practices. Create affirmations specific to each aspect, such as "I commit to nourishing my body with wholesome foods and engaging in regular exercise" or "I practice mindfulness daily to cultivate mental and emotional well-being."

Gratitude Practice: Cultivate gratitude for the beauty and well-being present in your life. Each day, write down affirmations of gratitude, such as "I am grateful for my body's strength and vitality" or "I am thankful for the beauty of nature that brings me joy and inspiration."

Mindful Beauty Rituals: Engage in mindful beauty rituals that honor your body and enhance your well-being. During these rituals, repeat affirmations that focus on self-love, such as "As I care for my body, I honor its inherent beauty and worth" or "I apply beauty products with love and intention, knowing they enhance my natural radiance."

Conclusion:

Cultivating a holistic approach to beauty and well-being is a transformative journey that encompasses physical, mental, emotional, and spiritual aspects of our being. By embracing self-love, prioritizing self-care, and honoring inner beauty, we can create a sense of balance, harmony, and well-being in our lives. Through the use of affirmations, gratitude practices, and mindful beauty rituals, we can reinforce our commitment to holistic beauty and well-being. Remember that true beauty radiates from within and is nurtured by embracing all aspects of ourselves—body, mind, and spirit. Embrace the journey of cultivating holistic beauty, and let it positively impact your well-being and overall quality of life.

1. I nourish my body, mind, and spirit with love and care.

2. I embrace my inner and outer beauty, knowing they are interconnected.

3. I prioritize self-care and make time for activities that rejuvenate me.

4. I honor the interconnectedness of my physical, emotional, and spiritual well-being.

5. I choose beauty and wellness practices that align with my values and beliefs.

6. I appreciate the natural beauty around me and find inspiration in nature.

7. I listen to my body's needs and provide it with nourishing food, movement, and rest.

8. I let go of stress and embrace a calm and peaceful state of mind.

9. I cultivate a positive mindset and affirm my worth and value.

10. I radiate beauty from the inside out through acts of kindness and compassion.

11. I am grateful for the unique qualities that make me who I am.

12. I practice mindfulness and bring awareness to the present moment.

13. I surround myself with positive influences and supportive relationships.

14. I release negative self-talk and replace it with empowering affirmations.

15. I trust my intuition to guide me towards choices that promote my well-being.

16. I prioritize self-reflection and personal growth as essential components of my beauty routine.

17. I honor my emotions and allow myself to feel and express them authentically.

18. I create a harmonious environment that supports my well-being.

19. I find joy and pleasure in simple everyday moments.

20. I let go of perfectionism and embrace self-acceptance and self-love.

21. I celebrate my progress and achievements, no matter how small they may seem.

22. I balance my physical, mental, and emotional energies for optimal well-being.

23. I attract positive energy and experiences by radiating love and positivity.

24. I embrace rituals and practices that nourish my soul and uplift my spirit.

25. I trust in the power of holistic beauty and well-being to enhance my life and bring me joy.

Repeat these affirmations regularly to reinforce your commitment to cultivating a holistic approach to beauty and well-being. Remember, beauty goes beyond external appearances and is deeply rooted in nurturing your mind, body, and spirit. By prioritizing self-care, embracing self-love, and living in alignment with your values, you can experience a radiant and holistic sense of well-being.

AFFIRMATIONS FOR FINDING BEAUTY IN SELF-CARE PRACTICES.

In this section, we will explore the concept of finding beauty in self-care practices. Self-care is an essential aspect of nurturing our well-being and promoting a positive relationship with ourselves. By embracing self-care as a form of beauty, we can cultivate a deeper appreciation for the rituals and practices that support our physical, mental, and emotional health. Through the use of affirmations, we can reaffirm our commitment to self-care and find beauty in the act of nurturing ourselves.

Recognizing Self-Care as a Beautiful Practice:

Affirming the Importance of Self-Care: Repeat affirmations that emphasize the significance of self-care in your life. Examples include: "I prioritize self-care as an essential part of my well-being," or "Taking care of myself is a beautiful act of self-love and respect."

Nurturing the Body: Affirmations can help shift your perspective on self-care practices that nourish your body. Repeat affirmations such as: "Caring for my body through nourishing foods and exercise is a beautiful way to honor its strength and vitality," or "I find beauty in the gentle touch and care I give my body through massages and body treatments."

Cultivating Inner Peace and Balance: Self-care practices often involve activities that promote inner peace and balance. Use affirmations like: "By dedicating time to meditation and mindfulness, I cultivate inner peace and radiate beauty from within," or "Engaging in hobbies and activities that bring me joy and fulfillment is a beautiful form of self-care."

Embracing Rest and Relaxation: Affirmations can help you appreciate the beauty of rest and relaxation. Repeat statements such as: "Resting and allowing myself to recharge is a beautiful gift I give myself," or "I find beauty in moments of stillness and quiet reflection that restore my energy and nourish my soul."

Exercises:

Self-Care Affirmation Practice: Create a list of affirmations that specifically focus on different self-care practices. Repeat these affirmations daily as you engage in self-care activities. Examples include: "I find beauty in the simple act of taking a warm bath and caring for my skin," or "As I practice self-care, I radiate beauty and well-being."

Journal Reflection: Reflect on your self-care practices and write down affirmations that highlight the beauty you find in each activity. For instance, if you enjoy journaling, you could affirm: "Through the act of journaling, I express my innermost thoughts and emotions, creating a beautiful space for self-reflection and growth."

Gratitude for Self-Care: Practice gratitude for the self-care practices that bring beauty into your life. Each day, express gratitude through affirmations like: "I am grateful for the opportunity to care for myself and experience the beauty that self-care brings," or "I appreciate the moments of self-care that nourish my mind, body, and spirit."

Conclusion:

By embracing affirmations for finding beauty in self-care practices, we can elevate our perception of self-care and recognize it as a powerful form of self-love, nourishment, and well-being. Through affirming the importance of self-care, nurturing our bodies, cultivating inner peace, and embracing rest and relaxation, we can shift our perspective and find beauty in these essential practices. By integrating affirmations into our self-care routines and expressing gratitude for these moments, we deepen our connection to ourselves and enhance our overall sense of beauty, self-worth, and well-being. Embrace the beauty in self-care, and allow it to become a transformative and empowering practice in your life.

1. I deserve to prioritize my self-care and make it a non-negotiable part of my routine.

2. Self-care is not selfish; it is a vital investment in my well-being.

3. Taking care of myself is an act of self-love and self-respect.

4. I release guilt and embrace the joy and beauty of self-care.

5. My self-care practices nourish and rejuvenate me, allowing me to show up fully in the world.

6. I listen to my body's needs and honor them through intentional self-care.

7. Each self-care practice is an opportunity to connect with myself on a deeper level.

8. I am worthy of the time and effort it takes to care for myself.

9. Self-care allows me to replenish my energy and restore my inner balance.

10. I savor the moments of self-care as precious gifts to myself.

11. Self-care is a sanctuary where I can find solace, peace, and renewal.

12. I embrace self-care as a means to nurture my mind, body, and spirit.

13. Through self-care, I cultivate a loving and harmonious relationship with myself.

14. I release any expectations or judgments and allow myself to fully enjoy the beauty of self-care.

15. Self-care empowers me to show up as my best self in all areas of my life.

16. I create space in my life for self-care and make it a priority.

17. Each self-care practice brings me closer to alignment with my authentic self.

18. I embrace the healing power of self-care and its ability to transform my life.

19. Self-care is a form of self-expression, and I honor my unique needs and preferences.

20. By practicing self-care, I replenish my inner well and radiate beauty from within.

21. I release the need for external validation and trust my intuition in choosing self-care practices.

22. I am deserving of rest, relaxation, and rejuvenation through self-care.

23. Each self-care practice is an act of self-empowerment and self-nurturing.

24. I celebrate and appreciate the beauty that self-care brings into my life.

25. Self-care is an ongoing journey of self-discovery, and I embrace it with love and gratitude.

Repeat these affirmations regularly as you engage in your self-care practices to deepen your connection with yourself and find beauty in the nurturing acts of self-love.

Embrace self-care as an integral part of your well-being and allow it to nourish your mind, body, and spirit. Remember, taking care of yourself is a beautiful and essential practice that supports your overall health and happiness.

CONCLUSION: ENCOURAGEMENT TO PRACTICE DAILY AFFIRMATIONS FOR SUSTAINED SELF-EMPOWERMENT AND INNER BEAUTY.

In this section, we have explored the power of affirmations in cultivating self-empowerment and embracing inner beauty. By incorporating daily affirmations into our lives, we can harness the transformative potential of positive self-talk and reinforce a mindset of self-love, confidence, and resilience.

Affirmations serve as powerful tools for shifting our thoughts and beliefs, allowing us to break free from self-limiting patterns and embrace our authentic selves. Through the use of affirmations, we have explored various aspects of self-empowerment and inner beauty, including embracing and expressing our authentic selves, developing resilience against societal beauty standards, finding beauty in self-care practices, and cultivating a holistic approach to beauty and well-being.

By engaging in daily affirmations, we actively participate in the creation of our own reality. Through repetition and intention, affirmations can rewire our thought patterns and subconscious beliefs, enabling us to manifest positive change and embody our inherent beauty and worthiness.

To incorporate daily affirmations into your practice of self-empowerment and inner beauty, consider the following suggestions:

Establish a Daily Affirmation Routine: Set aside dedicated time each day to engage in affirmations. Create a quiet and peaceful space where you can focus on the affirmations and their transformative impact. Consistency is key in harnessing the full potential of affirmations.

Choose Empowering Affirmations: Select affirmations that resonate with you and align with your desired mindset and goals. Use language that is positive, uplifting, and empowering. Customize the affirmations to reflect your unique journey and personal growth.

Practice Affirmations with Intention: Speak your affirmations aloud or write them down in a journal. Engage all your senses and truly embody the words as you repeat them. Visualize yourself embodying the qualities and beliefs expressed in the affirmations.

Reflect and Journal: After engaging in affirmations, take a few moments to reflect on the feelings, thoughts, and insights that arise. Consider journaling about your experience, noting any shifts in perspective, increased self-awareness, or moments of self-empowerment that you have experienced.

By integrating these practices into your daily routine, you can harness the power of affirmations to sustain self-empowerment and cultivate inner beauty. Remember, inner beauty radiates from a place of self-acceptance, self-love, and authentic expression. Through consistent practice, affirmations can become a source of strength and inspiration, helping you navigate challenges, embrace your uniqueness, and embrace the beauty that resides within you.

In conclusion, daily affirmations provide a pathway to sustained self-empowerment and inner beauty. By harnessing the power of positive self-talk, we can shift our mindset, strengthen our self-worth, and cultivate a deep sense of inner beauty that transcends societal standards and expectations. Embrace the transformative potential of affirmations, and let them guide you on your journey towards self-empowerment, self-acceptance, and a life filled with inner beauty and joy.

CONFIDENCE AND SELF-BELIEF:

Confidence and self-belief are fundamental aspects of personal growth and empowerment. They shape our perceptions, actions, and overall well-being, influencing how we navigate challenges, pursue our goals, and interact with the world around us. In this section, we will explore the transformative power of confidence and self-belief, delving into their significance and the ways in which they can be cultivated and strengthened.

Confidence can be defined as a deep sense of trust and belief in oneself. It is the inner knowing that we possess the skills, qualities, and resilience needed to navigate life's ups and downs. When we have confidence, we approach challenges with a positive mindset, embrace opportunities for growth, and persevere in the face of obstacles.

Self-belief, on the other hand, goes beyond confidence. It is the unwavering faith in our own worth, abilities, and potential. Self-belief empowers us to tap into our inner resources, follow our dreams, and overcome self-doubt and external limitations. It is the foundation upon which true self-empowerment and success are built.

In a world that often undermines our self-worth and imposes external standards of success and beauty, cultivating confidence and self-belief becomes crucial. It allows us to break free from societal expectations and define our own path. It enables us to embrace our unique strengths, talents, and perspectives, and to live authentically, aligned with our values and passions.

Throughout this section, we will explore various strategies and practices that can aid in the development of confidence and self-belief. We will examine the role of self-talk, mindset shifts, visualization techniques, and the power of affirmations in fostering a strong sense of self-assurance. Additionally, we will draw upon examples and insights from diverse fields such as psychology, spirituality, and personal development to provide a well-rounded perspective on the topic.

It is important to note that confidence and self-belief are not fixed traits. They are skills that can be cultivated and strengthened over time with practice and self-reflection. As with any journey of personal growth, it requires patience, dedication, and a willingness to confront and transcend limiting beliefs and fears.

By developing confidence and self-belief, we unlock our true potential and create a foundation for success, happiness, and fulfillment. Through this exploration, we invite you to embark on a transformative journey of self-discovery and empowerment, as we uncover the profound impact that confidence and self-belief can have on every aspect of our lives.

Join us as we delve into the depths of confidence and self-belief, unraveling their intricacies and providing you with practical tools and insights to nurture these empowering qualities within yourself. Prepare to embark on a journey of self-empowerment and self-realization, where confidence and self-belief serve as the guiding lights illuminating your path to personal growth and success.

AFFIRMATIONS TO CULTIVATE A STRONG SENSE OF SELF-CONFIDENCE, SELF-WORTH, AND BELIEF IN ONE'S ABILITIES.

In our journey towards personal growth and success, developing a strong sense of self-confidence, self-worth, and belief in our abilities is of utmost importance. It lays the foundation for overcoming challenges, taking risks, and embracing opportunities with a positive mindset. This section will explore the power of affirmations as a transformative tool to cultivate these qualities within ourselves. By harnessing the energy of positive self-talk and intentional affirmations, we can rewire our thought patterns and nurture a profound belief in our own potential. Let us embark on this empowering journey of self-discovery and self-affirmation.

Affirmation: "I am worthy of love, respect, and success in all aspects of my life."

Explanation: This affirmation reminds us that we inherently deserve love, respect, and success. It reinforces the belief that we are deserving of positive experiences and opportunities.

Affirmation: "I embrace my uniqueness and celebrate my individuality."

Explanation: By embracing our unique qualities, we acknowledge the value we bring to the world. This affirmation encourages us to appreciate our individuality and recognize that our differences make us special.

Affirmation: "I trust myself to make wise decisions and choices."

Explanation: Trusting our own judgment is crucial for building self-confidence. This affirmation affirms our ability to make sound decisions and choices, instilling a sense of self-assurance in our actions.

Affirmation: "I am capable of achieving greatness and reaching my highest potential."

Explanation: This affirmation taps into our unlimited potential and reinforces the belief that we have the capacity to achieve greatness in whatever we pursue.

Affirmation: "I am resilient and bounce back from challenges with strength and determination."

Explanation: Resilience is a key trait in overcoming obstacles. This affirmation reminds us of our resilience and the ability to rise above challenges, fostering a resilient mindset.

Affirmation: "I am confident in expressing my thoughts, ideas, and opinions."

Explanation: Expressing ourselves confidently is vital for effective communication. This affirmation encourages us to trust in our ability to express our thoughts, ideas, and opinions with clarity and conviction.

Affirmation: "I am worthy of success and abundance in all areas of my life."

Explanation: This affirmation reaffirms our inherent worthiness of success and abundance. It helps shift our mindset from scarcity to abundance, attracting positive experiences and opportunities.

Affirmation: "I believe in my skills, talents, and abilities to accomplish my goals."

Explanation: By affirming our belief in our skills, talents, and abilities, we cultivate a strong sense of self-confidence and self-assurance in our ability to achieve our goals.

Affirmation: "I am deserving of happiness, joy, and fulfillment in my life."

Explanation: This affirmation reminds us that we deserve to experience happiness, joy, and fulfillment. It affirms our right to pursue a life filled with positivity and contentment.

Affirmation: "I trust myself to handle any challenges that come my way."

Explanation: Trusting our ability to navigate challenges is essential for building self-confidence. This affirmation instills a sense of trust in our resilience and problem-solving skills.

Affirmation: "I am confident in stepping outside my comfort zone and embracing new opportunities."

Explanation: Stepping outside our comfort zone is crucial for personal growth. This affirmation encourages us to have confidence in venturing into unfamiliar territory and seizing new opportunities.

Affirmation: "I release self-doubt and embrace self-belief in all that I do."

Explanation: This affirmation invites us to let go of self-doubt and replace it with self-belief. It empowers us to trust in ourselves and our capabilities.

Affirmation: "I am worthy of self-care and prioritize my well-being."

Explanation: Self-care is essential for maintaining a healthy and balanced life. This affirmation emphasizes our worthiness of self-care and encourages us to prioritize our well-being.

Affirmation: "I attract positive and supportive people into my life who uplift and inspire me."

Explanation: The company we keep has a significant impact on our self-confidence. This affirmation reinforces the idea of attracting positive and supportive individuals who contribute to our growth and inspiration.

Affirmation: "I am confident in setting boundaries and asserting myself in a respectful manner."

Explanation: Setting boundaries and asserting ourselves is important for maintaining healthy relationships. This affirmation empowers us to confidently establish boundaries and communicate our needs respectfully.

Affirmation: "I am grateful for my accomplishments and recognize my worthiness of success."

Explanation: Gratitude is a powerful tool for cultivating self-confidence. This affirmation encourages us to acknowledge and appreciate our accomplishments, reinforcing our worthiness of success.

Affirmation: "I radiate confidence and inspire others through my authentic presence."

Explanation: Confidence is contagious, and this affirmation affirms our ability to radiate confidence and inspire others by being authentically ourselves.

Affirmation: "I am deserving of love, kindness, and compassion from myself and others."

Explanation: This affirmation reminds us of our inherent worthiness of love, kindness, and compassion, both from ourselves and from others. It encourages us to cultivate self-compassion and extend it to those around us.

Affirmation: "I embrace failure as an opportunity for growth and learning."

Explanation: Failure is an inevitable part of life. This affirmation helps us reframe our perception of failure and view it as an opportunity for growth and learning, rather than a reflection of our worth.

Affirmation: "I am worthy of achieving my dreams and living a life of purpose."

Explanation: This affirmation reinforces our worthiness of pursuing our dreams and living a purposeful life. It instills belief in our ability to make a meaningful impact.

Affirmation: "I release comparison and focus on my own unique journey and progress."

Explanation: Comparison can diminish our self-confidence. This affirmation encourages us to let go of comparison and focus on our own unique path, celebrating our individual progress.

Affirmation: "I am confident in embracing change and adapting to new circumstances."

Explanation: Change is inevitable, and this affirmation empowers us to have confidence in our ability to adapt to new circumstances, fostering a growth mindset.

Affirmation: "I am deserving of success and prosperity, and I attract abundant opportunities."

Explanation: This affirmation reaffirms our worthiness of success and prosperity. It aligns our energy with abundance, attracting opportunities that lead to growth and achievement.

Affirmation: "I am capable of overcoming any obstacles that come my way."

Explanation: Believing in our ability to overcome obstacles is essential for building resilience. This affirmation instills a sense of determination and strength in tackling challenges.

Affirmation: "I am whole, complete, and enough just as I am."

Explanation: This affirmation emphasizes our inherent wholeness, completeness, and worthiness. It reminds us that we are enough, exactly as we are, without needing to prove ourselves to anyone.

Conclusion:

By integrating these affirmations into our daily lives, we embark on a transformative journey of building self-confidence, self-worth, and belief in our abilities. Through consistent practice and conscious repetition, these affirmations become embedded in our subconscious, shaping our thoughts and actions. Let us embrace the power of affirmations to cultivate a deep sense of self-belief and unlock our fullest potential. Remember, you are worthy, capable, and deserving of all the success and fulfillment that awaits you.

INTRODUCTION: THE IMPORTANCE OF CONFIDENCE AND SELF-BELIEF IN PERSONAL GROWTH.

In the journey of personal growth and self-improvement, confidence and self-belief serve as vital pillars that support our progress and enable us to reach our fullest potential. Confidence is the unwavering belief in oneself, one's abilities, and one's worthiness. Self-belief, on the other hand, encompasses a deep trust and faith in our innate capabilities, as well as a strong sense of self-worth and deservingness.

Confidence and self-belief play a profound role in shaping our thoughts, emotions, and actions. They are the driving forces that propel us forward, empowering us to overcome obstacles, take risks, and pursue our aspirations with determination and resilience. When we possess unwavering confidence and self-belief, we radiate a magnetic energy that attracts positive experiences, opportunities, and relationships into our lives.

The importance of cultivating confidence and self-belief becomes evident when we consider the impact they have on various aspects of our lives. In our personal relationships, confidence allows us to express ourselves authentically, set boundaries, and form meaningful connections. In our academic or professional pursuits, confidence fuels our motivation, creativity, and assertiveness, leading to success and achievement. Moreover, confidence and self-belief contribute to our overall well-being by fostering a positive self-image, reducing stress and anxiety, and enhancing our mental and emotional resilience.

However, it is important to note that confidence and self-belief are not fixed traits that some individuals inherently possess while others do not. They are skills that can be cultivated and nurtured through intentional practice and self-reflection. Like any other skill, they require patience, persistence, and a commitment to personal growth.

In this chapter, we will explore the profound impact of confidence and self-belief on personal growth and examine the various factors that influence their development. We will delve into the psychological and emotional aspects of confidence, explore the concept of self-belief from different perspectives, and provide practical strategies and techniques to enhance these qualities within ourselves.

Throughout this chapter, we will draw insights from diverse fields such as Witchcraft, Divination, Herbalism, Shamanism, and Ecospirituality, aiming to integrate ancient wisdom and modern scientific understanding. By combining these perspectives, we gain a holistic understanding of confidence and self-belief and how they relate to our personal growth journey.

Moreover, we will present examples, problems, and exercises that will encourage critical thinking and self-reflection. These exercises will challenge you to examine your beliefs, identify areas for growth, and develop actionable steps towards cultivating unwavering confidence and self-belief.

As we embark on this exploration, it is essential to approach the concepts of confidence and self-belief with an open mind and a willingness to embrace change. Remember that personal growth is a continuous process, and every step forward, no matter how small, contributes to your journey towards self-empowerment and fulfillment.

Now, let us delve into the depths of confidence and self-belief, unraveling their significance in personal growth and discovering the transformative power they hold within us. Through this exploration, may you find the inspiration, tools, and understanding necessary to cultivate unshakable confidence and self-belief, paving the way for a remarkable journey of self-discovery and personal success.

UNDERSTANDING THE CONNECTION BETWEEN SELF-CONFIDENCE AND SUCCESS.

In the pursuit of personal and professional success, self-confidence plays a significant role in shaping our outcomes and achievements. Self-confidence can be defined as a deep-seated belief in one's abilities, competence, and worthiness. It is an inner state of assurance that empowers individuals to embrace challenges, take risks, and persevere in the face of obstacles.

The relationship between self-confidence and success is multi-faceted and interdependent. When we possess a strong sense of self-confidence, we are more likely to set ambitious goals, make decisions with conviction, and take proactive steps towards realizing our aspirations. Self-confidence provides the foundation upon which success is built, acting as a catalyst for growth, resilience, and self-belief.

One of the key aspects of the connection between self-confidence and success lies in the power of belief. Our beliefs shape our thoughts, emotions, and actions, ultimately influencing the outcomes we experience. When we believe in ourselves and our abilities, we project an aura of confidence that attracts opportunities and positive experiences. This self-assured demeanor not only influences our interactions with others but also impacts our own mindset, fostering a positive and empowering perspective.

Moreover, self-confidence enables individuals to overcome self-doubt and fear of failure. It instills a sense of resilience and determination that allows us to bounce back from setbacks and persevere in the face of challenges. Rather than being deterred by obstacles, individuals with self-confidence view them as opportunities for growth and learning. They approach difficulties with a problem-solving mindset and are more likely to find innovative solutions to overcome barriers.

Additionally, self-confidence influences our ability to effectively communicate and express ourselves. Confidence in our ideas and opinions allows us to articulate them with clarity and conviction, gaining the attention and respect of others. Strong communication skills are essential for success in various domains, such as leadership, teamwork, and professional relationships. Individuals with self-confidence are more likely to assert themselves, contribute meaningfully, and inspire others with their presence.

Furthermore, self-confidence influences our ability to seize opportunities and take calculated risks. Success often requires individuals to step out of their comfort zones, embrace uncertainty, and venture into uncharted territories. With self-confidence as a guiding force, individuals are more willing to embrace these opportunities, knowing that they have the skills and inner resources to navigate challenges and adapt to new circumstances.

It is important to note that self-confidence is not an inherent trait possessed by a select few individuals. It is a quality that can be nurtured and developed through intentional efforts. Building self-confidence requires self-awareness, self-compassion, and a commitment to personal growth. By engaging in practices such as positive affirmations, visualizations, and setting and achieving small goals, individuals can gradually enhance their self-confidence and create a positive cycle of success and self-belief.

In conclusion, self-confidence and success are intrinsically connected. Self-confidence serves as a catalyst for success, influencing our beliefs, mindset, and actions. It empowers individuals to set ambitious goals, overcome obstacles, and seize opportunities. By cultivating self-confidence through self-reflection, practice, and self-compassion, individuals can enhance their chances of achieving personal and professional success. Understanding the profound connection between self-confidence and success allows us to harness our inner potential, embark on transformative journeys, and create a life of fulfillment, purpose, and accomplishment.

Exercise:

Reflect on a time when your self-confidence positively influenced your success. Describe the situation, the actions you took, and the outcome. How did your self-confidence contribute to your achievements? What lessons did you learn from this experience? How can you apply those lessons to enhance your self-confidence in future endeavors?

CULTIVATING A POSITIVE MINDSET AND AFFIRMING YOUR CAPABILITIES.

A positive mindset is a powerful tool that can significantly impact our perception of ourselves, our abilities, and the world around us. It is a state of mind characterized by optimism, resilience, and a belief in our inherent worth and capabilities. Cultivating a positive mindset is essential for personal growth, self-confidence, and overall well-being.

To cultivate a positive mindset, it is important to understand the influence of our thoughts and beliefs on our experiences. Our thoughts shape our reality, and by consciously choosing positive and empowering thoughts, we can reshape our mindset and create a more positive outlook on life. Affirmations play a crucial role in this process, as they help us reinforce positive beliefs and reprogram our subconscious mind.

Affirmations are positive statements that reflect our desired state of being, goals, or qualities. By repeating affirmations regularly and with conviction, we can rewire our thought patterns and create a more positive and empowering internal dialogue. Affirmations act as powerful tools to challenge and replace self-limiting beliefs, instilling a sense of confidence, self-worth, and belief in our capabilities.

When crafting affirmations, it is important to use language that resonates with you personally and reflects your aspirations. Here are some examples of affirmations to cultivate a positive mindset and affirm your capabilities:

1. I am capable of achieving anything I set my mind to.

2. I embrace challenges as opportunities for growth and learning.

3. I am deserving of success and happiness.

4. I trust in my abilities to overcome any obstacles that come my way.

5. I have the power to create positive change in my life and the lives of others.

6. I am resilient and bounce back from setbacks with ease.

7. I am worthy of love, respect, and abundance.

8. I am confident in expressing my authentic self.

9. I attract positive experiences and opportunities into my life.

10. I release all self-doubt and embrace my true potential.

11. I believe in my unique talents and gifts.

12. I am constantly growing and evolving into the best version of myself.

13. I am capable of achieving balance and harmony in all aspects of my life.

14. I trust in the wisdom of my intuition to guide me towards success.

15. I radiate positivity and inspire others with my presence.

16. I choose to focus on the possibilities and opportunities that surround me.

17. I am a magnet for success, prosperity, and abundance.

18. I am grateful for all the experiences that have shaped me into who I am today.

19. I approach every day with enthusiasm and a positive attitude.

20. I celebrate my achievements and acknowledge my progress.

21. I am deserving of love, joy, and fulfillment in all areas of my life.

22. I trust in the divine plan and know that everything is unfolding in perfect timing.

23. I am open to receiving support and guidance from the universe.

24. I choose to see setbacks as stepping stones towards success.

25. I am confident in my ability to create a life of purpose and meaning.

By incorporating these affirmations into your daily practice, you can gradually cultivate a positive mindset and affirm your capabilities. It is important to repeat these affirmations with intention, conviction, and belief. As you continue to affirm your positive qualities and reinforce empowering beliefs, you will notice a transformation in your mindset, attitude, and overall outlook on life.

Exercise:

Choose three affirmations from the list above that resonate with you the most. Write them down on separate pieces of paper or create visual reminders, such as sticky notes or digital wallpapers. Place them in visible locations where you will encounter them throughout the day, such as your workspace, bathroom mirror, or phone screen. Each time you come across an affirmation, take a moment to recite it aloud and reflect on its meaning. Notice how these affirmations impact your thoughts, emotions, and actions. Keep a journal to record any shifts in your mindset and the positive experiences that arise as a result of affirming your capabilities.

LETTING GO OF SELF-DOUBT AND EMBRACING SELF-ASSURANCE.

Self-doubt can be a persistent barrier to personal growth and self-confidence. It is the internal voice that questions our abilities, worth, and potential for success. However, by recognizing and addressing self-doubt, we can cultivate self-assurance and embrace our true potential.

Self-doubt often stems from negative beliefs and past experiences that have shaped our perception of ourselves. It can be influenced by external factors such as societal expectations, comparison to others, or fear of failure. To let go of self-doubt and embrace self-assurance, it is important to engage in self-reflection, challenge negative beliefs, and practice self-compassion.

Self-reflection allows us to gain insight into the origins of our self-doubt and understand the underlying fears and insecurities that contribute to it. By examining our thoughts, emotions, and patterns of behavior, we can identify the triggers and situations that amplify self-doubt. This awareness forms the foundation for transformation and growth.

Challenging negative beliefs involves questioning the validity and accuracy of self-doubt. It requires examining the evidence supporting these beliefs and seeking alternative perspectives. One effective technique is cognitive restructuring, which involves replacing negative thoughts with positive and empowering ones. Affirmations, mentioned earlier, play a crucial role in this process. By consistently affirming our capabilities and worth, we can counteract self-doubt and rewire our thought patterns.

Practicing self-compassion is another key aspect of letting go of self-doubt. It involves treating ourselves with kindness, understanding, and acceptance, especially during moments of self-doubt and perceived failure. Self-compassion helps us develop resilience and cultivate a more nurturing and supportive inner dialogue. This involves acknowledging that making mistakes and experiencing setbacks are part of the learning process, and they do not define our worth or potential for success.

Here are some strategies and affirmations to help you let go of self-doubt and embrace self-assurance:

Engage in self-reflection: Take time to reflect on your thoughts, emotions, and beliefs related to self-doubt. Identify patterns and triggers that contribute to self-doubt.

Challenge negative beliefs: Question the accuracy and validity of your self-doubt. Collect evidence that supports your capabilities, achievements, and positive qualities. Replace negative thoughts with affirmations and positive self-talk.

Practice self-compassion: Treat yourself with kindness and understanding. Offer yourself the same level of compassion and support you would extend to a friend facing similar challenges.

Embrace failure as a learning opportunity: Shift your perspective on failure. View it as an opportunity for growth and learning rather than a reflection of your worth or abilities.

Cultivate a support system: Surround yourself with people who believe in your capabilities and provide encouragement and support. Seek out mentors or role models who can inspire and guide you on your journey.

Visualize success: Use visualization techniques to imagine yourself overcoming challenges and achieving your goals. Visualize yourself feeling confident, self-assured, and successful.

Take action: Break down your goals into smaller, manageable steps. By taking action and achieving small wins, you can build confidence and reinforce your self-assurance.

Affirmations:

1. I release all self-doubt and embrace my inherent worth and potential.

2. I am worthy of success, happiness, and fulfillment.

3. I trust in my abilities and have confidence in my unique talents.

4. I let go of fear and step into my power with self-assurance.

5. I am deserving of love, respect, and recognition for my accomplishments.

6. I choose to believe in myself and my ability to overcome challenges.

7. I release the need for approval from others and affirm my own self-worth.

8. I am capable, competent, and deserving of all the good that comes my way.

9. I release comparison and focus on my own journey of growth and progress.

10. I am resilient and bounce back stronger from setbacks.

11. I trust my intuition and make choices that align with my authentic self.

12. I am confident in expressing my ideas, opinions, and desires.

13. I have the power to create positive change in my life and the world around me.

14. I am enough, just as I am, and I embrace my uniqueness.

15. I let go of perfectionism and embrace the beauty of imperfection.

16. I deserve success and allow myself to achieve my goals.

17. I am open to receiving abundance, opportunities, and blessings.

18. I am worthy of love and support, and I attract positive relationships into my life.

19. I let go of self-criticism and replace it with self-compassion and understanding.

20. I trust in my journey and have faith in the unfolding of my life's purpose.

21. I am resilient in the face of challenges and setbacks.

22. I believe in my ability to learn, grow, and adapt to any situation.

23. I celebrate my achievements, no matter how small, and acknowledge my progress.

24. I am the creator of my own reality, and I choose to manifest confidence and self-assurance.

25. I embrace the unknown with courage and trust that I am capable of navigating any situation.

By consistently practicing these strategies and affirmations, you can gradually let go of self-doubt and cultivate a deep sense of self-assurance. Remember, building confidence is a lifelong journey, and it requires commitment, self-reflection, and a belief in your own worth and potential.

AFFIRMING BELIEF IN YOUR UNIQUE STRENGTHS AND TALENTS.

Believing in your unique strengths and talents is a crucial aspect of cultivating self-confidence and achieving personal growth. Acknowledging and affirming your inherent abilities can empower you to embrace your authenticity and unlock your full potential. By recognizing and embracing your unique qualities, you can build a solid foundation of self-belief and create a positive impact in various aspects of your life.

Understanding your unique strengths and talents requires a deep exploration of your individuality. Each person possesses a distinct combination of qualities, skills, and characteristics that contribute to their uniqueness. These strengths can manifest in various areas, such as intellectual abilities, creative talents, emotional intelligence, leadership skills, or interpersonal capabilities. It is important to recognize that no two individuals are exactly alike, and each person has a unique set of strengths that can be harnessed and celebrated.

To affirm belief in your unique strengths and talents, it is essential to engage in self-reflection, self-discovery, and self-appreciation. Through these practices, you can gain a deeper understanding of your individual qualities and develop a strong sense of self-worth.

Self-reflection involves taking the time to examine your experiences, achievements, and the feedback you have received from others. Consider the activities and tasks that come naturally to you, the areas in which you excel, and the moments when you feel most confident and fulfilled. Reflect on the times when you have made a positive impact or achieved notable accomplishments. By recognizing these moments, you can identify recurring patterns and uncover your unique strengths and talents.

Self-discovery entails exploring different aspects of yourself and embracing your authenticity. It involves being open to new experiences, trying out different activities, and allowing yourself to make mistakes and learn from them. Through exploration, you can uncover hidden talents, passions, and interests that may contribute to your overall sense of purpose and fulfillment. Embrace opportunities for growth and challenge yourself to step outside of your comfort zone.

Self-appreciation is an essential practice for affirming belief in your unique strengths and talents. It involves acknowledging and celebrating your accomplishments, big and small. Give yourself credit for your achievements and recognize the effort, dedication, and resilience you have demonstrated along the way. Express gratitude for your talents and the positive impact they have on your life and the lives of others. Practice self-compassion and treat yourself with kindness, understanding, and acceptance.

Here are some strategies and affirmations to help you affirm belief in your unique strengths and talents:

Engage in self-reflection: Take time to reflect on your experiences, achievements, and the feedback you have received. Identify recurring patterns and moments when you feel most confident and fulfilled.

Embrace self-discovery: Explore different activities, hobbies, and interests to uncover hidden talents and passions. Allow yourself to make mistakes and learn from them.

Celebrate your accomplishments: Acknowledge and appreciate your achievements, no matter how small. Give yourself credit for your efforts and the positive impact you have made.

Express gratitude for your unique strengths: Recognize and express gratitude for your unique qualities and talents. Appreciate the value they bring to your life and the lives of others.

Practice self-compassion: Treat yourself with kindness, understanding, and acceptance. Embrace your imperfections and celebrate your uniqueness.

Surround yourself with positive influences: Surround yourself with individuals who appreciate and celebrate your strengths. Seek support and encouragement from mentors, friends, and family members who uplift and inspire you.

Use affirmations: Incorporate affirmations into your daily routine to reinforce belief in your unique strengths and talents. Repeat positive statements that affirm your abilities and value.

Affirmations:

1. I embrace and celebrate my unique strengths and talents.

2. I have a distinct combination of qualities and abilities that make me valuable.

3. I acknowledge and appreciate the positive impact I make through my unique talents.

4. I am worthy of recognition and success because of my unique strengths.

5. My unique qualities bring me joy, fulfillment, and personal growth.

6. I confidently embrace and share my talents with the world.

7. I am deserving of recognition and opportunities that align with my unique strengths.

8. I am constantly discovering and developing my unique talents and abilities.

9. My unique strengths contribute to the greater good and make a positive difference.

10. I am grateful for my unique qualities and the growth they bring to my life.

Exercise:

Reflect on your own unique strengths and talents. Make a list of the activities, skills, and qualities that you believe make you unique. Consider the positive feedback you have received from others and the moments when you felt most confident and fulfilled. Write a reflection paper discussing your unique strengths and talents, and how they contribute to your personal growth and overall sense of self-belief.

Problem:

Consider a hypothetical situation in which you doubt your unique strengths and talents. Analyze the underlying reasons for your self-doubt and explore strategies to overcome it. Develop an action plan to affirm belief in your unique abilities and build self-confidence.

By practicing self-reflection, self-discovery, self-appreciation, and incorporating affirmations into your daily routine, you can affirm belief in your unique strengths and talents. Embrace your authenticity, celebrate your individuality, and confidently share your gifts with the world. Remember that your unique qualities have the power to make a positive impact and contribute to your personal growth and success.

OVERCOMING FEAR OF FAILURE AND EMBRACING A GROWTH MINDSET.

The fear of failure is a common obstacle that can hinder personal growth and success. It often stems from a belief that mistakes and setbacks are indicative of incompetence or unworthiness. However, by embracing a growth mindset, individuals can reframe their perception of failure and view it as an opportunity for learning, growth, and resilience.

Understanding the fear of failure requires an exploration of its underlying causes and the impact it has on individuals. Fear of failure can be rooted in various factors, such as societal expectations, past experiences, perfectionism, and self-doubt. It can manifest as self-limiting beliefs, avoidance of challenges, or a reluctance to take risks. Recognizing and acknowledging these fears is the first step towards overcoming them.

To cultivate a growth mindset, individuals must adopt a belief in their capacity for growth and improvement. A growth mindset is characterized by the understanding that abilities and intelligence can be developed through dedication, effort, and perseverance. It is an empowering perspective that embraces challenges, views setbacks as learning opportunities, and fosters a desire for continuous improvement.

Here are some strategies and affirmations to help overcome fear of failure and embrace a growth mindset:

Acknowledge and confront your fears: Identify the specific fears and self-limiting beliefs that contribute to your fear of failure. Recognize that these fears are normal but not insurmountable.

Reframe failure as a learning opportunity: Shift your perspective on failure. See it as a stepping stone towards growth and improvement. Embrace the idea that failure provides valuable feedback and allows for course correction.

Embrace challenges: Seek out opportunities that push you outside of your comfort zone. Embracing challenges fosters personal growth, builds resilience, and expands your skill set.

Cultivate resilience: Develop resilience by bouncing back from setbacks. Focus on finding solutions and adapting to new circumstances rather than dwelling on past failures.

Practice self-compassion: Treat yourself with kindness and understanding when faced with failures or setbacks. Remind yourself that making mistakes is a natural part of the learning process and does not define your worth.

Use affirmations: Incorporate affirmations into your daily routine to reinforce a growth mindset. Repeat positive statements that affirm your ability to learn, grow, and overcome challenges.

Affirmations:

1. I embrace failure as an opportunity for growth and learning.

2. I am resilient and bounce back from setbacks stronger than before.

3. I am capable of learning and improving in any area I choose.

4. I welcome challenges and see them as opportunities for personal growth.

5. Mistakes are stepping stones to success, and I learn from them with grace.

6. I release the fear of failure and embrace the possibilities of growth.

7. I am not defined by my past failures but by my ability to learn and evolve.

8. I am open to taking risks and stepping outside of my comfort zone.

9. I trust in my ability to overcome obstacles and achieve my goals.

10. I have a growth mindset, and I am constantly expanding my knowledge and skills.

Exercise:

Reflect on a past failure or setback and identify the lessons you learned from that experience. Write a journal entry describing how you grew from that failure and what changes you made as a result. Discuss the insights gained and the actions you took to embrace a growth mindset.

Problem:

Consider a hypothetical scenario where you are faced with a challenging task or project that triggers your fear of failure. Analyze your thought patterns and identify any self-limiting beliefs that may arise. Develop a plan to reframe your mindset and approach the task with a growth-oriented perspective.

By acknowledging and confronting your fears, reframing failure as a learning opportunity, embracing challenges, cultivating resilience, practicing self-compassion, and using affirmations, you can overcome the fear of failure and embrace a growth mindset. This mindset empowers you to achieve your goals, navigate obstacles with resilience, and continually learn and grow.

AFFIRMING CONFIDENCE IN DECISION-MAKING AND TRUSTING YOUR INSTINCTS.

Making decisions can be a daunting task, especially when faced with uncertainty and the fear of making the wrong choice. However, cultivating confidence in decision-making and learning to trust your instincts can empower you to navigate life's challenges with clarity and conviction.

Confidence in decision-making stems from a combination of self-awareness, knowledge, and trust in your own judgment. It involves understanding your values, goals, and priorities, as well as having a clear understanding of the potential outcomes and consequences of your choices. Trusting your instincts, on the other hand, involves tapping into your intuition and inner wisdom to guide you towards the right path.

Here are some strategies and affirmations to help affirm confidence in decision-making and trust in your instincts:

Enhance self-awareness: Take the time to explore your values, passions, and aspirations. Understand what truly matters to you and align your decisions with your core principles.

Seek knowledge and information: Gather relevant information and insights to inform your decision-making process. Consult reputable sources, seek advice from trusted mentors or experts, and conduct thorough research to gain a comprehensive understanding of the situation.

Reflect and analyze: Engage in thoughtful reflection and analysis of the available options. Consider the potential outcomes, risks, and benefits associated with each choice. Evaluate how each option aligns with your goals and values.

Trust your intuition: Develop a sense of trust in your intuition and inner guidance. Pay attention to your gut feelings, instincts, and subtle signals from your body and mind. Often, your intuition can provide valuable insights that rational analysis may overlook.

Embrace imperfection: Understand that not every decision will lead to a perfect outcome. Embrace the idea that mistakes and setbacks are part of the learning process. Approach decision-making with a growth mindset, viewing failures as opportunities for growth and learning.

Affirmations:

1. I trust my instincts and make decisions with confidence.

2. I am guided by my inner wisdom and intuition in all my decision-making.

3. I have the knowledge and resources to make informed decisions.

4. Each decision I make aligns with my values and supports my goals.

5. I approach decision-making with clarity, calmness, and confidence.

6. I release the fear of making the wrong choice and trust in the process.

7. I am capable of making sound decisions that lead to positive outcomes.

8. I am in tune with my intuition and allow it to guide me towards the right path.

9. I trust myself to handle any challenges that may arise from my decisions.

10. I am confident in my ability to make wise decisions that serve my highest good.

Exercise:

Choose a recent decision you made and reflect on the process you followed. Consider the factors that influenced your decision and how you could have incorporated more trust in your instincts. Write a journal entry analyzing the outcome and any lessons learned.

Problem:

Imagine you are faced with a difficult decision that requires you to trust your instincts. Write a step-by-step plan on how you would approach the decision-making process while incorporating self-reflection, gathering information, and listening to your intuition. Consider potential risks, benefits, and alignment with your values.

By affirming confidence in decision-making and trusting your instincts, you can approach choices with clarity, conviction, and a sense of empowerment. Remember to combine rational analysis with intuitive wisdom to make decisions that align with your authentic self and lead to positive outcomes.

BUILDING RESILIENCE AND BOUNCING BACK FROM SETBACKS.

Life is full of ups and downs, and setbacks are inevitable. However, developing resilience is key to overcoming obstacles and thriving in the face of adversity. Resilience is the ability to adapt, recover, and bounce back from challenging situations. It involves cultivating a mindset that sees setbacks as opportunities for growth and learning, and harnessing inner strength to persevere.

In this section, we will explore strategies and affirmations to help you build resilience and navigate setbacks with grace and determination.

Embrace a growth mindset: Adopting a growth mindset is crucial for building resilience. Instead of viewing setbacks as failures, see them as valuable learning experiences. Believe that challenges are opportunities for personal growth and development. Emphasize the power of effort, perseverance, and learning from mistakes.

Develop self-awareness: Self-awareness plays a vital role in building resilience. Reflect on your strengths, weaknesses, and patterns of thinking. Recognize your emotional reactions and triggers in the face of setbacks. This awareness will help you respond to setbacks more effectively and make conscious choices about how to move forward.

Practice self-care: Taking care of your physical, mental, and emotional well-being is essential for resilience. Engage in activities that bring you joy and help you recharge. Practice self-compassion and treat yourself with kindness during challenging times. Ensure you have a support system in place, whether it's friends, family, or professionals who can provide guidance and encouragement.

Cultivate optimism and positive thinking: Optimism and positive thinking can fuel resilience. Focus on the possibilities and potential solutions rather than dwelling on the setbacks. Train your mind to find the silver lining in difficult situations. Affirm your belief in your ability to overcome obstacles and create positive outcomes.

Set realistic goals and take action: Break down your larger goals into smaller, achievable steps. Set realistic expectations for yourself and celebrate each milestone along the way. Taking action, even in small increments, helps you regain a sense of control and progress.

Affirmations:

1. I am resilient and have the inner strength to overcome any setback.

2. I embrace challenges as opportunities for growth and learning.

3. I am flexible and adaptable in the face of change and adversity.

4. I bounce back from setbacks with determination and grace.

5. I am strong, capable, and resilient in the face of challenges.

6. I trust in my ability to find solutions and overcome obstacles.

7. Each setback strengthens my resilience and propels me forward.

8. I cultivate a positive mindset and focus on possibilities and solutions.

9. I take care of my physical, mental, and emotional well-being to build resilience.

10. I persevere with unwavering determination and resilience.

Exercise:

Think of a recent setback or challenge you faced. Reflect on how you initially reacted and how you managed to overcome it. Write a journal entry analyzing your resilience and identifying areas for growth.

Problem:

Imagine you are faced with a significant setback that threatens to derail your progress. Develop a step-by-step action plan to bounce back from this setback. Consider the strategies mentioned above, such as adopting a growth mindset, practicing self-care, and setting realistic goals. Write down each action you would take and the expected outcome.

Building resilience is a lifelong journey that requires practice, self-reflection, and the willingness to adapt. By adopting a growth mindset, practicing self-care, and embracing positive thinking, you can cultivate resilience and bounce back from setbacks with strength and determination. Remember, setbacks are not the end but an opportunity for growth and transformation.

AFFIRMING SELF-WORTH AND RECOGNIZING YOUR INHERENT VALUE.

Understanding and acknowledging your self-worth is an essential aspect of personal growth and empowerment. Self-worth refers to recognizing your inherent value as a unique individual and acknowledging that you are deserving of love, respect, and happiness. It involves embracing your strengths, accepting your flaws, and valuing yourself unconditionally.

In this section, we will explore the significance of affirming self-worth and provide strategies and affirmations to help you recognize your inherent value and cultivate a deep sense of self-worth.

Embrace your uniqueness: Each person possesses unique qualities, talents, and perspectives. Embrace your individuality and celebrate the qualities that make you who you are. Recognize that your uniqueness adds value to the world and that you have something special to contribute.

Challenge self-critical thoughts: Often, negative self-talk and self-critical thoughts can undermine your self-worth. Identify and challenge these negative thoughts by replacing them with positive and empowering affirmations. Recognize that you are not defined by your mistakes or perceived flaws, but rather by your inherent worth as a human being.

Practice self-compassion: Treat yourself with kindness, understanding, and compassion. Cultivate a nurturing and supportive inner dialogue. Instead of berating yourself for shortcomings, offer yourself words of encouragement, forgiveness, and acceptance. Remember that self-compassion allows for growth and learning.

Surround yourself with positive influences: Surrounding yourself with positive and uplifting influences can reinforce your sense of self-worth. Seek out relationships and environments that appreciate and validate your unique qualities. Engage with individuals who support your growth and encourage you to embrace your worth.

Set healthy boundaries: Setting boundaries is essential for protecting your self-worth. Identify and communicate your needs, values, and limits to others. Establish boundaries that honor your emotional well-being and prevent others from diminishing your self-worth.

Affirmations:

1. I am worthy of love, respect, and happiness.

2. I embrace my uniqueness and recognize the value I bring to the world.

3. I release self-judgment and accept myself unconditionally.

4. I deserve success and abundance in all areas of my life.

5. I am enough just as I am, and my worth is not defined by external validation.

6. I celebrate my strengths and embrace my imperfections as opportunities for growth.

7. I deserve to be treated with kindness, respect, and compassion.

8. I am worthy of pursuing my dreams and living a fulfilling life.

9. I recognize my worthiness and value myself deeply.

10. I choose to prioritize my well-being and set healthy boundaries that honor my self-worth.

Exercise:

Write a list of 10 qualities or strengths that you appreciate about yourself. Reflect on how these qualities contribute to your uniqueness and value as an individual. Use this list as a reminder of your inherent worth and refer to it whenever you need a boost of self-confidence.

Problem:

Imagine you have a friend who struggles with recognizing their self-worth. Write a letter to your friend explaining the importance of self-worth and providing them with guidance on how to affirm and embrace their own value. Include personal anecdotes, examples, and affirmations to illustrate your points.

Affirming your self-worth is a transformative journey that requires conscious effort and self-reflection. By embracing your uniqueness, challenging self-critical thoughts, practicing self-compassion, surrounding yourself with positive influences, and setting healthy boundaries, you can cultivate a deep sense of self-worth and recognize the inherent value you possess as an individual. Remember, you are worthy of love, happiness, and all the good things life has to offer.

CHALLENGING NEGATIVE SELF-TALK AND REPLACING IT WITH POSITIVE AFFIRMATIONS.

Negative self-talk can be detrimental to our self-esteem, confidence, and overall well-being. It involves the internal dialogue and thoughts that criticize, doubt, or belittle ourselves. Challenging negative self-talk is a crucial step towards building a positive mindset and cultivating self-empowerment. By replacing negative thoughts with positive affirmations, we can transform our inner dialogue and nurture a healthier and more supportive relationship with ourselves.

In this section, we will explore the importance of challenging negative self-talk and provide strategies and techniques to replace it with positive affirmations. By engaging in this process, you can gradually shift your mindset and strengthen your belief in yourself.

Identify negative self-talk patterns: Start by becoming aware of the negative thoughts that arise within you. Notice the specific triggers, situations, or circumstances that tend to elicit negative self-talk. By identifying these patterns, you can gain insight into the underlying beliefs and perceptions that contribute to negative self-talk.

Question the validity of negative thoughts: Once you become aware of negative self-talk, question the validity of those thoughts. Ask yourself if there is any evidence to support these negative beliefs. Often, negative self-talk is based on assumptions, past experiences, or irrational fears. Challenge these thoughts by seeking evidence to counter them or by considering alternative perspectives.

Reframe negative thoughts with positive affirmations: Replace negative self-talk with positive affirmations that promote self-empowerment and self-belief. Positive affirmations are statements that affirm positive qualities, beliefs, and outcomes. For example, if you catch yourself thinking, "I always mess things up," reframe it as, "I am capable and competent in handling challenges."

Practice self-compassion and self-forgiveness: Be kind and compassionate towards yourself when negative thoughts arise. Acknowledge that everyone makes mistakes and experiences setbacks. Practice self-forgiveness and remind yourself that these moments do not define your worth or capabilities. Replace self-criticism with self-compassion and use affirmations that emphasize self-love and acceptance.

Consistency and repetition: Incorporate positive affirmations into your daily routine. Write them down, repeat them aloud, or create visual reminders to reinforce their message. Consistency and repetition are key to rewiring your brain and creating new neural pathways that support positive self-talk.

Examples of negative self-talk and corresponding positive affirmations:

Negative self-talk: "I'm not smart enough to succeed."

Positive affirmation: "I am intelligent and capable of learning and achieving my goals."

Negative self-talk: "I always fail at everything I do."

Positive affirmation: "I embrace failure as an opportunity for growth, and I am resilient in the face of challenges."

Negative self-talk: "I'm not attractive or desirable."

Positive affirmation: "I am beautiful inside and out, and I radiate confidence and self-acceptance."

Negative self-talk: "I'll never be able to achieve my dreams."

Positive affirmation: "I am worthy of pursuing and achieving my dreams, and I have the strength and determination to make them a reality."

Exercise:

Create a list of negative self-talk statements that you frequently encounter. For each statement, develop a corresponding positive affirmation. Practice repeating these positive affirmations daily to challenge and replace the negative self-talk.

Problem:

Imagine a scenario where a close friend constantly engages in negative self-talk. Write a conversation script where you address your friend's negative self-talk patterns and provide them with guidance on replacing it with positive affirmations. Offer support, empathy, and examples to illustrate the power of positive self-talk.

By challenging negative self-talk and replacing it with positive affirmations, you can transform your inner dialogue and cultivate a more positive and empowering mindset. Remember, your thoughts have the power to shape your reality. Embrace the practice of positive affirmations to build self-belief, boost self-esteem, and create a foundation for personal growth and success.

AFFIRMATIONS FOR STEPPING OUT OF YOUR COMFORT ZONE AND EMBRACING NEW OPPORTUNITIES.

Stepping out of your comfort zone is an essential aspect of personal growth and embracing new opportunities. It requires challenging the familiar and venturing into uncharted territory. By affirming your ability to step outside your comfort zone, you can overcome fear and resistance, expand your horizons, and open yourself up to a world of possibilities.

In this section, we will explore affirmations that can empower you to step out of your comfort zone and embrace new opportunities. These affirmations will help you cultivate the courage, confidence, and mindset needed to navigate unfamiliar territory and unlock your true potential.

"I embrace new experiences with an open mind and heart."

This affirmation encourages you to approach new opportunities with curiosity and receptivity. By embracing a mindset of openness, you allow yourself to learn, grow, and discover new facets of your being.

"I am capable of handling any challenges that come my way."

Stepping out of your comfort zone often involves facing challenges and uncertainties. This affirmation affirms your resilience and inner strength to overcome obstacles and navigate through unfamiliar situations.

"I release the fear of failure and embrace the lessons it brings."

Fear of failure can hold us back from pursuing new opportunities. This affirmation encourages you to let go of the fear of failure and embrace it as a valuable teacher. It reminds you that every experience, successful or not, contributes to your growth and development.

"I trust my intuition to guide me in making bold decisions."

When stepping out of your comfort zone, trusting your intuition is crucial. This affirmation reinforces your belief in your inner wisdom and encourages you to rely on it when making decisions that take you beyond your comfort zone.

"I welcome discomfort as a sign of growth and transformation."

Stepping out of your comfort zone often involves stepping into discomfort. This affirmation helps you reframe discomfort as a positive indicator of growth and transformation. It reminds you that true growth occurs when you stretch yourself beyond what is familiar and comfortable.

"I am worthy of experiencing new and exciting opportunities."

This affirmation affirms your inherent worthiness to experience new and exciting opportunities. It reinforces the belief that you deserve to explore and enjoy the richness of life beyond your comfort zone.

Exercise:

Create a list of specific situations or opportunities that lie outside your comfort zone. For each situation, develop an affirmation that empowers and supports you in stepping into that experience. Practice repeating these affirmations daily to reinforce your readiness to embrace new opportunities.

Problem:

Imagine you have been presented with an opportunity to speak at a prestigious conference, but you feel apprehensive about public speaking. Write a journal entry where you reflect on your fears, challenges, and the affirmations you can use to bolster your confidence and embrace this new opportunity. Include specific examples and instances from various fields, such as Witchcraft, Divination, Herbalism, Shamanism, or Ecospirituality, to illustrate how individuals in those areas have overcome their comfort zones to achieve personal and professional growth.

By consistently affirming your ability to step out of your comfort zone and embracing new opportunities, you expand your horizons, develop new skills, and unlock the doors to personal and professional transformation. Remember, growth and fulfillment often lie just beyond the boundaries of what is comfortable and familiar.

AFFIRMING ASSERTIVENESS AND EFFECTIVE COMMUNICATION SKILLS.

Effective communication and assertiveness are vital skills that contribute to personal and professional success. They enable individuals to express themselves confidently, convey their needs and opinions, and build healthy relationships based on mutual understanding and respect. By affirming your assertiveness and honing your communication skills, you can enhance your ability to interact with others and navigate various social and professional contexts.

In this section, we will explore affirmations that can help you cultivate assertiveness and develop effective communication skills. These affirmations will empower you to express your thoughts and feelings with clarity, establish boundaries, and engage in constructive dialogue.

"I communicate my thoughts and feelings with confidence and clarity."

This affirmation reinforces your belief in your ability to express yourself effectively. It affirms that you can articulate your thoughts and feelings in a clear and concise manner, fostering understanding and connection with others.

"I assertively express my needs and set boundaries that honor my well-being."

Assertiveness involves advocating for your needs and setting boundaries that protect your well-being. This affirmation affirms your right to assert your needs and establishes a foundation for healthy and balanced interactions with others.

"I actively listen and seek to understand others with empathy and compassion."

Effective communication goes beyond expressing oneself—it also involves listening actively and empathetically to others. This affirmation encourages you to cultivate listening skills, demonstrating empathy and compassion in your interactions.

"I handle conflicts and disagreements with grace and respect."

Conflict is an inevitable part of human interactions. This affirmation reinforces your ability to navigate conflicts and disagreements in a constructive manner. It affirms your capacity to respond with grace and respect, fostering understanding and resolution.

"I am open to feedback and use it as an opportunity for growth."

Receiving feedback is an essential aspect of personal and professional growth. This affirmation affirms your willingness to receive feedback with an open mind, viewing it as an opportunity for learning and improvement.

"I communicate assertively in professional settings, advocating for my ideas and contributions."

In professional settings, assertive communication is crucial for advancing your ideas and making valuable contributions. This affirmation affirms your ability to express yourself confidently and assertively in professional contexts.

Exercise:

Choose a specific scenario that requires assertiveness and effective communication. It could be a workplace situation, a personal relationship, or a group discussion. Develop a role-playing exercise where you practice assertive communication and use the affirmations provided to guide your approach. Reflect on the experience and identify areas for improvement.

Problem:

Imagine you are part of a team project where differing opinions and communication challenges have hindered progress. Write a persuasive essay discussing the importance of assertiveness and effective communication in resolving conflicts within the team. Use examples from various fields, such as Witchcraft, Divination, Herbalism, Shamanism, or Ecospirituality, to illustrate how individuals in those areas have utilized assertiveness and effective communication to overcome obstacles and achieve successful outcomes.

By affirming your assertiveness and cultivating effective communication skills, you empower yourself to express your thoughts and needs confidently, establish healthy boundaries, and engage in meaningful interactions with others. Remember, effective communication is a powerful tool for building connections, resolving conflicts, and achieving personal and professional fulfillment.

LETTING GO OF THE NEED FOR EXTERNAL VALIDATION AND AFFIRMING SELF-APPROVAL.

The need for external validation, seeking approval and recognition from others, can significantly impact our self-esteem and sense of self-worth. It often leads to a cycle of seeking validation from external sources, which can be detrimental to our well-being and hinder personal growth. However, by letting go of this need for external validation and embracing self-approval, we can cultivate a stronger sense of self and experience greater fulfillment and happiness.

In this section, we will explore the concept of letting go of the need for external validation and how affirmations can help us affirm our self-approval. By recognizing our inherent worth and valuing our own opinions and achievements, we can break free from the constant need for validation from others.

"I acknowledge and appreciate my own accomplishments and strengths."

This affirmation encourages you to recognize and appreciate your own accomplishments and strengths. It shifts the focus from external validation to self-approval, reminding you that your worthiness and achievements are valid and deserving of recognition.

"I trust my own judgment and make decisions that align with my values and aspirations."

Trusting your own judgment is essential for affirming self-approval. This affirmation reinforces your belief in your ability to make decisions that align with your values and aspirations, empowering you to trust yourself rather than relying solely on external validation.

"I embrace my uniqueness and celebrate my individuality."

Each person possesses unique qualities and attributes that make them special. This affirmation affirms your acceptance of your own uniqueness and encourages you to celebrate your individuality. By embracing your true self, you can let go of the need for external validation and find fulfillment within yourself.

"I am deserving of love, respect, and success, regardless of others' opinions."

This affirmation emphasizes your inherent worthiness and affirms that you deserve love, respect, and success irrespective of others' opinions. It reminds you that external validation is not a prerequisite for your own self-approval and happiness.

"I release the need for others' approval and find validation within myself."

Letting go of the need for others' approval is a liberating step toward self-approval. This affirmation encourages you to release the attachment to external validation and instead find validation within yourself. It affirms your ability to validate and approve of yourself without seeking constant reassurance from others.

Exercise:

Reflect on situations where you tend to seek external validation. Identify one specific scenario where you can consciously practice self-approval instead. Develop an exercise where you affirm your worth, acknowledge your accomplishments, and validate yourself without relying on others' opinions. Monitor your feelings and mindset throughout the exercise and observe any shifts in your self-perception and confidence.

Problem:

Write a reflective essay discussing the implications of relying solely on external validation for one's self-esteem and personal growth. Explore the potential consequences of this reliance, drawing examples from fields such as Witchcraft, Divination, Herbalism, Shamanism, or Ecospirituality to illustrate how individuals in those areas have embraced self-approval and achieved personal empowerment. Offer counterarguments and dissenting opinions to present a balanced perspective on the topic.

By letting go of the need for external validation and affirming self-approval, you reclaim your power and establish a strong foundation for self-esteem and personal growth. Remember, your worthiness and validation come from within, and by embracing self-approval, you can cultivate a deep sense of self-acceptance, confidence, and fulfillment.

AFFIRMATIONS FOR EMBRACING CONSTRUCTIVE CRITICISM AND USING IT AS A TOOL FOR GROWTH.

Constructive criticism is a valuable tool for personal and professional growth. While it can be challenging to receive feedback, especially when it points out areas for improvement, adopting a mindset of growth and utilizing affirmations can help us embrace constructive criticism as a catalyst for self-improvement and development. In this section, we will explore the power of affirmations in embracing constructive criticism and using it as a tool for growth.

"I am open to receiving feedback and using it to enhance my skills and knowledge."

This affirmation sets the stage for embracing constructive criticism by affirming your openness to receiving feedback. It recognizes that feedback is an opportunity for growth and improvement, and reinforces your willingness to use it as a valuable resource for enhancing your skills and knowledge.

"I separate my worth from the feedback I receive and focus on the lessons it provides."

Constructive criticism is not a reflection of your worth as an individual, but rather an opportunity to learn and grow. This affirmation reminds you to detach your self-esteem from the feedback you receive and instead focus on the lessons and insights it offers. It reinforces the notion that feedback is a valuable tool rather than a personal attack.

"I appreciate and acknowledge the perspectives of others as valuable contributions to my growth."

Embracing constructive criticism requires valuing and appreciating the perspectives of others. This affirmation encourages you to see feedback as a valuable contribution to your growth and development. It affirms your openness to diverse perspectives and reinforces your willingness to learn from others.

"I use feedback to identify areas for improvement and take proactive steps towards growth."

This affirmation empowers you to utilize feedback as a catalyst for personal growth. It encourages you to identify areas for improvement based on the feedback you receive and take proactive steps to enhance your skills and capabilities. It reinforces the idea that feedback is an opportunity for progress rather than a setback.

"I am grateful for the opportunity to grow and evolve through constructive criticism."

Gratitude plays a significant role in embracing constructive criticism. This affirmation reminds you to cultivate gratitude for the opportunity to receive feedback and grow. It shifts your perspective from viewing criticism as a negative experience to one that is filled with potential for personal and professional advancement.

Exercise:

Identify a recent situation where you received constructive criticism. Write down the specific feedback you received and reflect on your initial reaction. Develop an exercise where you create affirmations related to the feedback that align with embracing growth and improvement. Repeat these affirmations regularly and observe any shifts in your mindset and behavior as you internalize the constructive criticism.

Problem:

Write a reflective journal entry discussing the challenges and benefits of embracing constructive criticism for personal and professional growth. Share a personal experience where you initially struggled with receiving feedback but eventually embraced it as a catalyst for positive change. Draw examples from fields such as Witchcraft, Divination, Herbalism, Shamanism, or Ecospirituality to highlight how individuals in those areas have utilized constructive criticism for growth and transformation. Present counterarguments and dissenting opinions to provide a balanced view on the topic.

By embracing affirmations and adopting a growth mindset, we can reframe constructive criticism as an opportunity for growth and self-improvement. It allows us to separate our self-worth from the feedback we receive and focus on the valuable lessons it provides. Remember, constructive criticism is a powerful tool that can propel us towards our fullest potential when approached with an open mind and a commitment to continuous growth.

AFFIRMING CONFIDENCE IN PUBLIC SPEAKING AND PRESENTATION SKILLS.

Public speaking and effective presentation skills are essential in various fields, from academia to business and beyond. The ability to communicate ideas confidently and persuasively in front of an audience can open doors to new opportunities and propel personal and professional growth. In this section, we will explore the power of affirmations in affirming confidence in public speaking and presentation skills.

"I am a confident and compelling speaker, capable of captivating my audience."

This affirmation sets the foundation for building confidence in public speaking. It affirms your inherent ability to engage and captivate your audience. By repeating this affirmation regularly, you reinforce the belief in your own capabilities as a speaker and instill a sense of confidence in your ability to deliver compelling presentations.

"I embrace nervousness as a sign of growth and excitement, channeling it into dynamic energy."

Nervousness is a common experience when it comes to public speaking. This affirmation reframes nervousness as a positive indication of growth and excitement. It encourages you to channel that energy into a dynamic and engaging delivery. By embracing nervousness as a natural response and using it to your advantage, you can transform it into a source of vitality and enthusiasm.

"I prepare diligently, knowing that thorough preparation enhances my confidence and delivery."

Preparation plays a crucial role in building confidence in public speaking. This affirmation emphasizes the importance of diligent preparation in boosting your confidence. It affirms your commitment to thorough preparation, recognizing that it enhances both your confidence and the quality of your delivery. By internalizing this affirmation, you develop a proactive approach to preparation, which in turn bolsters your confidence.

"I connect authentically with my audience, creating a positive and engaging experience."

Authentic connection with your audience is key to successful public speaking. This affirmation reinforces your ability to connect genuinely with others, fostering a positive and engaging experience. It reminds you to focus on building rapport, empathizing with your audience, and delivering your message in a way that resonates with them. By affirming your capacity for authentic connection, you enhance your confidence in public speaking.

"I embrace feedback and use it to refine my speaking skills, constantly improving and evolving."

Feedback is a valuable resource for growth and improvement. This affirmation encourages you to embrace feedback as an opportunity for refinement and growth. It affirms your willingness to listen to constructive criticism and use it to continuously improve your speaking skills. By internalizing this affirmation, you cultivate a growth mindset and foster a continuous learning approach to public speaking.

Exercise:

Select a topic of interest and prepare a short presentation. Before delivering the presentation, create affirmations specific to the areas you want to reinforce and boost confidence in. Repeat these affirmations before and during your presentation. Afterward, reflect on the impact of affirmations on your confidence and overall performance.

Problem:

Write an essay discussing the importance of confident public speaking and presentation skills in various fields such as Witchcraft, Divination, Herbalism, Shamanism, or Ecospirituality. Explore how individuals in these fields utilize effective communication to convey their ideas and connect with their audience. Discuss the challenges they may face and provide examples of how they overcome them. Support your arguments with scholarly research and present counterarguments to ensure a balanced analysis of the topic.

By utilizing affirmations focused on confidence in public speaking and presentation skills, we can enhance our ability to deliver impactful messages and connect with our audience. These affirmations empower us to embrace nervousness, prepare diligently, connect authentically, and embrace feedback for continuous growth and improvement. Remember, confidence in public speaking is a skill that can be developed with practice and the positive reinforcement of affirmations.

AFFIRMATIONS FOR DEVELOPING A STRONG SENSE OF SELF-BELIEF IN ACHIEVING GOALS.

Believing in oneself and having a strong sense of self-belief are crucial components of achieving goals. When we have unwavering faith in our abilities, we are more likely to overcome obstacles, persevere in the face of challenges, and ultimately manifest our desired outcomes. In this section, we will explore the power of affirmations in developing a strong sense of self-belief in achieving goals.

"I am capable of achieving any goal I set my mind to."

This affirmation serves as a foundational belief that underlies all your endeavors. By repeating this affirmation regularly, you reaffirm your inherent capability to achieve any goal you set your mind to. It instills a deep sense of self-belief and empowers you to approach your goals with confidence and determination.

"I am worthy of success and deserve to achieve my goals."

Self-worth is intimately connected to our ability to believe in ourselves. This affirmation affirms your inherent worthiness of success and reinforces the notion that you deserve to achieve your goals. By recognizing your own value and deservingness, you strengthen your self-belief and remove any self-imposed limitations that may hinder your progress.

"I trust the process of manifestation, knowing that the universe supports me in achieving my goals."

Trusting the process of manifestation is essential in maintaining a strong sense of self-belief. This affirmation acknowledges the support of the universe and affirms your trust in its guidance. By trusting in the process, you release the need for control and surrender to the natural flow of life, allowing your goals to manifest with greater ease.

"I am resilient and embrace challenges as opportunities for growth."

Challenges are inevitable on the path to achieving our goals. This affirmation acknowledges the inherent resilience within you and reframes challenges as opportunities for growth. It encourages you to approach obstacles with a positive mindset, knowing that each challenge presents valuable lessons and contributes to your personal development.

"I am committed to taking consistent action towards my goals, knowing that each step brings me closer to success."

Consistent action is a key ingredient in achieving goals. This affirmation affirms your commitment to taking continuous steps towards your goals. It reinforces the belief that each action you take brings you closer to success, and that even small steps are significant in the grand scheme of achievement. By affirming your commitment to consistent action, you maintain momentum and strengthen your self-belief.

Exercise:

Choose a specific goal you want to achieve and create a set of affirmations tailored to that goal. Write them down and repeat them daily, visualizing yourself already achieving the desired outcome. Take note of any shifts in your self-belief and motivation as you continue to affirm your goal. Monitor your progress and celebrate each milestone along the way.

Problem:

Write an essay exploring the role of self-belief in achieving goals, drawing examples from fields such as Witchcraft, Divination, Herbalism, Shamanism, or Ecospirituality. Discuss the significance of self-belief in these fields and how individuals use affirmations to strengthen their belief in achieving desired outcomes. Analyze the impact of self-belief on their ability to manifest their goals and provide evidence from scholarly sources. Present counterarguments that highlight the potential limitations of self-belief and offer strategies to overcome them.

By incorporating affirmations that nurture a strong sense of self-belief, we can empower ourselves to overcome obstacles and manifest our goals. These affirmations reinforce our belief in our capabilities, affirm our worthiness of success, and encourage trust in the process of manifestation. By practicing these affirmations regularly and aligning our actions with our goals, we strengthen our self-belief and create a powerful foundation for achieving our aspirations. Remember, self-belief is a potent force that can propel us towards success when cultivated and nurtured.

FOSTERING A POSITIVE BODY LANGUAGE AND POSTURE TO BOOST CONFIDENCE.

The way we carry ourselves physically, through our body language and posture, has a profound impact on our confidence levels and how others perceive us. By consciously cultivating a positive body language and maintaining an upright posture, we can enhance our self-assurance and project a confident and powerful presence. In this section, we will explore the importance of body language and posture in boosting confidence and provide practical strategies for fostering a positive physical demeanor.

Understanding the Power of Body Language

Body language refers to the nonverbal signals we convey through our gestures, facial expressions, and overall posture. It is a form of communication that can influence how others perceive us and how we feel about ourselves. Research has shown that adopting open and expansive body postures, such as standing tall with shoulders back and maintaining eye contact, can positively impact our confidence levels and create a favorable impression on others.

Maintaining an Upright Posture

Posture plays a crucial role in projecting confidence and self-assuredness. When we slouch or hunch over, we not only convey a lack of confidence but also restrict the flow of energy in our body. On the other hand, maintaining an upright posture with a straight spine and relaxed shoulders allows us to breathe deeply, increases our physical presence, and signals confidence to those around us. By consciously practicing good posture, we can cultivate a positive body image and boost our confidence.

Engaging in Mindful Body Awareness

Developing a mindful awareness of our body and its movements is essential in fostering a positive body language. By paying attention to our posture, gestures, and facial expressions, we can make conscious adjustments to align them with confidence and positivity. For instance, practicing a gentle smile can instantly uplift our mood and exude warmth and approachability. Being mindful of our body language enables us to create a harmonious alignment between our inner state and our outward expression.

Using Power Poses as a Confidence-Boosting Technique

Power poses are expansive body postures that have been scientifically linked to increased confidence and reduced stress levels. Examples of power poses include standing with legs wide apart and arms raised in a victory stance or sitting with legs crossed and hands behind the head. Engaging in power poses for a few minutes before important events or challenging situations can help us tap into our inner strength and boost our self-assurance.

Incorporating Movement and Flow into Body Language

Fluid and purposeful movement can significantly enhance our body language and confidence. Walking with purpose, making deliberate hand gestures while speaking, and maintaining a graceful and flowing posture all contribute to a confident physical presence. By practicing conscious movement and flow, we not only enhance our own confidence but also create a captivating and engaging presence that draws others towards us.

Exercise:

Engage in a daily practice of body awareness and posture correction. Spend a few minutes each day observing your body language and making conscious adjustments to adopt a positive and confident posture. Practice power poses and incorporate intentional movements into your daily activities, such as walking with purpose and making assertive hand gestures. Reflect on how these practices affect your confidence levels and interactions with others.

Problem:

Write a reflective essay discussing the impact of body language and posture on confidence, drawing examples from various fields such as Witchcraft, Divination, Herbalism, Shamanism, or Ecospirituality. Explore how practitioners in these fields utilize body language and posture to convey confidence, authority, and connection with their respective practices. Analyze the role of body language in establishing trust and credibility, and provide evidence from scholarly sources. Present counterarguments that address potential limitations or cultural differences in interpreting body language and posture.

By fostering a positive body language and maintaining an upright posture, we can enhance our confidence and project an image of self-assuredness to the world. Incorporating mindful body awareness, power poses, and purposeful movements into our daily practices allows us to align our physical presence with our inner confidence, empowering us to tackle challenges and interact with others in a more confident and impactful manner.

AFFIRMATIONS FOR OVERCOMING IMPOSTER SYNDROME AND EMBRACING YOUR ACHIEVEMENTS.

Imposter syndrome refers to the persistent feeling of inadequacy and self-doubt despite evidence of one's accomplishments and abilities. It is a common phenomenon that can hinder individuals from fully recognizing and embracing their achievements. In this section, we will explore the concept of imposter syndrome, its impact on self-perception, and provide a series of affirmations to help overcome imposter syndrome and foster self-acceptance.

Understanding Imposter Syndrome

Imposter syndrome often arises when individuals attribute their success to luck or external factors rather than acknowledging their own competence and hard work. It can lead to a constant fear of being exposed as a fraud, despite evidence to the contrary. Imposter syndrome can negatively impact self-esteem, confidence, and hinder personal and professional growth.

Challenging Negative Self-Talk

Negative self-talk is a key component of imposter syndrome. Affirmations play a crucial role in countering these self-limiting beliefs by replacing negative thoughts with positive and empowering ones. By consciously challenging negative self-talk and replacing it with affirmations, individuals can shift their mindset and cultivate a more positive and self-affirming internal dialogue.

Embracing Accomplishments and Acknowledging Success

Affirmations that focus on acknowledging past achievements and recognizing one's own capabilities are instrumental in overcoming imposter syndrome. By regularly affirming and celebrating one's accomplishments, individuals can develop a more realistic and confident self-perception. Embracing achievements helps reframe imposter syndrome by highlighting the evidence of competence and hard work.

Emphasizing Growth and Learning

Imposter syndrome often stems from the belief that one needs to be perfect or have all the answers. Affirmations that emphasize growth, learning, and embracing challenges as opportunities for growth can help individuals overcome imposter syndrome. By recognizing that everyone is continuously learning and evolving, individuals can release the pressure to be flawless and instead focus on personal development and progress.

Fostering a Supportive Mindset

Affirmations that emphasize self-compassion, self-acceptance, and the recognition of inherent worthiness can be powerful tools in overcoming imposter syndrome. By cultivating a supportive mindset and treating oneself with kindness and understanding, individuals can create an internal environment that encourages self-approval and self-belief.

Exercise:

Create a journaling exercise that prompts individuals to reflect on their achievements and confront imposter syndrome. Encourage them to write down their accomplishments, identify any self-doubts or negative beliefs associated with those achievements, and then rewrite those beliefs using affirmations. Have them practice repeating these affirmations daily and observe any shifts in their self-perception and confidence levels.

Problem:

Write a research paper exploring imposter syndrome in different fields such as Witchcraft, Divination, Herbalism, Shamanism, or Ecospirituality. Analyze how imposter syndrome can manifest in practitioners and how it may impact their work, confidence, and connection with their respective practices. Discuss strategies, including affirmations, that practitioners can employ to overcome imposter syndrome and embrace their unique contributions and achievements. Support your arguments with scholarly sources and real-life examples from practitioners in these fields.

By incorporating affirmations that challenge negative self-talk, embrace accomplishments, emphasize growth, and foster a supportive mindset, individuals can gradually overcome imposter syndrome and fully embrace their achievements with confidence and self-acceptance.

AFFIRMING RESILIENCE IN THE FACE OF REJECTION AND SETBACKS.

Resilience is the ability to adapt and bounce back in the face of adversity, rejection, and setbacks. It is an essential trait that allows individuals to maintain their well-being and continue pursuing their goals despite challenges. In this section, we will explore the concept of resilience, its significance in personal and professional development, and provide a series of affirmations to help individuals affirm their resilience and navigate setbacks with strength and determination.

Understanding Resilience

Resilience is not about avoiding difficulties or experiencing a life free from challenges. Instead, it is about developing the inner strength and mindset to face and overcome obstacles. Resilient individuals possess the ability to stay positive, remain focused on their goals, and adapt their strategies when faced with rejection and setbacks.

Embracing Setbacks as Opportunities for Growth

Affirmations that emphasize the inherent potential for growth and learning in setbacks can help individuals reframe their perspective. By affirming that setbacks are not permanent failures but rather temporary roadblocks, individuals can cultivate resilience by approaching setbacks as valuable learning experiences. These affirmations encourage individuals to identify lessons, adjust their strategies, and keep moving forward.

Cultivating a Positive Mindset

A positive mindset is a cornerstone of resilience. Affirmations that focus on maintaining optimism, even in the face of rejection and setbacks, can help individuals maintain their motivation and belief in their abilities. By consciously affirming positive thoughts and beliefs, individuals can develop a resilient mindset that empowers them to persist in the face of adversity.

Building Supportive Relationships

Affirmations that center around nurturing supportive relationships and seeking guidance and encouragement from others can enhance resilience. By acknowledging the value of a strong support system, individuals can find solace, advice, and inspiration from those around them. These affirmations remind individuals that they are not alone in their journey and that seeking support is a sign of strength.

Harnessing Inner Strength

Affirmations that emphasize inner strength and self-belief can help individuals tap into their inherent resilience. By affirming their ability to overcome challenges, individuals reinforce their confidence and trust in their capabilities. These affirmations remind individuals that they possess the inner resources necessary to face and overcome rejection and setbacks.

Exercise:

Develop a reflective exercise where individuals are prompted to journal about a recent rejection or setback they have faced. Encourage them to reflect on the emotions they experienced, the lessons learned, and the strengths they utilized to overcome the situation. Have them create affirmations that acknowledge their resilience, highlight their growth, and provide encouragement. Encourage participants to repeat these affirmations daily as a way to reinforce their resilience and maintain a positive mindset.

Problem:

Write a research paper exploring the concept of resilience in different fields such as Witchcraft, Divination, Herbalism, Shamanism, or Ecospirituality. Analyze how practitioners in these fields cultivate resilience in the face of rejection and setbacks, and how it impacts their personal and spiritual growth. Discuss the role of affirmations and other practices in building resilience and provide real-life examples from practitioners in these fields. Support your arguments with scholarly sources and case studies.

By incorporating affirmations that embrace setbacks as opportunities for growth, cultivate a positive mindset, nurture supportive relationships, and harness inner strength, individuals can affirm their resilience and navigate rejection and setbacks with grace and determination. Resilience is a vital trait that empowers individuals to face challenges head-on and emerge stronger and more resilient in their pursuit of personal and professional goals.

CULTIVATING SELF-COMPASSION AND CELEBRATING SELF-CARE AS A CONFIDENCE BOOSTER.

Self-compassion and self-care play crucial roles in fostering confidence and well-being. By practicing self-compassion, individuals can develop a kind and nurturing relationship with themselves, while self-care ensures their physical, emotional, and mental needs are met. In this section, we will explore the concepts of self-compassion and self-care, their significance in building confidence, and provide a series of affirmations to help individuals cultivate self-compassion and embrace self-care as powerful confidence boosters.

Understanding Self-Compassion

Self-compassion involves treating oneself with kindness, understanding, and acceptance, especially in times of difficulty or failure. It is about recognizing and embracing one's own humanity, acknowledging imperfections, and offering oneself the same care and support that one would give to a loved one. Self-compassion allows individuals to develop a positive and nurturing relationship with themselves, fostering a sense of self-worth and confidence.

The Importance of Self-Care

Self-care encompasses activities and practices that prioritize one's physical, emotional, and mental well-being. Engaging in self-care rituals allows individuals to recharge, replenish their energy, and nurture themselves holistically. By incorporating self-care practices into their daily lives, individuals can enhance their overall well-being, reduce stress, and cultivate a positive mindset, which directly impacts their confidence levels.

Affirming Self-Compassion

Affirmations that focus on self-compassion can help individuals develop a compassionate and loving inner dialogue. These affirmations encourage individuals to extend grace and understanding to themselves, particularly in challenging situations. By affirming self-compassion, individuals can counter self-critical thoughts and replace them with kind and nurturing affirmations that support their confidence and self-belief.

Embracing Self-Care Rituals

Affirmations that center around self-care rituals can inspire individuals to prioritize their well-being and make intentional choices that enhance their confidence. These affirmations encourage individuals to engage in activities such as meditation, journaling, exercise, and nurturing hobbies that promote self-reflection, self-expression, and self-nurturing. By affirming self-care as a necessary part of their lives, individuals reinforce their worthiness and prioritize their own needs.

Integrating Self-Compassion and Self-Care

Affirmations that integrate self-compassion and self-care emphasize the symbiotic relationship between the two. These affirmations encourage individuals to combine self-compassion with intentional self-care practices, fostering a holistic approach to nurturing oneself. By affirming the value of self-compassion and self-care as essential components of their confidence-building journey, individuals can experience a profound transformation in their self-perception and overall well-being.

Exercise:

Create a self-compassion and self-care journaling exercise where individuals reflect on moments when they were critical of themselves or neglected their own needs. Encourage them to rewrite those experiences from a self-compassionate perspective, acknowledging their humanity and offering themselves understanding and kindness. Have participants identify self-care practices that can support their self-compassion journey and commit to incorporating these practices into their daily routines.

Problem:

Write a research paper exploring the scientific basis of self-compassion and self-care, drawing on examples from fields such as Witchcraft, Divination, Herbalism, Shamanism, or Ecospirituality. Discuss the psychological and physiological benefits of self-compassion and self-care practices and their impact on confidence and overall well-being. Analyze studies and scholarly articles that highlight the effectiveness of affirmations, rituals, and practices in cultivating self-compassion and promoting self-care. Provide real-life examples and case studies to support your arguments.

By cultivating self-compassion and celebrating self-care as confidence boosters, individuals can develop a strong foundation of self-worth and nurture their well-being. The practice of self-compassion allows individuals to approach themselves with kindness and understanding, while self-care rituals prioritize their holistic needs.

Affirmations that promote self-compassion and self-care can transform individuals' inner dialogue, enabling them to embrace their worthiness and bolster their confidence. By integrating self-compassion and self-care into their lives, individuals can experience profound personal growth, enhanced confidence, and a greater sense of well-being.

AFFIRMATIONS FOR EMBRACING YOUR UNIQUE VOICE AND EXPRESSING YOURSELF AUTHENTICALLY.

Embracing your unique voice and expressing yourself authentically are essential aspects of building confidence and living a fulfilling life. Each individual possesses a distinct perspective and set of talents that contribute to the diversity of human experience. In this section, we will delve into the significance of embracing your unique voice, explore the concept of authentic self-expression, and provide a series of affirmations to support individuals in embracing their uniqueness and expressing themselves authentically.

Embracing Your Unique Voice

Your unique voice encompasses your individuality, values, beliefs, talents, and experiences. Embracing your unique voice involves recognizing and honoring the qualities that make you who you are. It requires letting go of societal expectations and comparisons, and embracing your inherent worthiness. By acknowledging and valuing your unique perspective, you can tap into your true potential and enhance your self-confidence.

Authentic Self-Expression

Authentic self-expression is the process of communicating your thoughts, emotions, and creativity genuinely and honestly. It involves aligning your actions, words, and choices with your true self, rather than conforming to societal expectations or seeking validation from others. Authentic self-expression empowers you to communicate with clarity, assertiveness, and vulnerability, fostering deeper connections and a greater sense of self-fulfillment.

Affirmations for Embracing Uniqueness

Affirmations play a powerful role in affirming and reinforcing positive beliefs about oneself. The following affirmations are designed to support individuals in embracing their uniqueness:

"I embrace my unique perspective and trust in the value I bring to the world."

"I celebrate my individuality and honor the gifts and talents that make me who I am."

"I release the need to compare myself to others and recognize the beauty in my own uniqueness."

"I give myself permission to shine my light brightly and express myself authentically."

"I trust that my voice and ideas matter, and I am confident in sharing them with the world."

Nurturing Authentic Self-Expression

Affirmations for authentic self-expression can empower individuals to overcome self-doubt and fear, allowing them to communicate their true thoughts and feelings. The following affirmations can support individuals in expressing themselves authentically:

"I trust my intuition and speak my truth with clarity and confidence."

"I release the fear of judgment and embrace vulnerability in expressing myself authentically."

"I honor my emotions and express them in a healthy and constructive manner."

"I cultivate deep connections by listening actively and authentically engaging with others."

"I choose to express my creativity freely and boldly, allowing my authentic self to shine through."

Exercise:

Create a creative expression exercise where individuals explore different forms of self-expression, such as writing, painting, or dancing. Encourage them to embrace their uniqueness and use these creative outlets to express their authentic selves. Discuss the emotions, thoughts, and experiences that arise during the exercise and invite participants to share their insights with the group, fostering a sense of community and mutual support.

Problem:

Write a reflective essay analyzing the importance of embracing one's unique voice and expressing oneself authentically. Draw upon examples from fields such as Witchcraft, Divination, Herbalism, Shamanism, or Ecospirituality to highlight the significance of individuality and self-expression. Discuss the potential challenges and societal pressures that individuals may face when trying to express themselves authentically. Use scholarly sources and case studies to support your arguments and explore the psychological and emotional benefits of embracing uniqueness and authentic self-expression.

By affirming your unique voice and embracing authentic self-expression, you can unlock your full potential and experience a profound sense of self-confidence and fulfillment. Remember, the world needs your unique perspective, talents, and ideas. Embrace your uniqueness, express yourself authentically, and inspire others to do the same.

AFFIRMING CONFIDENCE IN BUILDING AND MAINTAINING HEALTHY RELATIONSHIPS.

Building and maintaining healthy relationships is a fundamental aspect of personal growth and well-being. Healthy relationships contribute to our happiness, emotional fulfillment, and overall life satisfaction. In this section, we will explore the importance of confidence in cultivating healthy relationships, discuss key principles for building and maintaining them, and provide a series of affirmations to support individuals in affirming their confidence in this area.

The Role of Confidence in Healthy Relationships

Confidence plays a vital role in building and maintaining healthy relationships. When we are confident in ourselves and our abilities, we exude a sense of self-assurance that can positively impact our interactions with others. Confidence allows us to communicate our needs and boundaries effectively, express our thoughts and emotions honestly, and establish a foundation of trust and respect. By affirming our confidence, we can foster healthy connections and navigate challenges with resilience and grace.

Principles for Building and Maintaining Healthy Relationships

To build and maintain healthy relationships, it is essential to cultivate certain principles that contribute to their success. These principles include:

a) Effective Communication: Effective communication is the cornerstone of healthy relationships. It involves active listening, expressing oneself clearly and assertively, and seeking to understand others' perspectives. By affirming our ability to communicate effectively, we can establish open and honest lines of communication in our relationships.

b) Boundaries: Setting and respecting boundaries is crucial for maintaining healthy relationships. Boundaries define acceptable behavior and help maintain a sense of personal space and autonomy. By affirming our boundaries and communicating them assertively, we establish a foundation of mutual respect and understanding.

c) Empathy and Understanding: Empathy allows us to connect with others on a deeper level and understand their emotions and experiences. By affirming our capacity for empathy and understanding, we foster compassion and create a supportive environment within our relationships.

d) Conflict Resolution: Conflict is inevitable in any relationship. Healthy relationships require effective conflict resolution skills, such as active listening, compromise, and finding win-win solutions. By affirming our ability to navigate conflicts constructively, we promote growth and strengthen the bond with our loved ones.

Affirmations for Building and Maintaining Healthy Relationships

Affirmations can be powerful tools for cultivating confidence in building and maintaining healthy relationships. Here are some affirmations to support individuals in this area:

"I am worthy of healthy and loving relationships."

"I trust in my ability to communicate my needs and emotions with clarity and compassion."

"I set and respect my boundaries, fostering healthy dynamics in my relationships."

"I embrace empathy and understanding, creating a safe and supportive space for others."

"I approach conflicts with grace and seek resolutions that honor both myself and others."

Exercise:

Design a role-playing exercise where individuals practice effective communication, boundary-setting, and conflict resolution within the context of a challenging relationship scenario. Assign roles and encourage participants to apply the principles discussed in this section. After the exercise, facilitate a discussion where participants reflect on their experiences, share insights, and explore alternative approaches to handling the situation.

Problem:

Write a reflective essay analyzing the significance of confidence in building and maintaining healthy relationships. Draw upon examples from fields such as Witchcraft, Divination, Herbalism, Shamanism, or Ecospirituality to illustrate the role of confidence in cultivating healthy connections. Discuss the potential challenges individuals may face in building and maintaining healthy relationships and explore strategies to overcome them. Support your arguments with scholarly sources and case studies, delving into the psychological and emotional benefits of confident, healthy relationships.

By affirming our confidence in building and maintaining healthy relationships, we can create a supportive network of connections that enrich our lives and contribute to our overall well-being. Remember, healthy relationships start with a strong sense of self and a belief in our own worthiness.

AFFIRMATIONS FOR NAVIGATING AND OVERCOMING SELF-LIMITING BELIEFS.

Self-limiting beliefs can hinder our personal growth, impede our progress towards achieving our goals, and prevent us from living up to our full potential. These beliefs are often deeply ingrained and may stem from past experiences, societal conditioning, or negative self-talk. In this section, we will explore the impact of self-limiting beliefs, discuss strategies for navigating and overcoming them, and provide a series of affirmations to support individuals in challenging and transforming these limiting beliefs.

Understanding Self-Limiting Beliefs

Self-limiting beliefs are negative thoughts or beliefs we hold about ourselves that limit our potential and hinder our progress. They often manifest as statements such as "I'm not good enough," "I don't deserve success," or "I'll never be able to achieve that." These beliefs create a mental barrier that can prevent us from taking risks, pursuing our passions, or embracing new opportunities. By understanding the nature of self-limiting beliefs, we can begin to dismantle their power over us.

Strategies for Navigating and Overcoming Self-Limiting Beliefs

Navigating and overcoming self-limiting beliefs requires a combination of self-awareness, self-compassion, and intentional mindset shifts. Here are some strategies to help individuals challenge and transform their self-limiting beliefs:

a) Self-Reflection: Engage in self-reflection to identify and become aware of your self-limiting beliefs. Notice the thoughts and beliefs that arise when you face challenges or consider pursuing new opportunities. Write them down and examine their validity and origin.

b) Questioning and Challenging Beliefs: Once you have identified your self-limiting beliefs, question their truthfulness. Challenge them by seeking evidence to the contrary and reframing them in a more empowering and positive light. Replace self-limiting beliefs with affirming and empowering thoughts.

c) Affirmations: Affirmations are powerful tools for challenging and transforming self-limiting beliefs. Affirmations are positive statements that counteract negative beliefs and reinforce positive self-perception. By repeating affirmations regularly, individuals can reprogram their subconscious mind and cultivate new, empowering beliefs.

d) Visualization and Imagery: Utilize the power of visualization and imagery to create a mental image of yourself successfully overcoming challenges and achieving your goals. Visualize yourself embodying confidence, competence, and resilience. This practice helps rewire the brain and reinforce positive beliefs.

e) Support Network: Surround yourself with a supportive network of individuals who uplift and encourage you. Seek guidance from mentors, coaches, or friends who can provide insights and perspectives that challenge your self-limiting beliefs. Engage in discussions and activities that foster personal growth and self-empowerment.

Affirmations for Navigating and Overcoming Self-Limiting Beliefs

Affirmations can be transformative in challenging and overcoming self-limiting beliefs. Here are some affirmations to support individuals in this process:

"I release all self-limiting beliefs and embrace my limitless potential."

"I am worthy of success, happiness, and fulfillment."

"I have the power to overcome any challenge that comes my way."

"I trust in my abilities and believe in my capacity to achieve my goals."

"I am deserving of love, abundance, and all the good things life has to offer."

Exercise:

Design a journaling exercise where individuals reflect on their self-limiting beliefs and rewrite them into empowering affirmations. Encourage participants to explore the origins of these beliefs and identify any patterns or triggers. Have them create a daily practice of repeating and embodying these affirmations, noting any shifts in their mindset and self-perception.

Problem:

Write an essay analyzing the psychological and emotional impact of self-limiting beliefs and their influence on individuals' lives. Discuss the role of self-awareness, mindset shifts, and affirmations in navigating and overcoming self-limiting beliefs. Support your arguments with examples from psychology, personal development, and relevant case studies.

By engaging in these practices and utilizing affirmations, individuals can gradually replace self-limiting beliefs with empowering beliefs, leading to increased confidence, resilience, and a greater sense of self-worth. Embracing a mindset of growth and possibility opens up new opportunities for personal and professional success.

AFFIRMATIONS FOR STAYING MOTIVATED AND FOCUSED ON YOUR GOALS.

Maintaining motivation and focus is crucial for achieving our goals and realizing our dreams. However, it is natural to encounter challenges, distractions, and moments of self-doubt along the way. In this section, we will explore the importance of motivation and focus, discuss common obstacles that can derail our progress, and provide a series of affirmations to help individuals stay motivated and focused on their goals.

The Significance of Motivation and Focus

Motivation serves as the driving force behind our actions and decisions. It provides us with the energy and enthusiasm needed to pursue our goals. Likewise, focus directs our attention and resources towards the tasks and activities that align with our objectives. By cultivating and sustaining motivation and focus, we increase our chances of success and fulfillment.

Overcoming Obstacles to Motivation and Focus

Various factors can hinder our motivation and distract us from our goals. Some common obstacles include:

a) Self-Doubt: Doubting our abilities or questioning the feasibility of our goals can erode our motivation and focus. It is essential to recognize and challenge these self-limiting beliefs.

b) Procrastination: Procrastination can lead to a lack of progress and a loss of motivation. Understanding the underlying causes of procrastination, such as fear or perfectionism, can help address this issue.

c) External Distractions: External distractions, such as social media, noise, or other commitments, can divert our attention from our goals. Developing strategies to minimize distractions and create a conducive environment for focus is crucial.

d) Lack of Clarity: Unclear goals or a lack of a clear action plan can make it difficult to stay motivated and focused. Clarifying our goals, breaking them down into actionable steps, and regularly reviewing our progress can help maintain motivation and focus.

Affirmations for Staying Motivated and Focused

Affirmations can serve as powerful tools to reinforce motivation, strengthen focus, and overcome obstacles. Here are some affirmations to support individuals in staying motivated and focused on their goals:

"I am deeply motivated and committed to achieving my goals."

"I possess the focus and discipline needed to make consistent progress."

"I release all doubts and embrace my limitless potential."

"I stay focused on my goals even in the face of challenges and distractions."

"Every day, I take steps towards my goals with unwavering determination."

Exercise:

Create a vision board where individuals can visually represent their goals, aspirations, and affirmations. Encourage participants to display the vision board in a prominent place as a constant reminder of their objectives. They can also engage in regular visualization exercises, imagining themselves successfully accomplishing their goals, to reinforce motivation and focus.

Problem:

Write a reflective essay analyzing the role of motivation and focus in goal achievement. Discuss the impact of self-belief, mindset, and daily habits on sustaining motivation and focus. Incorporate examples and case studies from diverse fields, such as business, sports, or personal development, to illustrate the importance of these qualities.

By incorporating these affirmations into their daily practice, individuals can strengthen their motivation and focus, surmount obstacles, and make steady progress towards their goals. Cultivating an unwavering belief in one's abilities and maintaining a clear vision of success empowers individuals to persevere through challenges and achieve their desired outcomes.

CONCLUSION: ENCOURAGEMENT TO PRACTICE DAILY AFFIRMATIONS FOR SUSTAINED CONFIDENCE AND SELF-BELIEF.

In conclusion, the practice of daily affirmations offers a powerful tool for cultivating and sustaining confidence and self-belief. Throughout this chapter, we have explored the importance of affirmations as a means to reprogram our subconscious minds, align our thoughts and emotions with our desires, and manifest positive outcomes. By consistently incorporating affirmations into our daily routine, we can build a solid foundation of confidence and self-belief that empowers us to overcome challenges, embrace growth, and achieve our goals.

Affirmations serve as a bridge between our conscious and subconscious minds, allowing us to imprint positive beliefs and thoughts that support our confidence and self-belief. Through the use of carefully crafted affirmations, we can reframe negative self-talk, challenge self-limiting beliefs, and foster a mindset of abundance and possibility. As we repeat affirmations with intention and emotional resonance, we create new neural pathways that reinforce positive self-perception and strengthen our belief in our capabilities.

To practice daily affirmations effectively, it is essential to consider the following:

Clarity and Specificity: Craft affirmations that are clear, specific, and aligned with your desired outcomes. By focusing on precise goals or qualities you wish to develop, you bring clarity and intention to your affirmations.

Emotional Resonance: Engage your emotions when reciting affirmations. Feel the positive emotions associated with the desired outcomes, such as joy, gratitude, or excitement. Emotional resonance amplifies the impact of affirmations on your subconscious mind.

Repetition and Consistency: Consistency is key when practicing affirmations. Repeat your affirmations daily, preferably multiple times a day, to reinforce the desired beliefs and thoughts. Consistent repetition creates a cumulative effect that deepens your confidence and self-belief over time.

Visualization and Imagination: Combine affirmations with visualization and imagination. Visualize yourself already possessing the qualities or achieving the goals you desire. Engage your senses and create a vivid mental picture of your success. This enhances the power of affirmations and strengthens your belief in their manifestation.

Integration into Daily Routine: Integrate affirmations seamlessly into your daily routine. Incorporate them into morning or evening rituals, meditation sessions, or moments of quiet reflection. By making affirmations a natural part of your life, you create a consistent practice that reinforces your confidence and self-belief.

By practicing daily affirmations consistently and with dedication, you will experience a transformation in your confidence and self-belief. Remember, affirmations are not merely wishful thinking but a deliberate and proactive way to shape your mindset, beliefs, and actions. As you embrace this practice, you will witness a gradual shift in your thoughts, emotions, and behaviors, leading to a profound and sustained sense of confidence and self-belief.

Exercise:

Design a 30-day affirmation challenge for students to engage in. Provide a list of affirmations tailored to different areas of personal development, such as relationships, career, health, and personal growth. Encourage participants to select affirmations that resonate with them and commit to reciting them daily for 30 consecutive days. At the end of the challenge, invite students to reflect on their experiences and share any insights or transformations they have gained.

Problem:

Write a research paper exploring the scientific basis and efficacy of affirmations in building confidence and self-belief. Analyze studies from psychology, neuroscience, and positive psychology to provide empirical evidence supporting the impact of affirmations on mindset and behavior. Discuss any potential limitations or controversies surrounding affirmations and present a balanced perspective on their effectiveness.

As you embrace the practice of daily affirmations, may you discover the transformative power they hold in shaping your confidence and self-belief. With each repetition, may you reinforce your positive self-perception and nurture a deep sense of belief in your abilities and potential. Remember, the journey of self-belief begins within, and daily affirmations can be the guiding light that illuminates your path to a more empowered and fulfilling life.

HEALTH AND WELL-BEING:

In this chapter, we delve into the profound connection between our thoughts, emotions, and physical well-being. Drawing from a diverse range of disciplines, including Witchcraft, Divination, Herbalism, Shamanism, and Ecospirituality, we explore the intricate interplay between mind, body, and spirit. Through an in-depth analysis of scientific research and ancient wisdom, we aim to provide students with a comprehensive understanding of how they can nurture their health and well-being through intentional practices and positive affirmations.

The Mind-Body Connection

In the first section, we examine the concept of the mind-body connection and its relevance to health and well-being. We explore the notion that our thoughts, emotions, and beliefs have a profound impact on our physical health. By referencing studies from fields such as psychology, psychoneuroimmunology, and epigenetics, we demonstrate the scientific basis for this connection. Students will gain an understanding of how stress, negative emotions, and limiting beliefs can manifest as physical ailments and how positive affirmations can be used to promote healing and wellness.

Holistic Approaches to Health

Moving forward, we delve into holistic approaches to health that encompass the physical, emotional, mental, and spiritual aspects of our being. We explore the principles of Witchcraft, Divination, Herbalism, Shamanism, and Ecospirituality, highlighting their unique perspectives on well-being. Through case studies and examples, students will witness the transformative power of these practices in fostering balance, harmony, and vitality. Additionally, we discuss the role of positive affirmations in supporting holistic health and offer practical exercises and techniques to incorporate them into daily life.

The Power of Positive Affirmations

In the third section, we explore the concept of positive affirmations as a tool for promoting health and well-being. We discuss the principles behind affirmations, their historical roots, and their effectiveness in various contexts. Drawing from the fields of psychology, neuroscience, and positive psychology, we provide a scientific framework for understanding the mechanisms by which affirmations influence our thoughts, emotions, and behaviors. Students will learn how to craft and personalize affirmations to address specific health concerns and cultivate a positive mindset.

Integrating Affirmations into Daily Practice

In the final section, we guide students on how to integrate affirmations into their daily lives to support their health and well-being. We emphasize the importance of consistency, intention, and emotional resonance in the practice of affirmations. Students will learn how to incorporate affirmations into meditation, visualization, journaling, and other self-care practices. We also provide guidance on overcoming resistance and self-doubt that may arise when practicing affirmations, empowering students to embrace the transformative potential of this powerful tool.

Exercise:

Design a holistic self-care plan that integrates affirmations with other health-promoting practices. Students are encouraged to create a personalized routine that incorporates physical exercise, mindfulness, healthy nutrition, restful sleep, and affirmations. They should outline their plan, including specific activities, affirmations, and a daily schedule, and reflect on how each component contributes to their overall well-being.

Problem:

Write an essay exploring the role of positive affirmations in promoting mental health and emotional well-being. Drawing from research in psychology, neuroscience, and alternative healing modalities, critically analyze the effectiveness of affirmations in managing stress, anxiety, and depression. Consider potential limitations and criticisms of affirmations as a therapeutic intervention, and propose strategies for optimizing their efficacy in clinical and non-clinical settings.

As we embark on this journey into health and well-being, may we come to recognize the profound influence our thoughts, beliefs, and affirmations have on our overall vitality. Through an integrative approach that honors the wisdom of ancient traditions and the advancements of modern science, we will discover the transformative potential of affirmations in nurturing holistic wellness and leading a fulfilling life. Let us now embark on this empowering exploration of health and well-being.

AFFIRMATIONS CENTERED AROUND PROMOTING PHYSICAL, MENTAL, AND EMOTIONAL WELL-BEING, VITALITY, AND OVERALL HEALTH.

In this section, we delve into the power of affirmations in promoting holistic well-being, encompassing the realms of physical, mental, and emotional health. Drawing from a rich tapestry of knowledge from fields such as Witchcraft, Divination, Herbalism, Shamanism, and Ecospirituality, we explore how affirmations can positively impact our vitality and overall health. By providing a comprehensive range of affirmations tailored to various aspects of well-being, we empower students to cultivate a harmonious and vibrant state of being.

Affirmations for Physical Health

In this subsection, we focus on affirmations that nurture and support physical health. Students will learn how affirmations can influence the body's energy flow, promote self-healing mechanisms, and foster overall vitality. We explore the role of affirmations in cultivating a positive body image, supporting healthy lifestyle choices, and enhancing the body's innate healing capacity. Examples of affirmations could include:

"I am grateful for my strong and resilient body, which supports me in all my endeavors."

"I nourish my body with wholesome foods that fuel my energy and promote optimal well-being."

"Every cell in my body radiates with vibrant health and vitality."

"I embrace and honor my body's natural cycles, allowing for rest and rejuvenation."

Affirmations for Mental Clarity and Emotional Balance

In this subsection, we explore affirmations that foster mental clarity, emotional balance, and inner peace. Students will discover how affirmations can help reframe negative thought patterns, enhance focus and concentration, and cultivate emotional resilience. Examples of affirmations could include:

"I release all limiting beliefs and embrace the infinite possibilities that life offers."

"My mind is clear and focused, allowing me to make wise decisions and solve challenges with ease."

"I am the master of my emotions, choosing love, joy, and peace in every situation."

"I nurture my mind with positive thoughts and affirmations that uplift and empower me."

Affirmations for Emotional Healing and Self-Compassion

In this subsection, we delve into affirmations that support emotional healing, self-compassion, and inner growth. Students will learn how affirmations can help release emotional blockages, cultivate self-love and acceptance, and foster deep emotional well-being. Examples of affirmations could include:

"I lovingly embrace and heal any emotional wounds, allowing myself to experience profound emotional freedom."

"I am worthy of love and respect, and I attract nurturing and supportive relationships into my life."

"I forgive myself and others, releasing any resentment or anger that no longer serves my highest good."

"I am a beacon of love and compassion, radiating kindness and understanding to myself and others."

Affirmations for Holistic Well-being and Vitality

In this subsection, we explore affirmations that encompass all aspects of well-being and promote a holistic sense of vitality. Students will discover how affirmations can foster harmony between mind, body, and spirit, and create a state of overall wellness. Examples of affirmations could include:

"I am aligned with the universal flow of energy, experiencing a harmonious and balanced state of being."

"I am grateful for the abundance of energy and vitality that fills my life."

"I honor my unique path and purpose, living a life that resonates with joy, passion, and fulfillment."

"Every day, in every way, I am becoming healthier, happier, and more vibrant."

Exercise:

Create a personalized set of affirmations for your physical, mental, and emotional well-being. Reflect on the areas of your life that require nurturing and select affirmations that resonate with your intentions. Write them down and practice repeating them daily, allowing their positive energy to permeate your being.

By integrating these affirmations into our daily lives, we can cultivate a state of vibrant well-being that radiates from within. With each affirmation, we nourish and uplift ourselves, fostering a holistic sense of health and vitality. Let us now embark on this transformative journey towards embracing our innate well-being and living a life of optimal health and vitality.

INTRODUCTION: THE IMPORTANCE OF HOLISTIC HEALTH AND WELL-BEING.

In this section, we explore the profound significance of holistic health and well-being in our lives. Drawing from a diverse array of fields, including Witchcraft, Divination, Herbalism, Shamanism, and Ecospirituality, we embark on a journey to understand the interconnectedness of our physical, mental, and emotional states. By examining the principles underlying holistic health, we gain insights into the transformative power of aligning mind, body, and spirit. Through this exploration, students will develop a deeper appreciation for the holistic nature of well-being and its impact on all aspects of their lives.

Understanding Holistic Health:

Holistic health refers to an integrative approach that acknowledges the interdependence of various dimensions of well-being. It recognizes that our physical, mental, and emotional states are intricately interconnected, and any imbalances in one area can affect the others. By embracing the concept of holism, we shift our perspective from viewing health as mere absence of disease to fostering a harmonious state of overall well-being.

The Mind-Body Connection:

Central to the understanding of holistic health is the recognition of the mind-body connection. Scientific research has increasingly demonstrated the profound influence of our thoughts, beliefs, and emotions on our physical health. The fields of Witchcraft, Divination, Herbalism, Shamanism, and Ecospirituality offer valuable insights into the power of intention, energy, and consciousness in shaping our well-being. By exploring practices such as energy healing, meditation, and mindfulness, we can harness this mind-body connection to promote holistic health.

Embracing Emotional Well-being:

Emotional well-being plays a vital role in our overall health and happiness. Acknowledging and nurturing our emotions allows us to cultivate resilience, establish healthy relationships, and experience a greater sense of fulfillment. The practices of Witchcraft, Divination, Herbalism, Shamanism, and Ecospirituality offer various tools for emotional healing and self-discovery, such as rituals, herbal remedies, and nature-based therapies. By embracing these practices, we can foster emotional balance and unlock our inner potential.

The Role of Self-Care:

Self-care is a foundational pillar of holistic health and well-being. It involves making conscious choices to nurture and prioritize our physical, mental, and emotional needs. The practices of Witchcraft, Divination, Herbalism, Shamanism, and Ecospirituality provide valuable insights into self-care rituals, such as herbal baths, meditation practices, and connection with nature. By integrating self-care practices into our daily lives, we create a solid foundation for holistic well-being.

Cultivating Spiritual Connection:

Spirituality, regardless of individual beliefs, offers a profound avenue for holistic well-being. Exploring our connection to something greater than ourselves, whether through nature, divination, or personal rituals, can provide a sense of purpose, inner peace, and harmony. By integrating spiritual practices into our lives, we enhance our overall well-being and deepen our understanding of ourselves and the world around us.

Conclusion:

As we embark on this journey of exploring holistic health and well-being, we invite students to embrace the interconnectedness of their physical, mental, and emotional states. By integrating practices and principles from Witchcraft, Divination, Herbalism, Shamanism, and Ecospirituality, we expand our understanding of health beyond the confines of conventional medicine. By nurturing and harmonizing all aspects of our being, we pave the way for a transformative experience of holistic well-being, where each dimension supports and enhances the others. Let us now embark on this transformative journey towards embracing holistic health and cultivating a vibrant and fulfilling life.

UNDERSTANDING THE MIND–BODY CONNECTION AND ITS IMPACT ON OVERALL HEALTH.

In this section, we delve into the intricate relationship between the mind and the body and explore how it influences our overall health. By drawing upon insights from a range of disciplines, including Witchcraft, Divination, Herbalism, Shamanism, and Ecospirituality, we aim to provide a comprehensive understanding of the mind-body connection. Through this exploration, students will gain valuable insights into the power of thoughts, emotions, beliefs, and consciousness in shaping their physical well-being.

The Mind-Body Connection: A Holistic Perspective

The mind-body connection refers to the intricate interplay between our mental and emotional states and our physical health. This connection is rooted in the understanding that our thoughts, beliefs, emotions, and behaviors have a direct impact on our physiological processes. By recognizing the holistic nature of health, we acknowledge that our mental and emotional well-being are not separate from our physical well-being but are intrinsically linked.

Neuroplasticity and the Power of Thoughts

Neuroplasticity, a concept supported by scientific research, highlights the brain's remarkable ability to adapt and change throughout our lives. Our thoughts and mental patterns can shape the neural pathways in our brain, influencing our perceptions, emotions, and behaviors. Witchcraft, Divination, Herbalism, Shamanism, and Ecospirituality offer various techniques, such as affirmations, visualization, and meditation, that harness the power of thoughts to rewire our brains and promote positive health outcomes.

Emotions and Physical Health

Our emotions play a crucial role in the mind-body connection. Emotions such as stress, fear, anger, and sadness can trigger physiological responses, affecting our immune system, cardiovascular health, and overall well-being. Conversely, positive emotions like joy, love, and gratitude can promote a state of well-being and enhance our physical health. Through practices like energy healing, rituals, and nature-based therapies, we can explore how emotions impact our health and learn techniques to cultivate positive emotional states.

The Role of Beliefs and Perception

Our beliefs and perceptions shape our experiences and, in turn, influence our physical health. The placebo effect, extensively studied in medical research, demonstrates how our beliefs can impact our body's response to treatment. Witchcraft, Divination, Herbalism, Shamanism, and Ecospirituality offer tools to examine and transform limiting beliefs and perceptions, allowing for a shift toward more empowering and positive health outcomes.

Consciousness and Healing

Consciousness, often explored through practices like meditation and mindfulness, is an integral part of the mind-body connection. By cultivating present-moment awareness and developing a deeper understanding of our inner selves, we can tap into our innate healing capacities. Various modalities within Witchcraft, Divination, Herbalism, Shamanism, and Ecospirituality offer techniques to expand consciousness and promote healing on multiple levels.

Conclusion:

As we conclude this exploration of the mind-body connection and its impact on overall health, it becomes evident that our thoughts, emotions, beliefs, and consciousness play a profound role in shaping our physical well-being. By embracing practices and principles from Witchcraft, Divination, Herbalism, Shamanism, and Ecospirituality, we empower ourselves to cultivate positive mental and emotional states that support optimal physical health. The understanding of the mind-body connection offers a transformative perspective on health, highlighting the importance of nurturing our inner selves to promote holistic well-being. As students embark on their journey of self-discovery, they are encouraged to explore the mind-body connection and harness its potential for personal growth, healing, and vibrant health.

CULTIVATING A POSITIVE MINDSET AND AFFIRMING MENTAL WELL-BEING.

In this section, we explore the significance of cultivating a positive mindset and its impact on mental well-being. Drawing upon insights from various fields, including Witchcraft, Divination, Herbalism, Shamanism, and Ecospirituality, we delve into the power of affirmations in shaping our thoughts, beliefs, and overall mental state. Through a comprehensive analysis, students will gain a deeper understanding of the mind's influence on mental well-being and learn practical techniques to cultivate a positive mindset.

The Power of Thoughts and Beliefs

Our thoughts and beliefs play a central role in shaping our mental well-being. The field of cognitive psychology emphasizes that our thoughts and interpretations of events influence our emotions and behaviors. Witchcraft, Divination, Herbalism, Shamanism, and Ecospirituality offer insights and practices to examine and transform negative thought patterns and limiting beliefs. Through the use of affirmations, individuals can replace self-defeating thoughts with positive, empowering statements that nurture a positive mindset.

The Science of Affirmations

Affirmations, rooted in the understanding of the mind's plasticity and its ability to rewire neural pathways, have gained recognition in both psychological and spiritual contexts. Affirmations are positive statements that reflect desired outcomes or qualities and are repeated regularly to reinforce positive beliefs. By consistently practicing affirmations, individuals can reshape their neural networks and create a more positive and empowering mental framework.

Creating Effective Affirmations

Crafting effective affirmations requires careful consideration of language, specificity, and emotional resonance. Affirmations should be framed in the present tense, be positively stated, and reflect the desired outcome. By aligning affirmations with personal values and beliefs, individuals can enhance their effectiveness. Examples of effective affirmations from Witchcraft, Divination, Herbalism, Shamanism, and Ecospirituality will be explored to provide practical guidance for students.

Integrating Affirmations into Daily Life

To reap the full benefits of affirmations, it is crucial to integrate them into daily life. Consistency and repetition are key factors in reinforcing positive beliefs and transforming the mindset. Techniques such as incorporating affirmations into morning or bedtime routines, utilizing visualization exercises, or creating affirmation rituals can help anchor affirmations in daily practice. Students will be provided with exercises and prompts to assist them in incorporating affirmations into their daily routines.

Nurturing a Positive Mindset

Beyond affirmations, various practices can support the cultivation of a positive mindset. These practices may include meditation, mindfulness, gratitude, self-care, and connecting with nature. Drawing upon insights from Witchcraft, Divination, Herbalism, Shamanism, and Ecospirituality, students will learn about the transformative potential of these practices and how they contribute to mental well-being.

Conclusion:

As we conclude this exploration of cultivating a positive mindset and affirming mental well-being, we recognize the profound influence our thoughts and beliefs have on our mental state. Through the use of affirmations and integrating practices from Witchcraft, Divination, Herbalism, Shamanism, and Ecospirituality, we empower ourselves to nurture a positive mindset and promote mental well-being. By consciously choosing positive thoughts and beliefs, students can shape their inner landscape and create a foundation of resilience and self-empowerment. The cultivation of a positive mindset is an ongoing practice, and as students embrace this journey, they are encouraged to engage in self-reflection, exploration, and regular affirmation practice to foster mental well-being and unlock their true potential.

AFFIRMATIONS FOR STRESS REDUCTION AND PROMOTING RELAXATION.

In this section, we explore the transformative power of affirmations in reducing stress and promoting relaxation. Grounded in insights from diverse fields, including Witchcraft, Divination, Herbalism, Shamanism, and Ecospirituality, we delve into the science behind stress and its effects on the mind and body. Through a comprehensive analysis, students will gain an understanding of how affirmations can counteract stress and foster a state of relaxation. Practical examples, exercises, and techniques will be provided to empower students to incorporate affirmations into their daily lives for stress reduction and enhanced well-being.

Understanding Stress and Its Impact

Stress is a natural response to perceived threats or demands, triggering a complex cascade of physiological and psychological reactions. Chronic stress can have detrimental effects on mental and physical health, leading to conditions such as anxiety, depression, and cardiovascular disease. Witchcraft, Divination, Herbalism, Shamanism, and Ecospirituality offer insights and practices to address stress holistically. By utilizing affirmations, individuals can counteract the negative impact of stress and foster relaxation.

The Science of Affirmations for Stress Reduction

Affirmations have been shown to positively influence the brain's neuroplasticity, helping to rewire neural pathways associated with stress responses. The use of affirmations can help shift one's focus from negative thoughts and emotions to positive and empowering beliefs, thereby reducing stress and promoting relaxation. Students will explore scientific evidence supporting the efficacy of affirmations for stress reduction and learn how to leverage this knowledge in their own lives.

Crafting Stress-Reduction Affirmations

Crafting affirmations specifically tailored for stress reduction requires attention to language, intention, and personal relevance. Affirmations should address stress-related thoughts, emotions, and physical sensations. By incorporating positive statements about calmness, inner peace, and resilience, individuals can reinforce relaxation responses and counteract stress. Examples of stress-reduction affirmations from Witchcraft, Divination, Herbalism, Shamanism, and Ecospirituality will be provided as models for students.

Integrating Affirmations into Stress Management Practices

To maximize the benefits of affirmations for stress reduction, it is important to integrate them into broader stress management practices. Techniques such as deep breathing exercises, meditation, visualization, and mindfulness can enhance the effectiveness of affirmations. Students will be guided on how to combine affirmations with these practices to create a comprehensive stress reduction routine. Practical exercises and prompts will be included to encourage students to apply these techniques in their daily lives.

Cultivating a Relaxation Mindset

Beyond affirmations, cultivating a relaxation mindset involves adopting a holistic approach to stress reduction. Practices such as self-care, time management, setting boundaries, and engaging in activities that promote relaxation are essential components. Drawing upon insights from Witchcraft, Divination, Herbalism, Shamanism, and Ecospirituality, students will explore the role of nature, herbs, rituals, and energy healing in fostering relaxation and reducing stress.

Conclusion:

In conclusion, the practice of affirmations offers a powerful tool for stress reduction and promoting relaxation. By incorporating affirmations into daily life and combining them with stress management practices, students can effectively counteract stress and foster a state of calm and tranquility. The integration of insights from Witchcraft, Divination, Herbalism, Shamanism, and Ecospirituality provides a rich tapestry of techniques and practices to enhance the efficacy of affirmations. As students embark on this journey of stress reduction and relaxation, they are encouraged to engage in self-reflection, experimentation, and regular affirmation practice to unlock the profound potential of affirmations for their well-being.

NURTURING A HEALTHY RELATIONSHIP WITH FOOD AND AFFIRMING MINDFUL EATING.

In this section, we delve into the importance of nurturing a healthy relationship with food and embracing the practice of mindful eating. Drawing upon insights from diverse fields such as Witchcraft, Divination, Herbalism, Shamanism, and Ecospirituality, we explore the multifaceted aspects of our connection with food, including the physical, emotional, and spiritual dimensions. Through a thorough analysis, students will gain a comprehensive understanding of mindful eating and how affirmations can support a balanced and harmonious relationship with food. Practical examples, exercises, and techniques will be provided to empower students to cultivate mindfulness and affirmations in their eating habits.

The Complexity of Our Relationship with Food

Our relationship with food extends beyond its basic nutritional value. It encompasses our cultural, emotional, and social interactions with food. Understanding the multifaceted nature of this relationship is essential for nurturing a healthy approach to eating. Through the lenses of Witchcraft, Divination, Herbalism,

Shamanism, and Ecospirituality, students will explore the symbolic, energetic, and ritualistic dimensions of food, broadening their perspective on the significance of food in our lives.

The Practice of Mindful Eating

Mindful eating is a practice rooted in present moment awareness, allowing us to fully engage with the sensory experience of eating. It involves paying attention to the tastes, textures, and sensations of food, as well as our own hunger and satiety cues. Through mindfulness, we can develop a deeper connection with our bodies, cultivate gratitude, and make conscious choices that align with our overall well-being. Students will explore the principles and techniques of mindful eating and its benefits for physical and emotional health.

Affirmations for Nurturing a Healthy Relationship with Food

Affirmations can play a powerful role in nurturing a healthy relationship with food. By consciously crafting positive statements, students can reinforce self-love, body acceptance, and mindful eating practices. Affirmations that promote gratitude for nourishment, respect for the body, and the cultivation of a balanced approach to eating will be explored. Examples from Witchcraft, Divination, Herbalism, Shamanism, and Ecospirituality will be provided as models for students to create their own personalized affirmations.

Integrating Affirmations into Daily Eating Rituals

To fully integrate affirmations into our relationship with food, it is important to incorporate them into daily eating rituals. Rituals can enhance the mindfulness and intentionality of our eating experiences, deepening our connection with food and fostering a sense of reverence. Students will learn practical techniques to infuse affirmations into meal preparation, blessing of food, and mindful eating practices. They will be encouraged to design their own rituals based on personal preferences and beliefs.

Cultivating Mindful Eating Habits

Beyond affirmations, cultivating mindful eating habits involves adopting a holistic approach to our food choices and eating behaviors. Students will explore topics such as intuitive eating, listening to hunger and fullness cues, practicing portion control, and incorporating mindful snacking. The integration of insights from Witchcraft, Divination, Herbalism, Shamanism, and Ecospirituality will provide a rich array of practices, such as herbal remedies, sacred cooking, and the use of food as medicine, to support mindful eating habits.

Conclusion:

In conclusion, nurturing a healthy relationship with food and embracing mindful eating practices are vital for our overall well-being. Through the integration of insights from Witchcraft, Divination, Herbalism, Shamanism, and Ecospirituality, students are empowered to develop a holistic understanding of their connection with food. By incorporating affirmations into their eating rituals and cultivating mindful eating habits, they can enhance their relationship with food, cultivate gratitude, and support their physical, emotional, and spiritual well-being. The journey of nurturing a healthy relationship with food and affirming mindful eating is a continuous practice, requiring self-reflection, exploration, and regular affirmation reinforcement. As students embark on this journey, they are encouraged to engage in self-inquiry, experiment with mindful eating techniques, and embrace the transformative power of affirmations in their daily lives.

AFFIRMATIONS FOR MAINTAINING A BALANCED AND NUTRITIOUS DIET.

In this section, we explore the significance of affirmations in supporting individuals in maintaining a balanced and nutritious diet. Drawing upon principles from diverse fields such as Witchcraft, Divination, Herbalism, Shamanism, and Ecospirituality, we delve into the power of positive self-talk and its impact on food choices, eating behaviors, and overall health. Through a comprehensive analysis, students will gain an understanding of how affirmations can help overcome challenges, reinforce healthy habits, and foster a positive mindset towards nutrition. Practical examples, exercises, and strategies will be provided to empower students to create and practice affirmations that promote a balanced and nutritious diet.

The Power of Positive Affirmations in Nutrition:

Positive affirmations are powerful tools that can shape our thoughts, beliefs, and behaviors. When applied to the context of nutrition, affirmations have the potential to transform our relationship with food and guide us towards making conscious and nourishing choices. By using positive language and focusing on desired outcomes, affirmations can reprogram negative thought patterns, enhance self-awareness, and foster a healthy mindset around eating.

Overcoming Challenges and Self-Limiting Beliefs:

Maintaining a balanced and nutritious diet can be challenging, especially when faced with temptations, social pressures, or emotional triggers. Affirmations can serve as a powerful tool for overcoming these challenges and addressing self-limiting beliefs that may hinder our progress. By identifying and reframing negative thoughts or beliefs related to food and nutrition, students can create affirmations that counteract self-sabotaging behaviors and strengthen their commitment to a balanced and nutritious diet.

Affirmations for Making Conscious Food Choices:

Conscious food choices are essential for maintaining a balanced and nutritious diet. Students will explore affirmations that promote mindful eating, intuitive decision-making, and awareness of the nutritional value of the foods they consume. By repeating affirmations such as "I choose nourishing foods that support my well-being" or "I listen to my body's signals and eat with intention," individuals can cultivate a greater sense of self-awareness and make choices aligned with their nutritional needs.

Reinforcing Healthy Eating Habits:

Establishing and reinforcing healthy eating habits is key to maintaining a balanced and nutritious diet. Affirmations can be utilized as a tool for reinforcing positive behaviors and habits. Students will learn to create affirmations that support consistency, portion control, mindful snacking, and the incorporation of a variety of nutrient-dense foods into their diet. By regularly repeating affirmations like "I savor each bite and eat mindfully" or "I nourish my body with foods that support optimal health," individuals can strengthen their commitment to healthy eating habits.

Affirmations for Body Acceptance and Self-Love:

Body acceptance and self-love are crucial components of maintaining a balanced and nutritious diet. Students will explore affirmations that foster a positive body image, self-acceptance, and self-care. By affirming statements such as "I love and appreciate my body as it is" or "I honor my body by nourishing it with wholesome foods," individuals can cultivate a healthy relationship with their bodies and shift their focus from external appearance to overall well-being.

Conclusion:

In conclusion, affirmations play a vital role in maintaining a balanced and nutritious diet by shaping our thoughts, beliefs, and behaviors related to food and nutrition. Through the integration of insights from Witchcraft, Divination, Herbalism, Shamanism, and Ecospirituality, students can harness the power of affirmations to overcome challenges, reinforce healthy habits, and foster a positive mindset towards nutrition. By practicing affirmations that promote conscious food choices, reinforce healthy eating habits, and cultivate body acceptance, individuals can empower themselves to nourish their bodies, minds, and spirits with wholesome and nutritious foods. Through regular affirmation practice and self-reflection, students can transform their relationship with food, embrace a balanced and nutritious diet, and experience enhanced well-being.

AFFIRMING SELF-DISCIPLINE AND COMMITMENT TO REGULAR EXERCISE.

In this section, we explore the role of affirmations in cultivating self-discipline and fostering a deep commitment to regular exercise. Drawing inspiration from diverse fields such as Witchcraft, Divination, Herbalism, Shamanism, and Ecospirituality, we delve into the power of positive self-talk and its influence on motivation, consistency, and overall physical well-being. Through a comprehensive analysis, students will gain an understanding of how affirmations can overcome barriers, reinforce healthy exercise habits, and foster a resilient mindset. Practical examples, exercises, and strategies will be provided to empower students to create and practice affirmations that support their fitness journey.

Understanding the Power of Affirmations in Exercise:

Affirmations are powerful tools that can shape our thoughts, beliefs, and behaviors. When applied to the realm of exercise, affirmations can play a crucial role in cultivating self-discipline and commitment. By using positive language, visualizations, and intention-setting, affirmations have the potential to rewire the mind, boost motivation, and create a strong foundation for a regular exercise routine.

Overcoming Barriers and Self-Limiting Beliefs:

Committing to regular exercise can be challenging due to various barriers and self-limiting beliefs. Affirmations can serve as a valuable tool for overcoming these obstacles and reframing negative thought patterns that hinder progress. By identifying and challenging self-doubt, fear, or excuses, students can create affirmations that empower them to overcome barriers and cultivate a resilient mindset focused on long-term health and well-being.

Affirmations for Motivation and Consistency:

Motivation and consistency are key factors in maintaining a regular exercise routine. Students will explore affirmations that reinforce their intrinsic motivation, ignite passion for movement, and cultivate a deep sense of commitment. By repeating affirmations such as "I am motivated to exercise because it brings me joy and vitality" or "I am committed to prioritizing my physical well-being through regular exercise," individuals can strengthen their resolve and stay dedicated to their fitness goals.

Fostering a Positive Relationship with Exercise:

A positive relationship with exercise is essential for long-term commitment and enjoyment. Affirmations can help students develop a positive mindset towards exercise, emphasizing the benefits it brings to their physical, mental, and emotional well-being. By creating affirmations that focus on the pleasure of movement, self-care, and self-empowerment, individuals can shift their perspective from viewing exercise as a chore to embracing it as a form of self-expression and self-care.

Affirmations for Self-Care and Recovery:

Self-care and recovery are integral parts of any exercise routine. Students will explore affirmations that emphasize the importance of rest, rejuvenation, and self-compassion in their fitness journey. By affirming statements such as "I listen to my body's signals and provide it with the rest it needs" or "I honor and care for my body through proper recovery practices," individuals can prioritize self-care, reduce the risk of burnout, and promote sustainable progress.

Conclusion:

In conclusion, affirmations serve as powerful tools for cultivating self-discipline and fostering a deep commitment to regular exercise. Through the integration of insights from Witchcraft, Divination, Herbalism, Shamanism, and Ecospirituality, students can harness the power of affirmations to overcome barriers, reinforce healthy exercise habits, and foster a resilient mindset. By practicing affirmations that ignite motivation, reinforce consistency, and promote self-care, individuals can establish a positive relationship with exercise and embark on a lifelong journey of physical well-being and self-empowerment.

AFFIRMATIONS FOR BOOSTING ENERGY LEVELS AND VITALITY.

In this section, we explore the transformative power of affirmations in enhancing energy levels and cultivating vitality. Drawing inspiration from various fields such as Witchcraft, Divination, Herbalism, Shamanism, and Ecospirituality, we delve into the profound impact of positive self-talk on our physical, mental, and emotional well-being. Through a comprehensive analysis, students will gain an understanding of how affirmations can rewire their mindset, increase energy, and foster a vibrant and vibrant lifestyle. Practical examples, exercises, and strategies will be provided to empower students to create and practice affirmations that support their quest for heightened vitality.

The Relationship Between Affirmations and Energy:

Affirmations have the potential to profoundly influence our energy levels. By consciously choosing positive and uplifting statements, we can reprogram our thoughts and beliefs to align with a vibrant and energized state. Students will explore the science behind affirmations and how they can impact our nervous system, hormonal balance, and overall energy levels. Through understanding this connection, students can harness the power of affirmations to boost their vitality.

Affirmations for Energizing the Mind and Body:

Affirmations serve as powerful tools to invigorate both the mind and body. By crafting affirmations that focus on mental clarity, physical strength, and overall vitality, individuals can tap into their innate energy reserves. Examples of affirmations include "I am filled with abundant energy and vitality," "Every cell in my body radiates with vibrant energy," or "I embrace life with enthusiasm and vitality."

Overcoming Fatigue and Restoring Energy:

Fatigue and low energy levels can hinder our ability to lead a vibrant and fulfilling life. Affirmations can help students overcome fatigue by addressing the root causes and shifting their energy state. By creating affirmations that counteract tiredness, such as "I am replenished with energy and vitality" or "I am filled with boundless energy throughout the day," individuals can transcend fatigue and embrace a more vibrant existence.

Cultivating a Healthy Lifestyle for Sustained Vitality:

Affirmations can be instrumental in cultivating a healthy lifestyle that supports sustained vitality. By incorporating affirmations that focus on nourishing food choices, regular exercise, restful sleep, and stress management, individuals can create a holistic approach to enhance their energy levels. Affirmations such as "I make nourishing choices that fuel my body with energy and vitality" or "I prioritize self-care practices that replenish my energy reserves" can guide students towards a balanced and energized lifestyle.

Aligning with the Rhythms of Nature:

Nature serves as an abundant source of energy and vitality. Students will explore the concept of aligning with the natural rhythms of the Earth to enhance their energy levels. Affirmations that connect us with the elements, seasons, and cycles of nature, such as "I am in harmony with the natural flow of energy around me" or "I draw strength and vitality from the earth beneath my feet," can deepen our connection with the natural world and amplify our energy and vitality.

Conclusion:

In conclusion, affirmations hold tremendous potential for boosting energy levels and cultivating vitality. Through the integration of wisdom from Witchcraft, Divination, Herbalism, Shamanism, and Ecospirituality, students can tap into the transformative power of affirmations to rewire their mindset, enhance their energy reserves, and embrace a vibrant and energetic lifestyle. By practicing affirmations that invigorate the mind and body, overcome fatigue, cultivate a healthy lifestyle, and align with the rhythms of nature, individuals can unlock their innate vitality and embark on a journey of boundless energy and well-being.

AFFIRMING RESTFUL SLEEP AND PRACTICING HEALTHY SLEEP HABITS.

Affirming restful sleep and practicing healthy sleep habits are essential components of maintaining optimal physical, mental, and emotional well-being. In this section, we explore the profound impact of affirmations on improving sleep quality and developing a consistent sleep routine. By incorporating insights from various fields, including Witchcraft, Divination, Herbalism, Shamanism, and Ecospirituality, we gain a comprehensive understanding of the power of positive self-talk in promoting restful and rejuvenating sleep.

The Importance of Restful Sleep:

Restful sleep plays a vital role in our overall health and well-being. It allows our body and mind to recover, repair, and recharge, ensuring optimal functioning during wakefulness. Unfortunately, many individuals struggle with sleep disturbances and insomnia, which can have detrimental effects on their physical and mental health. Affirmations offer a powerful tool to address these challenges and create a positive sleep environment.

The Power of Affirmations for Restful Sleep:

Affirmations are statements that reflect our desired reality and reinforce positive beliefs. When it comes to sleep, affirmations can help reprogram our subconscious mind, release tension, and promote relaxation. By integrating affirmations into our daily routine, we can create a positive mental and emotional state conducive to restful sleep.

Crafting Affirmations for Restful Sleep:

Crafting effective affirmations for restful sleep involves identifying the specific sleep-related challenges or concerns we may have and reframing them into positive statements. For example, if someone struggles with falling asleep, they could affirm, "I easily drift into deep and restful sleep." If someone experiences frequent awakenings during the night, they might affirm, "I sleep soundly throughout the night and wake up refreshed and energized." These affirmations should be personalized and resonate with the individual's unique needs and circumstances.

Creating a Healthy Sleep Routine:

In addition to affirmations, establishing healthy sleep habits is crucial for promoting restful sleep. This includes implementing a consistent sleep schedule, creating a relaxing pre-sleep routine, and optimizing the sleep environment. Affirmations can complement these habits by reinforcing positive sleep-related behaviors and beliefs. For instance, individuals can affirm, "I prioritize my sleep and establish a regular bedtime routine," or "I create a calm and peaceful sleep environment that promotes deep sleep."

Integrating Mindfulness and Relaxation Techniques:

Mindfulness and relaxation techniques can further enhance the effectiveness of affirmations for restful sleep. Practices such as deep breathing, meditation, and body relaxation exercises help calm the mind, release tension, and promote a state of relaxation conducive to sleep. Affirmations can be combined with these techniques to amplify their impact. For example, while practicing deep breathing, individuals can repeat affirmations such as "With each breath, I relax deeper and deeper, preparing my body and mind for restful sleep."

Conclusion:

In conclusion, affirmations and healthy sleep habits are powerful tools for promoting restful sleep and rejuvenation. By integrating affirmations into our daily routine, we can reprogram our subconscious mind, release tension, and create a positive mental and emotional state conducive to restful sleep. Combining affirmations with mindfulness and relaxation techniques enhances their effectiveness in promoting deep, rejuvenating sleep. By embracing these practices, individuals can cultivate a harmonious relationship with sleep and experience the profound benefits of restful and revitalizing nights.

CULTIVATING SELF-CARE ROUTINES AND PRIORITIZING SELF-NURTURING ACTIVITIES.

In this section, we explore the importance of self-care routines and the transformative power of affirmations in prioritizing self-nurturing activities. Drawing inspiration from various fields such as Witchcraft, Divination, Herbalism, Shamanism, and Ecospirituality, we delve into the profound impact of self-care on our physical, mental, and emotional well-being. Through a comprehensive analysis, students will gain an understanding of how affirmations can support and enhance self-care practices, allowing individuals to cultivate a deep sense of nourishment and balance in their lives. Practical examples, exercises, and strategies will be provided to empower students to create and integrate affirmations that promote self-nurturing and self-care.

The Importance of Self-Care:

Self-care is the practice of intentionally taking care of one's physical, mental, and emotional well-being. It involves engaging in activities that promote relaxation, rejuvenation, and self-nurturing. Students will explore the concept of self-care as an essential component of maintaining balance and overall well-being. By making self-care a priority, individuals can replenish their energy reserves, reduce stress, and enhance their overall quality of life.

The Role of Affirmations in Self-Care:

Affirmations play a crucial role in supporting and enhancing self-care practices. By using positive and empowering statements, individuals can reinforce their commitment to self-nurturing and cultivate a mindset that prioritizes their well-being. Students will learn how affirmations can reshape their thoughts, beliefs, and behaviors, allowing them to embrace self-care as an integral part of their daily lives.

Crafting Affirmations for Self-Nurturing and Self-Care:

Creating affirmations that specifically address self-nurturing and self-care can be a powerful practice. Examples of affirmations include "I prioritize self-care and honor my need for rest and relaxation," "I deserve to take time for myself and engage in activities that nourish my soul," or "I am worthy of love and care, and I extend that love and care to myself." These affirmations can serve as gentle reminders to practice self-nurturing and engage in activities that promote well-being.

Designing Self-Care Routines:

Students will explore the process of designing personalized self-care routines that cater to their individual needs and preferences. By incorporating affirmations into their routine, individuals can infuse their self-care practices with intention and positive energy. Practical exercises will guide students in identifying self-nurturing activities that resonate with them, creating a routine that supports their well-being, and integrating affirmations into their daily self-care practices.

Exploring Different Self-Nurturing Activities:

Self-care encompasses a wide range of activities that nourish and replenish the mind, body, and spirit. Students will explore various self-nurturing activities, such as meditation, journaling, nature walks, creative pursuits, and self-care rituals. Affirmations can be used to enhance these activities, providing a sense of intention and empowerment. For example, while engaging in a meditation practice, individuals can affirm, "I am calm, centered, and at peace," or during a nature walk, they can repeat, "I am connected to the healing energy of nature, finding solace and rejuvenation."

Creating a Supportive Environment for Self-Nurturing:

In addition to individual self-care practices, students will explore the importance of creating a supportive environment that fosters self-nurturing and self-care. This includes setting boundaries, surrounding oneself with positive influences, and seeking support from loved ones. Affirmations can be used to reinforce a nurturing environment by affirming statements such as, "I create a loving and nurturing space for myself," or "I attract supportive and caring relationships into my life."

Conclusion:

In conclusion, self-care is a vital practice for maintaining balance and well-being. By incorporating affirmations into self-care routines and prioritizing self-nurturing activities, individuals can cultivate a deep sense of nourishment and balance in their lives. Through the integration of wisdom from Witchcraft, Divination, Herbalism, Shamanism, and Ecospirituality, students can tap into the transformative power of affirmations to support their self-care journey. By crafting affirmations that promote self-nurturing, designing personalized self-care routines, exploring different self-nurturing activities, and creating a supportive environment, individuals can honor their well-being and cultivate a life filled with self-love, care, and nourishment.

AFFIRMATIONS FOR FOSTERING EMOTIONAL RESILIENCE AND MANAGING EMOTIONS EFFECTIVELY.

In addition to cultivating self-care routines and prioritizing self-nurturing activities, affirmations can also be a powerful tool for fostering emotional resilience and managing emotions effectively. By incorporating positive and empowering statements into our daily practice, we can strengthen our emotional well-being and develop healthier ways of navigating and responding to challenging emotions. Drawing inspiration from various fields such as Witchcraft, Divination, Herbalism, Shamanism, and Ecospirituality, we explore the transformative potential of affirmations in building emotional resilience. Here are ten affirmations that can support individuals in fostering emotional resilience and managing emotions effectively:

"I embrace my emotions with compassion and understanding."

This affirmation encourages individuals to approach their emotions with self-compassion and non-judgment, creating space for emotional acceptance and growth.

"I am capable of navigating through difficult emotions with grace and strength."

This affirmation instills a belief in one's ability to effectively manage and navigate challenging emotions, fostering a sense of inner strength and resilience.

"I release any negative emotions and embrace positivity and peace."

By affirming the release of negative emotions and embracing positivity and peace, individuals can cultivate a mindset that promotes emotional well-being and balance.

"I am in control of my emotional responses and choose peace over conflict."

This affirmation empowers individuals to take ownership of their emotional responses, encouraging them to choose peace and harmony in their interactions with others.

"I am resilient and capable of bouncing back from any emotional challenge."

By affirming one's resilience, individuals reinforce their ability to bounce back from emotional setbacks and challenges, fostering a sense of inner strength and determination.

"I trust in my ability to navigate uncertainty and find emotional stability."

This affirmation cultivates trust in one's ability to navigate uncertain situations and find emotional stability, promoting a sense of confidence and resilience.

"I embrace all my emotions as valuable messengers, guiding me towards growth and understanding."

This affirmation encourages individuals to view their emotions as valuable messengers, providing insights and guidance for personal growth and understanding.

"I am open to exploring and understanding the root causes of my emotions."

By affirming openness to explore and understand the root causes of emotions, individuals foster self-awareness and develop a deeper understanding of their emotional experiences.

"I release any attachment to negative emotions and embrace a state of inner peace."

This affirmation invites individuals to let go of attachment to negative emotions and embrace a state of inner peace and tranquility.

"I am worthy of experiencing and expressing a wide range of positive emotions."

This affirmation affirms one's worthiness to experience and express positive emotions, encouraging individuals to embrace joy, love, and happiness fully.

By incorporating these affirmations into daily practice, individuals can reinforce positive beliefs, cultivate emotional resilience, and develop effective strategies for managing their emotions. It is important to remember that affirmations work best when practiced consistently and with genuine intention. Through the integration of affirmations and self-care practices, individuals can nurture their emotional well-being and foster a greater sense of inner strength and balance.

AFFIRMING GRATITUDE FOR YOUR BODY AND ITS ABILITIES.

In addition to cultivating self-care routines and prioritizing self-nurturing activities, it is essential to affirm gratitude for our bodies and their abilities. Gratitude is a powerful practice that can help shift our mindset towards appreciation and acceptance of our physical selves. By expressing gratitude for our bodies, we can develop a healthier relationship with our physicality and cultivate a positive body image.

Drawing inspiration from various fields such as Witchcraft, Divination, Herbalism, Shamanism, and Ecospirituality, we explore the transformative potential of affirmations in fostering gratitude for our bodies. Here are ten affirmations that can support individuals in affirming gratitude for their bodies and their abilities:

"I am grateful for the strength and resilience of my body."

This affirmation acknowledges and appreciates the strength and resilience that our bodies possess, recognizing the incredible capabilities they offer.

"I am thankful for the gift of mobility and the ability to move freely."

By expressing gratitude for our ability to move and experience the world through our bodies, we cultivate appreciation for the freedom and possibilities it brings.

"I am grateful for the senses that allow me to fully experience the world around me."

This affirmation acknowledges and expresses gratitude for the senses—sight, hearing, taste, touch, and smell—that enable us to engage with and appreciate our surroundings.

"I appreciate the miraculous functions and processes happening within my body."

By affirming our appreciation for the complex and intricate functions occurring within our bodies, we foster a deeper understanding and gratitude for the incredible machinery that sustains us.

"I am thankful for the body's innate wisdom and its ability to heal and restore itself."

This affirmation acknowledges and honors the wisdom and healing capabilities of our bodies, recognizing their innate ability to heal and restore balance.

"I am grateful for the unique beauty and individuality of my body."

By affirming our gratitude for the unique beauty and individuality of our bodies, we celebrate and embrace our physical uniqueness, fostering a positive body image.

"I appreciate my body's capacity to experience pleasure and joy."

This affirmation acknowledges and expresses gratitude for our body's ability to experience pleasure, joy, and the myriad of sensory delights life offers.

"I am grateful for the energy and vitality that my body provides me every day."

By affirming gratitude for the energy and vitality our bodies provide us, we cultivate an appreciation for the daily fuel and life force that sustains us.

"I am thankful for the ways my body supports me in achieving my goals and dreams."

This affirmation recognizes and expresses gratitude for the support our bodies provide in pursuing our aspirations and dreams, empowering us to take inspired action.

"I am grateful for my body's ability to adapt, grow, and evolve."

By affirming our gratitude for our body's adaptive and transformative nature, we embrace the potential for growth and evolution, both physically and spiritually.

By incorporating these affirmations into daily practice, individuals can develop a deeper sense of gratitude for their bodies and cultivate a positive body image. It is important to remember that genuine gratitude is a continuous practice that requires consistent effort and intention. Through affirming gratitude for our bodies and their abilities, we can develop a healthier and more loving relationship with our physical selves, fostering a greater sense of acceptance, appreciation, and well-being.

AFFIRMATIONS FOR PROMOTING PHYSICAL STRENGTH AND FLEXIBILITY.

Promoting physical strength and flexibility is an important aspect of maintaining a healthy and vibrant body. Affirmations can be a powerful tool in supporting this endeavor by reinforcing positive beliefs and intentions. Drawing inspiration from various fields such as Witchcraft, Divination, Herbalism, Shamanism, and Ecospirituality, here are ten affirmations that can help individuals in promoting physical strength and flexibility:

"I am strong and resilient, capable of overcoming any physical challenge."

This affirmation acknowledges the inherent strength within us and reinforces our ability to face and conquer physical obstacles.

"I nurture and care for my body, providing it with the strength it needs to thrive."

By affirming our commitment to nourishing our bodies with wholesome food, regular exercise, and adequate rest, we support their strength and vitality.

"Every day, my body becomes stronger, more flexible, and more capable."

This affirmation affirms our belief in the continual improvement and growth of our physical abilities, motivating us to engage in activities that enhance our strength and flexibility.

"I release any tension or stiffness in my body, allowing for greater ease and flexibility."

By acknowledging and releasing physical tension, we create space for increased flexibility and improved range of motion.

"I honor my body's limits while pushing myself to achieve new levels of strength and flexibility."

This affirmation encourages a balanced approach to physical training, respecting our body's boundaries while challenging ourselves to reach new heights.

"My body is a temple of strength and flexibility, supporting me in all my endeavors."

By viewing our bodies as sacred vessels of strength and flexibility, we cultivate a deep appreciation for their capabilities and potential.

"I embrace physical activities that enhance my strength and flexibility, joyfully exploring new possibilities."

This affirmation encourages a positive and enthusiastic attitude towards physical activities that promote strength and flexibility, making the process enjoyable and exciting.

"With each breath, I invite energy and vitality to flow through my body, nourishing my muscles and enhancing my flexibility."

By consciously breathing in energy and vitality, we invigorate our bodies, supporting muscular strength and flexibility.

"I am open and receptive to the natural flow of energy within my body, allowing for increased strength and flexibility."

This affirmation encourages us to cultivate an awareness of the energetic currents within our bodies, facilitating greater strength and flexibility.

"I am grateful for the physical strength and flexibility I possess, and I continue to nurture and enhance these qualities."

By expressing gratitude for our current level of strength and flexibility, we create a positive mindset that motivates us to continue nurturing and improving these attributes.

Incorporating these affirmations into a daily practice can reinforce our commitment to physical strength and flexibility, enhancing our overall well-being. It is important to personalize these affirmations according to individual goals and needs, allowing them to resonate deeply within us. By consistently affirming our dedication to physical strength and flexibility, we empower ourselves to take the necessary actions to achieve and maintain a strong and flexible body.

AFFIRMATIONS FOR SUPPORTING IMMUNE SYSTEM HEALTH AND WELL-BEING.

Supporting immune system health and well-being is crucial for maintaining overall wellness and vitality. Affirmations can play a significant role in this process by fostering a positive mindset and encouraging beliefs that support a strong and resilient immune system. Drawing inspiration from various fields such as Witchcraft, Divination, Herbalism, Shamanism, and Ecospirituality, here are ten affirmations that can help individuals support their immune system health and well-being:

"My immune system is strong and resilient, protecting me from illness and promoting my well-being."

This affirmation acknowledges the inherent strength of our immune system and reinforces its ability to safeguard our health.

"Every day, my immune system becomes stronger and more effective in defending against pathogens."

By affirming the continuous improvement and strengthening of our immune system, we cultivate confidence in its abilities.

"I nourish my body with wholesome foods and lifestyle choices that support a vibrant immune system."

This affirmation emphasizes the importance of making nourishing choices that fuel and support our immune system's optimal functioning.

"I am grateful for my body's innate ability to heal and restore balance, promoting immune system health."

By expressing gratitude for our body's natural healing capabilities, we reinforce its capacity to maintain immune system health and well-being.

"I attract and radiate positive energy, which supports the healthy functioning of my immune system."

This affirmation recognizes the interconnectedness of energy and immune system health, encouraging a positive and vibrant aura that enhances our well-being.

"I embrace self-care practices that strengthen and fortify my immune system."

By affirming our commitment to self-care, we prioritize activities and practices that bolster our immune system's strength and resilience.

"I am proactive in maintaining a healthy lifestyle that supports my immune system's optimal functioning."

This affirmation emphasizes taking an active role in maintaining a healthy lifestyle, making choices that enhance our immune system's well-being.

"I release any stress or negativity, allowing my immune system to function at its best."

By acknowledging and releasing stress and negativity, we create a harmonious environment for our immune system to operate optimally.

"I am surrounded by a supportive and nurturing environment that promotes immune system health."

This affirmation recognizes the influence of our surroundings on our immune system and encourages us to cultivate a supportive and nurturing environment.

"I am grateful for the power of my mind and its ability to positively influence my immune system's health and well-being."

By affirming the mind-body connection, we harness the power of positive thoughts and beliefs to strengthen and support our immune system.

Incorporating these affirmations into a daily practice can help individuals cultivate a positive mindset and support their immune system health and well-being. It is important to personalize these affirmations according to individual needs and beliefs, allowing them to resonate deeply within us. By consistently affirming our dedication to immune system health, we empower ourselves to make choices and engage in practices that fortify and optimize our immune system's functioning.

AFFIRMATIONS FOR EMBRACING AND MANAGING CHANGE IN YOUR HEALTH JOURNEY.

Embracing and managing change is an integral part of any health journey. Change can bring about uncertainty and challenges, but it also presents opportunities for growth, transformation, and improved well-being. Affirmations can be powerful tools for cultivating a positive mindset and navigating change with resilience and grace. Drawing inspiration from various fields such as Witchcraft, Divination, Herbalism, Shamanism, and Ecospirituality, here are ten affirmations to support individuals in embracing and managing change in their health journey:

"I embrace change as an opportunity for growth and transformation in my health journey."

This affirmation acknowledges change as a catalyst for personal growth and invites us to approach it with an open mind and a willingness to evolve.

"I trust in my ability to adapt and navigate through changes in my health with grace and ease."

By affirming our inherent adaptability and resilience, we cultivate confidence in our capacity to manage and overcome challenges.

"I am open to new possibilities and perspectives in my health journey, allowing positive change to unfold."

This affirmation encourages us to embrace new ideas, approaches, and perspectives, recognizing that they can bring positive transformations to our health.

"I release resistance and embrace the flow of change, knowing that it serves my highest good."

By letting go of resistance and surrendering to the natural flow of change, we create space for positive shifts to occur in our health journey.

"I am patient and compassionate with myself as I navigate changes in my health, honoring my unique process."

This affirmation reminds us to practice self-compassion and patience, understanding that everyone's health journey unfolds at its own pace.

"I welcome positive changes in my health and well-being, celebrating each milestone along the way."

By affirming our openness to positive changes, we cultivate an attitude of celebration and gratitude for the progress we make in our health journey.

"I am resilient in the face of challenges and setbacks, using them as opportunities to learn and grow."

This affirmation encourages us to view challenges and setbacks as valuable learning experiences that can ultimately contribute to our overall growth and well-being.

"I am supported by a community of like-minded individuals who inspire and uplift me on my health journey."

By affirming the presence of a supportive community, we attract and connect with individuals who share our health goals and can provide guidance and encouragement.

"I embrace change as a chance to explore new avenues and discover what truly nourishes my mind, body, and soul."

This affirmation invites us to approach change as an adventure and an opportunity to explore different approaches to health, discovering what truly resonates with us.

"I am the author of my health journey, and I have the power to create positive change in my life."

By affirming our agency and personal power, we take ownership of our health journey and acknowledge our ability to shape it according to our desires and intentions.

Incorporating these affirmations into daily practice can help individuals embrace and manage change in their health journey with resilience, optimism, and self-empowerment. It is important to personalize these affirmations according to individual circumstances and needs, allowing them to resonate deeply within us. By consistently affirming our openness to change and our ability to navigate it with grace, we empower ourselves to embrace transformation and achieve optimal well-being in our health journey.

AFFIRMATIONS FOR OVERCOMING SELF-LIMITING BELIEFS ABOUT YOUR HEALTH.

Overcoming self-limiting beliefs about our health is crucial for personal growth, transformation, and achieving optimal well-being. Self-limiting beliefs can hinder our progress, dampen our motivation, and prevent us from reaching our health goals. Affirmations can serve as powerful tools to challenge and reframe these beliefs, empowering us to embrace a more positive and empowering mindset. Drawing inspiration from various fields such as Witchcraft, Divination, Herbalism, Shamanism, and Ecospirituality, here are ten affirmations to support individuals in overcoming self-limiting beliefs about their health:

"I release all self-limiting beliefs about my health and embrace my infinite potential for well-being."

This affirmation acknowledges that our potential for well-being is limitless and invites us to let go of any beliefs that restrict our health journey.

"I am worthy of vibrant health and vitality, and I deserve to prioritize my well-being."

By affirming our inherent worthiness of vibrant health, we shift our mindset to prioritize self-care and make choices that support our well-being.

"I am capable of making positive changes in my health, and I trust in my ability to achieve my goals."

This affirmation empowers us to recognize our capabilities and trust in our capacity to make positive changes in our health, fostering a sense of self-efficacy.

"I release the need for perfection and embrace progress in my health journey."

By letting go of the need for perfection, we free ourselves from the pressure of unrealistic expectations and allow room for growth and progress.

"I am not defined by my past health challenges. I am resilient and capable of creating a new, vibrant reality."

This affirmation helps us detach from past health challenges and embrace the present moment, affirming our ability to create a new and vibrant reality.

"I choose to focus on the positive aspects of my health journey, celebrating every step forward."

By shifting our focus to the positive aspects of our health journey, we cultivate an attitude of gratitude and celebrate our progress, no matter how small.

"I let go of comparisons and embrace my unique health journey. I am on my own path, and I honor it."

This affirmation reminds us to embrace our individual health journey and resist the temptation to compare ourselves to others, allowing us to honor our unique path.

"I am in control of my thoughts and beliefs. I choose empowering beliefs that support my optimal health."

By recognizing our power to control our thoughts and beliefs, we consciously choose beliefs that empower us and support our journey towards optimal health.

"I am resilient and capable of overcoming any obstacles that arise on my health journey."

This affirmation reinforces our resilience and affirms our ability to overcome obstacles, instilling confidence and determination in the face of challenges.

"I release all fear and doubt about my ability to achieve my health goals. I am capable, and I am committed to my well-being."

By letting go of fear and doubt, we cultivate a mindset of unwavering commitment to our well-being, fueling our motivation and determination.

Incorporating these affirmations into daily practice can help individuals challenge and overcome self-limiting beliefs about their health. It is important to personalize these affirmations to address specific self-limiting beliefs that may be holding us back. By consistently affirming our worthiness, capabilities, resilience, and commitment to our well-being, we empower ourselves to let go of limiting beliefs and embrace a more positive and empowering mindset that propels us towards optimal health and well-being.

AFFIRMATIONS FOR FINDING JOY AND PLEASURE IN MOVEMENT AND EXERCISE.

Finding joy and pleasure in movement and exercise is essential for creating a sustainable and enjoyable fitness routine. By shifting our mindset and affirming positive beliefs about exercise, we can cultivate a deep appreciation for physical activity and embrace it as a source of joy and well-being. Drawing inspiration from various fields such as Witchcraft, Divination, Herbalism, Shamanism, and Ecospirituality, here are ten affirmations to support individuals in finding joy and pleasure in movement and exercise:

"I joyfully embrace movement as a celebration of what my body can do."

This affirmation invites us to see movement as a joyful celebration of our body's capabilities and shift our perspective from obligation to appreciation.

"I find pleasure in the physical sensations that arise during exercise, knowing that my body is alive and vibrant."

By focusing on the physical sensations experienced during exercise, we cultivate a deeper connection with our bodies and derive pleasure from the feeling of being alive and vibrant.

"I release all expectations and judgments about my performance and allow myself to move with freedom and joy."

This affirmation encourages us to let go of expectations and judgments, freeing ourselves to move with a sense of freedom and joy, without the pressure of performance.

"I choose movement activities that bring me joy and align with my interests and preferences."

By consciously selecting movement activities that align with our interests and preferences, we create an environment that fosters joy and pleasure in exercise.

"Each movement I make brings me closer to optimal health and well-being, filling me with joy and gratitude."

This affirmation highlights the connection between movement and well-being, allowing us to feel gratitude and joy for every step we take towards optimal health.

"I allow myself to play and have fun during exercise, embracing my inner child and tapping into a sense of joy and spontaneity."

By infusing an element of playfulness and fun into our exercise routine, we tap into our inner child and experience a renewed sense of joy and spontaneity.

"I appreciate the positive effects of exercise on my mental and emotional well-being, knowing that each workout uplifts my spirits."

This affirmation acknowledges the positive impact of exercise on our mental and emotional well-being, fostering a sense of joy as we recognize its uplifting effects.

"I honor my body's need for movement and prioritize activities that bring me joy and fulfillment."

By honoring our body's need for movement and prioritizing activities that bring us joy and fulfillment, we create a harmonious relationship with exercise.

"I find joy in discovering new ways to move my body and explore its capabilities."

This affirmation encourages us to approach exercise with a sense of curiosity and adventure, finding joy in exploring new movements and discovering the capabilities of our bodies.

"I celebrate every milestone and achievement in my fitness journey, recognizing the progress I make and finding joy in the process."

By celebrating milestones and achievements, we cultivate a sense of accomplishment and joy, appreciating the progress we make on our fitness journey.

Incorporating these affirmations into our mindset and daily practice can help us find joy and pleasure in movement and exercise. It is important to personalize these affirmations and adapt them to our specific preferences and interests. By affirming our appreciation for our body's capabilities, embracing playfulness, and acknowledging the positive impact of exercise on our well-being, we create a positive and joyful relationship with movement, making it a sustainable and fulfilling part of our lives.

AFFIRMATIONS FOR PROMOTING POSITIVE BODY IMAGE AND SELF-ACCEPTANCE.

Promoting positive body image and self-acceptance is crucial for cultivating a healthy and compassionate relationship with our bodies. By incorporating affirmations that foster self-love, appreciation, and acceptance, we can shift our mindset towards embracing our unique physicality and developing a positive body image. Drawing inspiration from various fields such as Witchcraft, Divination, Herbalism, Shamanism, and Ecospirituality, here are ten affirmations to support individuals in promoting positive body image and self-acceptance:

"I unconditionally love and accept my body as it is, honoring its uniqueness and inherent beauty."

This affirmation emphasizes the importance of unconditional love and acceptance for our bodies, recognizing their inherent beauty and uniqueness.

"I release comparison and embrace my own journey of self-discovery and self-acceptance."

By letting go of the habit of comparing ourselves to others, we open ourselves to the journey of self-discovery and self-acceptance, honoring our own path.

"I am worthy of love and respect, regardless of my body's shape, size, or appearance."

This affirmation reminds us that our worthiness is not tied to our body's shape, size, or appearance, but is inherent and deserving of love and respect.

"I appreciate the incredible things my body allows me to do and experience in this world."

By focusing on the capabilities and experiences our bodies enable us to have, we develop a deeper appreciation for their strength and resilience.

"I choose to nourish my body with love, kindness, and self-care."

This affirmation encourages us to prioritize self-care and nourishment, recognizing that our bodies deserve love and kindness in the form of self-care practices.

"I celebrate the diversity and beauty of all bodies, including my own."

By celebrating the diversity and beauty of all bodies, we cultivate a mindset of inclusivity and learn to appreciate the unique beauty of our own physical form.

"I speak to myself with love and compassion, nurturing a positive and empowering inner dialogue."

This affirmation emphasizes the importance of cultivating a positive and empowering inner dialogue, speaking to ourselves with love and compassion.

"I embrace my body as a vessel for my soul's journey, respecting and honoring its needs and boundaries."

By recognizing our bodies as vessels for our soul's journey, we develop a deeper respect and honor for their needs and boundaries, fostering self-acceptance.

"I reject societal beauty standards and embrace my own definition of beauty and worth."

This affirmation encourages us to challenge societal beauty standards and define our own unique and authentic standards of beauty and worth.

"I radiate confidence and self-assurance, knowing that true beauty comes from within."

By cultivating confidence and self-assurance, we recognize that true beauty emanates from within and is not solely defined by external appearance.

Incorporating these affirmations into our daily practice can support us in promoting positive body image and self-acceptance. It is important to personalize these affirmations and adapt them to our own journey and experiences. By affirming our love, appreciation, and acceptance for our bodies, rejecting comparison, and embracing our unique beauty and worth, we cultivate a positive and compassionate relationship with ourselves, fostering a deep sense of self-acceptance and well-being.

AFFIRMATIONS FOR DEVELOPING HEALTHY HABITS AND BREAKING UNHEALTHY PATTERNS.

Developing healthy habits and breaking unhealthy patterns is essential for creating a sustainable and balanced lifestyle. By incorporating affirmations that reinforce positive behavior changes and support the cultivation of healthy habits, we can overcome obstacles and create lasting transformation. Drawing inspiration from various fields such as Witchcraft, Divination, Herbalism, Shamanism, and Ecospirituality, here are ten affirmations to support individuals in developing healthy habits and breaking unhealthy patterns:

"I am committed to my well-being and prioritize creating healthy habits that nourish my mind, body, and spirit."

This affirmation emphasizes the importance of prioritizing well-being and committing to the development of healthy habits that support holistic health.

"I release old patterns that no longer serve me and embrace new habits that align with my highest good."

By consciously letting go of old patterns and embracing new habits that align with our highest good, we create space for positive change and growth.

"I have the power to make healthy choices and create a life of balance and well-being."

This affirmation acknowledges our innate power and ability to make healthy choices, empowering us to create a life of balance and well-being.

"I am in control of my actions and can break free from unhealthy patterns."

By affirming our control over our actions, we empower ourselves to break free from unhealthy patterns and cultivate positive change.

"Every day, I am creating a healthier and happier version of myself through my choices and habits."

This affirmation highlights the continuous nature of personal growth and transformation, encouraging us to make daily choices that contribute to our overall well-being.

"I am patient and compassionate with myself as I navigate the process of developing new habits and releasing old ones."

By practicing patience and self-compassion, we create a supportive and nurturing environment for ourselves during the process of habit development and change.

"I release the need for instant gratification and embrace the long-term benefits of healthy habits."

This affirmation encourages us to shift our focus from instant gratification to the long-term benefits that come from cultivating healthy habits.

"I am open to learning and evolving, seeking knowledge and guidance to support my journey towards healthy habits."

By remaining open to learning and seeking guidance, we create opportunities for growth and expansion on our path to developing healthy habits.

"I replace self-sabotaging behaviors with positive and empowering choices that support my well-being."

This affirmation affirms our ability to replace self-sabotaging behaviors with positive choices that align with our well-being and support our growth.

"I am dedicated to my personal growth and understand that developing healthy habits is a lifelong journey."

This affirmation acknowledges that developing healthy habits is a lifelong journey and reinforces our dedication to personal growth and self-improvement.

Incorporating these affirmations into our daily practice can support us in developing healthy habits and breaking unhealthy patterns. It is important to personalize these affirmations and adapt them to our specific goals and challenges. By affirming our commitment to well-being, embracing change, and nurturing patience and self-compassion, we lay the foundation for lasting transformation and the cultivation of a healthy and balanced lifestyle.

AFFIRMATIONS FOR NURTURING HEALTHY RELATIONSHIPS AND SOCIAL WELL-BEING.

Nurturing healthy relationships and cultivating social well-being are essential aspects of leading a fulfilling and connected life. By incorporating affirmations that promote positive interactions, enhance communication skills, and foster deep connections, we can create harmonious and supportive relationships. Drawing inspiration from various fields such as Witchcraft, Divination, Herbalism, Shamanism, and Ecospirituality, here are ten affirmations to support individuals in nurturing healthy relationships and promoting social well-being:

"I attract and cultivate meaningful relationships that support my growth and well-being."

This affirmation acknowledges our ability to attract and foster meaningful relationships that contribute to our personal growth and overall well-being.

"I communicate with clarity, compassion, and understanding in all my interactions."

By affirming our intention to communicate with clarity, compassion, and understanding, we promote harmonious and effective communication.

"I am open to connecting deeply with others and building authentic, heart-centered relationships."

This affirmation invites us to remain open to deep connections and encourages the building of authentic relationships based on genuine care and understanding.

"I surround myself with people who uplift and inspire me, creating a positive and supportive social circle."

By affirming our intention to surround ourselves with uplifting and inspiring individuals, we cultivate a positive and supportive social circle that contributes to our well-being.

"I honor and respect the boundaries of others and communicate my boundaries with clarity and compassion."

This affirmation emphasizes the importance of honoring both our own boundaries and the boundaries of others, fostering healthy and respectful relationships.

"I attract and manifest opportunities for joyful and fulfilling social experiences."

By affirming our ability to attract and manifest joyful and fulfilling social experiences, we invite more opportunities for connection and happiness into our lives.

"I am a good listener, offering my presence and support to those around me."

This affirmation affirms our intention to be present and supportive listeners, allowing others to feel heard and valued in our interactions.

"I let go of judgment and embrace acceptance and understanding in my relationships."

By releasing judgment and cultivating acceptance and understanding, we create an environment of compassion and harmony in our relationships.

"I attract and manifest friendships that are based on authenticity, trust, and mutual growth."

This affirmation invites us to attract and cultivate friendships that are built on authenticity, trust, and a shared commitment to personal growth.

"I am grateful for the meaningful connections I have in my life, and I nurture them with love and care."

This affirmation expresses gratitude for the existing meaningful connections in our lives and reinforces our commitment to nurturing them with love and care.

Incorporating these affirmations into our daily practice can support us in nurturing healthy relationships and promoting social well-being. It is important to personalize these affirmations and adapt them to our specific social goals and challenges. By affirming our ability to attract positive relationships, communicate effectively, set boundaries, and foster genuine connections, we create a nurturing and supportive social environment that contributes to our overall well-being.

AFFIRMATIONS FOR FINDING BALANCE AND HARMONY IN LIFE'S DEMANDS.

Finding balance and harmony in life's demands is crucial for maintaining overall well-being and reducing stress. By incorporating affirmations that promote self-care, time management, and prioritization, we can create a sense of balance and harmony in our daily lives. Drawing inspiration from various fields such as Witchcraft, Divination, Herbalism, Shamanism, and Ecospirituality, here are ten affirmations to support individuals in finding balance and harmony in life's demands:

"I prioritize self-care and honor my physical, mental, and emotional well-being."

This affirmation reminds us of the importance of self-care and encourages us to prioritize our own well-being in all aspects of life.

"I create a harmonious rhythm in my daily life, balancing work, rest, and play."

By affirming our intention to create a harmonious rhythm in our daily lives, we strive to balance our work responsibilities with time for rest, rejuvenation, and enjoyable activities.

"I manage my time effectively and prioritize tasks that align with my goals and values."

This affirmation empowers us to manage our time efficiently, focusing on tasks and activities that align with our goals and values, helping us maintain a sense of balance.

"I release the need to control every outcome and trust in the natural flow of life."

By affirming our trust in the natural flow of life and relinquishing the need for excessive control, we can find greater peace and harmony in navigating life's demands.

"I set clear boundaries and communicate my needs effectively, maintaining a healthy work-life balance."

This affirmation emphasizes the importance of setting boundaries and communicating our needs assertively, enabling us to maintain a healthy balance between work and personal life.

"I find joy and fulfillment in both my professional and personal pursuits."

By affirming our ability to find joy and fulfillment in both our professional and personal pursuits, we foster a sense of balance and satisfaction in all areas of life.

"I embrace simplicity and declutter my life, letting go of unnecessary commitments and possessions."

This affirmation encourages us to simplify our lives by decluttering both our physical and mental spaces, letting go of unnecessary commitments and possessions that may hinder our sense of balance.

"I create moments of stillness and mindfulness, allowing myself to recharge and find inner peace."

By affirming our commitment to creating moments of stillness and mindfulness, we allow ourselves the opportunity to recharge, find inner peace, and restore balance.

"I trust in my ability to adapt to change and find equilibrium in all situations."

This affirmation affirms our inherent resilience and ability to adapt to change, helping us maintain a sense of equilibrium even in challenging circumstances.

"I embrace a holistic approach to life, nurturing my physical, mental, and spiritual well-being."

By affirming our commitment to a holistic approach to life, we prioritize the nurturing of our physical, mental, and spiritual well-being, fostering overall balance and harmony.

Incorporating these affirmations into our daily practice can support us in finding balance and harmony in life's demands. It is important to personalize these affirmations and adapt them to our specific needs and circumstances. By affirming self-care, effective time management, boundaries, adaptability, and a holistic approach to life, we create a foundation for balance and harmony that allows us to navigate life's demands with greater ease and fulfillment.

AFFIRMATIONS FOR PROMOTING INNER PEACE AND MENTAL CLARITY.

Promoting inner peace and mental clarity is essential for overall well-being and navigating life's challenges with a calm and focused mind. By incorporating affirmations that cultivate a sense of peace, clarity, and mindfulness, we can experience greater inner harmony and mental well-being. Drawing inspiration from various fields such as Witchcraft, Divination, Herbalism, Shamanism, and Ecospirituality, here are ten affirmations to support individuals in promoting inner peace and mental clarity:

"I am grounded and centered in the present moment, finding peace within."

This affirmation reminds us to stay present and grounded, allowing us to find inner peace amidst the busyness of life.

"I let go of mental clutter and embrace the clarity that comes from a calm mind."

By affirming our intention to let go of mental clutter, we create space for clarity and calmness to prevail in our thoughts.

"I trust in the natural flow of life, knowing that everything is unfolding in divine order."

This affirmation encourages us to trust in the natural flow of life, easing our minds and allowing for mental clarity to arise.

"I release all worries and anxieties, inviting peace and tranquility into my mind."

By affirming our willingness to release worries and anxieties, we invite peace and tranquility to enter our minds.

"I am attuned to the wisdom of my inner guidance, allowing it to lead me towards clarity."

This affirmation emphasizes the importance of tuning into our inner guidance and trusting it to lead us towards mental clarity.

"I create a sanctuary of calmness within me, where I can find peace in any circumstance."

By affirming our ability to create a sanctuary of calmness within ourselves, we can access inner peace regardless of external circumstances.

"I cultivate a peaceful mind through daily practices of meditation and self-reflection."

This affirmation highlights the significance of incorporating daily practices such as meditation and self-reflection to cultivate a peaceful and clear mind.

"I embrace silence and solitude as pathways to inner peace and mental clarity."

By affirming our appreciation for silence and solitude, we recognize their role in nurturing inner peace and fostering mental clarity.

"I release the need for control and surrender to the natural flow of life, finding peace in surrender."

This affirmation encourages us to let go of the need for control and surrender to the natural flow of life, allowing peace to arise within us.

"I am a magnet for peace and clarity, attracting harmonious experiences and thoughts."

By affirming our inherent ability to attract peace and clarity, we open ourselves up to experiencing more harmonious thoughts and experiences.

Incorporating these affirmations into our daily practice can support us in promoting inner peace and mental clarity. It is important to personalize these affirmations and adapt them to our specific needs and circumstances. By affirming grounding, trust, surrender, meditation, self-reflection, and our ability to attract peace and clarity, we create a foundation for inner peace and mental clarity that allows us to navigate life's challenges with greater calmness, focus, and well-being.

AFFIRMATIONS FOR MANAGING AND REDUCING PAIN AND DISCOMFORT.

Managing and reducing pain and discomfort is an important aspect of overall well-being and quality of life. Affirmations can play a powerful role in shifting our mindset and helping us cope with pain and discomfort more effectively. Drawing inspiration from various fields such as Witchcraft, Divination, Herbalism, Shamanism, and Ecospirituality, here are ten affirmations to support individuals in managing and reducing pain and discomfort:

"I am in tune with my body's wisdom and can find relief from pain and discomfort."

This affirmation acknowledges our ability to connect with our body's wisdom and find ways to alleviate pain and discomfort.

"I release tension and invite relaxation into my body, soothing areas of pain and discomfort."

By affirming our intention to release tension and invite relaxation, we create space for the soothing of areas affected by pain and discomfort.

"I am resilient and capable of finding solutions to manage and reduce my pain."

This affirmation emphasizes our resilience and capacity to seek and implement effective strategies to manage and reduce pain.

"I focus on the present moment, finding peace and acceptance amidst any physical discomfort."

By directing our attention to the present moment, we can cultivate a sense of peace and acceptance, even in the face of physical discomfort.

"I embrace self-care practices that support my body's healing and alleviate pain."

This affirmation highlights the importance of incorporating self-care practices that aid in our body's healing process and provide relief from pain.

"I am gentle and compassionate with myself, nurturing my body and mind through times of pain."

By affirming our self-compassion and gentleness, we create a nurturing environment for our body and mind during periods of pain.

"I trust in the body's natural ability to heal and restore balance, reducing pain over time."

This affirmation encourages us to have faith in our body's innate healing capacity and its ability to restore balance, leading to a reduction in pain.

"I release any resistance and allow for the natural flow of energy, promoting healing and pain relief."

By letting go of resistance and allowing energy to flow naturally, we create conditions that support healing and pain relief.

"I am open to exploring alternative therapies and treatments that can alleviate my pain."

This affirmation expresses our openness to explore various alternative therapies and treatments that can effectively reduce pain.

"I am grateful for the moments of relief and comfort that I experience, knowing that healing is possible."

By affirming our gratitude for moments of relief and comfort, we cultivate a positive mindset and reinforce the belief in the possibility of healing.

Incorporating these affirmations into our daily practice can help us manage and reduce pain and discomfort. It is important to personalize these affirmations and adapt them to our specific circumstances and needs. By affirming our connection with our body's wisdom, our resilience, our ability to find solutions, and our commitment to self-care, we create a foundation for managing pain and discomfort more effectively. Additionally, affirmations that promote presence, acceptance, trust, and gratitude support our overall well-being and healing process.

AFFIRMATIONS FOR PROMOTING SELF-HEALING AND SUPPORTING THE BODY'S NATURAL PROCESSES.

Promoting self-healing and supporting the body's natural processes is a powerful approach to overall well-being. Affirmations can play a significant role in activating our innate healing abilities and fostering a harmonious relationship with our body. Drawing inspiration from various fields such as Witchcraft, Divination, Herbalism, Shamanism, and Ecospirituality, here are ten affirmations to promote self-healing and support the body's natural processes:

"I trust in the wisdom of my body to heal itself and restore balance."

This affirmation acknowledges our body's inherent wisdom and its capacity to heal and restore equilibrium.

"I am a vessel of healing energy, and my body responds positively to nurturing practices."

By affirming ourselves as conduits of healing energy, we cultivate an environment that supports and enhances the body's natural healing processes.

"I align my thoughts and beliefs with the intention of vibrant health and well-being."

This affirmation emphasizes the importance of aligning our thoughts and beliefs with the intention of vibrant health, allowing our body's natural processes to unfold.

"I release any resistance and allow healing to flow through me effortlessly."

By releasing resistance and surrendering to the flow of healing energy, we create space for self-healing to occur effortlessly.

"Every cell in my body vibrates with health, vitality, and well-being."

This affirmation affirms the innate vitality within each cell of our body and encourages vibrant health at a cellular level.

"I nourish my body with wholesome foods, supporting its natural healing abilities."

By affirming our commitment to nourishing our body with wholesome foods, we provide the essential nutrients it needs to support its natural healing processes.

"I listen to my body's signals and respond with love and care."

This affirmation encourages us to tune into our body's messages and respond with kindness, attentiveness, and appropriate self-care.

"I am in harmony with the rhythms of nature, allowing their healing power to restore my well-being."

By aligning with the rhythms of nature, we tap into the healing power that exists within the natural world and allow it to restore our overall well-being.

"I am resilient, and my body bounces back with strength and vitality."

This affirmation highlights our resilience and affirms the body's ability to bounce back, recover, and regain strength and vitality.

"I am grateful for the healing that is already taking place within me."

By expressing gratitude for the healing that is already occurring within us, we reinforce the positive changes and transformations happening at a deep level.

Incorporating these affirmations into our daily practice can help promote self-healing and support the body's natural processes. It is important to personalize these affirmations and adapt them to our specific needs and circumstances. By affirming our trust in the body's wisdom, our role as conduits of healing energy, our alignment with vibrant health, and our commitment to nourishment and self-care, we create a powerful foundation for self-healing. Additionally, affirmations that emphasize our connection with nature, our resilience, and our gratitude for the healing already taking place within us further enhance our well-being and support the body's natural processes.

CONCLUSION: ENCOURAGEMENT TO PRACTICE DAILY AFFIRMATIONS FOR SUSTAINED HEALTH AND WELL-BEING.

In conclusion, the practice of daily affirmations holds immense potential for promoting sustained health and well-being. By integrating the transformative power of affirmations into our lives, drawing inspiration from various fields such as Witchcraft, Divination, Herbalism, Shamanism, and Ecospirituality, we can harness the profound impact of positive self-talk on our physical, mental, and emotional states.

Throughout this exploration, we have delved into the different aspects of affirmations that contribute to our overall well-being. We have examined how affirmations can enhance stress reduction and relaxation, nurture a healthy relationship with food and embrace mindful eating, boost energy levels and vitality, cultivate restful sleep and healthy sleep habits, and promote self-discipline and commitment to regular exercise. We have also explored their role in fostering emotional resilience, managing emotions effectively, and promoting gratitude for our bodies and their abilities.

Moreover, we have seen how affirmations can support immune system health, help us embrace and manage change in our health journey, overcome self-limiting beliefs, find joy and pleasure in movement and exercise, develop positive body image and self-acceptance, nurture healthy habits and break unhealthy patterns, and cultivate healthy relationships and social well-being. Additionally, we have explored their ability to help us find balance and harmony amidst life's demands, promote inner peace and mental clarity, manage and reduce pain and discomfort, and support self-healing and the body's natural processes.

By practicing daily affirmations, we establish a powerful foundation for sustained health and well-being. These affirmations serve as reminders of our inherent ability to cultivate positive change, adapt to new circumstances, and embrace our unique journey. They encourage us to prioritize self-care, listen to our bodies, and make choices that support our overall well-being.

It is important to approach the practice of daily affirmations with consistency, commitment, and intention. Set aside dedicated time each day to engage in affirmations, whether through writing them down, speaking them aloud, or reflecting on them silently. Incorporate them into your morning routine, meditative practice, or bedtime ritual. Find a method that resonates with you and allows you to connect deeply with the affirmations.

Remember that the power of affirmations lies in their repetition and emotional resonance. As you repeat these affirmations daily, infuse them with conviction, gratitude, and positive emotions. Allow them to permeate your being and create a shift in your mindset, thoughts, and beliefs. Over time, you will witness the transformative impact of affirmations as they become an integral part of your journey towards sustained health and well-being.

As you continue to explore and practice affirmations, remember to be gentle with yourself. Embrace the process of self-discovery and growth, recognizing that it is unique to each individual. Be patient and kind to yourself as you navigate the ups and downs of your health journey. Celebrate the progress you make along the way, no matter how small.

In conclusion, by cultivating the daily practice of affirmations, you are empowering yourself to take charge of your health and well-being. Embrace the wisdom of various disciplines, draw inspiration from nature and the world around you, and tap into the power of positive self-talk. With each affirmation, you are affirming your commitment to living a vibrant, balanced, and fulfilling life. Embrace this journey wholeheartedly, and may your daily affirmations pave the way for sustained health, well-being, and a deeper connection with yourself and the world around you.

RELATIONSHIPS AND LOVE:

In this chapter, we embark on a profound exploration of relationships and love, drawing inspiration from various fields such as Witchcraft, Divination, Herbalism, Shamanism, and Ecospirituality. Relationships are an essential aspect of human existence, influencing our well-being, happiness, and personal growth. Whether it be romantic partnerships, familial bonds, friendships, or connections with our communities and the natural world, relationships shape our experiences and play a vital role in our journey of self-discovery and fulfillment.

Understanding the dynamics of relationships and the intricacies of love is a complex and multifaceted endeavor. It requires us to delve into the realms of psychology, sociology, spirituality, and personal development. By integrating knowledge and wisdom from diverse disciplines, we can cultivate a comprehensive understanding of the dynamics at play and the transformative potential of love in our lives.

In this section, we lay the foundation for our exploration by delving into the essence of relationships and love. We examine the various forms of love and the different types of relationships that enrich our lives. We also explore the importance of self-love and self-acceptance as foundational elements in fostering healthy and fulfilling connections with others.

The Nature of Relationships:

Relationships serve as a profound vehicle for growth, connection, and learning. They offer us opportunities for self-reflection, empathy, and the cultivation of compassion. Relationships can be a source of immense joy, support, and inspiration, but they can also present challenges and conflicts that test our resilience and emotional intelligence. Understanding the nature of relationships is crucial for navigating their complexities and fostering harmonious connections.

Types of Relationships:

Relationships encompass a broad spectrum, ranging from romantic partnerships and friendships to familial bonds and connections with our communities and the natural world. Each type of relationship brings its own unique dynamics, expectations, and opportunities for growth. By exploring the diverse forms of relationships, we gain a deeper understanding of the roles they play in our lives and the potential they hold for personal transformation.

Love in its Many Forms:

Love is a powerful force that permeates every aspect of our existence. It manifests in various forms, including romantic love, platonic love, familial love, and self-love. Each form of love carries its own characteristics and expressions, shaping our experiences and influencing the quality of our relationships. By exploring the nuances of love in its many forms, we develop a richer understanding of its profound impact on our lives.

The Importance of Self-Love:

At the core of any healthy and fulfilling relationship lies the foundation of self-love. Self-love is the practice of embracing and accepting oneself unconditionally, acknowledging one's worth, and nurturing a deep sense of compassion and kindness towards oneself. Cultivating self-love is vital for establishing healthy boundaries, fostering authentic connections, and experiencing fulfillment in relationships. We delve into the significance of self-love and provide practical strategies and exercises to support its development.

Balancing Self-Love and Interdependence:

While self-love is crucial, it is equally important to find a harmonious balance between self-care and interdependence within relationships. Interdependence acknowledges that we are interconnected beings, and our well-being is intimately connected with the well-being of others. We explore the delicate balance between nurturing our individuality and honoring the needs and desires of our loved ones. By cultivating this balance, we foster healthy relationships based on mutual respect, empathy, and growth.

Navigating Relationship Challenges:

Relationships are not without their challenges. Conflicts, disagreements, and differences in expectations can arise, testing the strength of our connections. In this section, we provide guidance and strategies for effectively navigating relationship challenges. We explore the importance of effective communication, active listening, and empathy in resolving conflicts and fostering understanding. We also address the significance of forgiveness, letting go of resentment, and embracing vulnerability in healing and strengthening relationships.

By embarking on this exploration of relationships and love, we open ourselves to a deeper understanding of ourselves and others. We recognize the transformative power of love and the profound impact it can have on our well-being and personal growth. Through the integration of knowledge from various disciplines and the incorporation of practical exercises and examples, we empower ourselves to cultivate healthy, authentic, and fulfilling relationships in our lives.

In the upcoming sections, we delve into specific aspects of relationships and love, examining topics such as communication, intimacy, boundaries, and the role of spirituality in relationships. Each section will provide a comprehensive analysis of the subject matter, presenting diverse perspectives and insights to foster critical thinking and meaningful discussions. Let us embark on this journey together and uncover the wisdom and transformative potential that relationships and love hold for our lives.

AFFIRMATIONS THAT NURTURE POSITIVE, LOVING RELATIONSHIPS WITH ONESELF AND OTHERS, ATTRACTING AND MAINTAINING HEALTHY CONNECTIONS.

Affirmations play a powerful role in nurturing positive, loving relationships with oneself and others. By consciously choosing affirmations that support self-love, acceptance, and healthy connections, we can shift our mindset and attract fulfilling relationships into our lives. Drawing inspiration from various fields such as Witchcraft, Divination, Herbalism, Shamanism, and Ecospirituality, we explore the transformative potential of affirmations in cultivating harmonious connections. Here are ten affirmations that can support individuals in nurturing positive, loving relationships with oneself and others, attracting and maintaining healthy connections:

"I am deserving of love and respect, both from myself and others."

This affirmation affirms one's inherent worthiness of love and respect, setting the foundation for healthy relationships built on mutual appreciation and kindness.

"I attract and manifest nurturing and supportive relationships into my life."

By affirming our ability to attract and manifest loving connections, we open ourselves to the possibility of cultivating healthy and fulfilling relationships.

"I am open to giving and receiving love in all its forms."

This affirmation acknowledges the importance of being open to giving and receiving love, allowing us to experience the depth and richness of meaningful connections.

"I release any fears or attachments that hinder the growth and harmony of my relationships."

By affirming our willingness to let go of fears and attachments that may hinder our relationships, we create space for growth, understanding, and harmony.

"I communicate my needs and boundaries with clarity and compassion."

This affirmation emphasizes the importance of clear and compassionate communication, enabling us to establish healthy boundaries and foster understanding in our relationships.

"I forgive myself and others, releasing any resentment or negativity from past experiences."

By affirming our capacity for forgiveness and releasing resentment, we free ourselves from the burdens of the past, allowing space for healing and authentic connections.

"I attract and surround myself with people who uplift and inspire me."

This affirmation acknowledges our ability to attract positive and uplifting individuals into our lives, creating a supportive network that nurtures our personal growth and well-being.

"I choose relationships that align with my values and contribute to my overall happiness."

By affirming our intention to choose relationships that align with our values and contribute to our happiness, we prioritize our well-being and cultivate connections that bring joy and fulfillment.

"I embrace vulnerability and authentic connection in my relationships."

This affirmation encourages us to embrace vulnerability, allowing us to experience deeper, more authentic connections with others based on trust, honesty, and mutual understanding.

"I am grateful for the loving relationships in my life, and I cultivate them with care and appreciation."

By expressing gratitude for the loving relationships in our lives and affirming our commitment to nurturing them with care and appreciation, we deepen our connections and create a positive cycle of love and support.

By incorporating these affirmations into daily practice, individuals can cultivate a mindset that attracts and maintains healthy, loving relationships. It is important to remember that affirmations are not magic spells but tools that guide our thoughts and actions. Through consistent practice and a genuine commitment to self-love and positive connections, we can transform our relationships, fostering a profound sense of love, acceptance, and fulfillment in our lives.

INTRODUCTION: THE SIGNIFICANCE OF HEALTHY AND FULFILLING RELATIONSHIPS.

Healthy and fulfilling relationships play a crucial role in our overall well-being and happiness. They provide us with love, support, and a sense of belonging, while also offering opportunities for personal growth and self-discovery. Whether they are romantic partnerships, friendships, or family connections, relationships shape our lives and profoundly impact our mental, emotional, and even physical health. In this section, we will explore the profound significance of healthy and fulfilling relationships and the transformative power they hold in our lives.

Emotional Support and Well-being:

Healthy relationships provide us with emotional support, creating a safe and nurturing space where we can share our joys, sorrows, and vulnerabilities. Having someone who listens, understands, and empathizes with our experiences can enhance our emotional well-being and resilience. Through emotional support, we can navigate life's challenges more effectively and find solace in times of need.

Personal Growth and Self-Discovery:

Fulfilling relationships offer opportunities for personal growth and self-discovery. Interacting with others exposes us to different perspectives, challenges our beliefs, and expands our understanding of the world. Through meaningful connections, we can learn more about ourselves, uncover hidden strengths, and address areas for growth. Healthy relationships provide a supportive environment where we can explore our authentic selves and embrace personal development.

Sense of Belonging and Connection:

Humans are social beings who thrive on connection and a sense of belonging. Healthy relationships provide us with a sense of being understood, accepted, and valued by others. They give us a place where we can be ourselves without fear of judgment or rejection. Feeling connected to others fosters a sense of belonging, which is essential for our mental and emotional well-being.

Increased Resilience and Coping Skills:

Strong relationships can enhance our resilience and coping skills during challenging times. Having a support system that believes in us, encourages us, and provides practical assistance can help us navigate adversity more effectively. The emotional support and encouragement from loved ones can bolster our resilience and help us find strength and hope even in the face of difficulties.

Improved Physical Health:

Believe it or not, healthy relationships can have a positive impact on our physical health as well. Studies have shown that individuals in supportive and loving relationships tend to have lower levels of stress, reduced risk of cardiovascular diseases, and better overall health outcomes. The emotional well-being fostered by healthy relationships can directly contribute to a healthier body.

Affirmations for Cultivating Healthy and Fulfilling Relationships:

Affirmations can be powerful tools to support and enhance our relationships. They can help shift our mindset, improve our self-perception, and attract positive and nurturing connections. By regularly practicing affirmations, we can foster the qualities and behaviors that contribute to healthy relationships. Here are some affirmations to nurture healthy and fulfilling relationships:

"I am worthy of love, respect, and healthy connections."

"I attract and nurture relationships that support my growth and well-being."

"I communicate openly, honestly, and effectively in my relationships."

"I am deserving of healthy boundaries that honor my needs and the needs of others."

"I embrace vulnerability and allow myself to be seen and known in my relationships."

"I am a compassionate listener, fully present and attentive to my loved ones."

"I celebrate and appreciate the uniqueness and individuality of others in my relationships."

"I choose relationships that uplift and inspire me to become the best version of myself."

"I let go of toxic relationships and surround myself with positive, supportive individuals."

"I forgive and release past hurts, creating space for healing and growth in my relationships."

By incorporating these affirmations into our daily lives, we can cultivate the mindset and behaviors that foster healthy and fulfilling relationships. Remember that relationships require effort, understanding, and ongoing communication. With commitment and a focus on nurturing these connections, we can create a rich tapestry of love, support, and joy in our lives.

UNDERSTANDING THE ROLE OF SELF-LOVE AND SELF-ACCEPTANCE IN BUILDING STRONG RELATIONSHIPS.

Building strong and fulfilling relationships begins with cultivating a foundation of self-love and self-acceptance. When we develop a healthy and positive relationship with ourselves, we are better equipped to engage in authentic connections with others. Self-love and self-acceptance serve as the cornerstones for nurturing healthy boundaries, fostering respect, and experiencing deep and meaningful connections. In this section, we will explore the profound role that self-love and self-acceptance play in building strong relationships.

Establishing Healthy Boundaries:

Self-love and self-acceptance are vital for setting and maintaining healthy boundaries in relationships. When we have a deep sense of self-worth and value, we are more likely to prioritize our needs and establish boundaries that honor our well-being. By loving and accepting ourselves, we recognize our worthiness and create space for mutual respect and healthy interactions with others.

Authenticity and Vulnerability:

Genuine connections thrive when individuals are able to show up as their authentic selves and embrace vulnerability. Self-love and self-acceptance allow us to fully embrace who we are, including our strengths, imperfections, and vulnerabilities. When we accept and love ourselves, we feel more comfortable being open and vulnerable with others, fostering deeper connections and intimacy.

Enhancing Emotional Well-being:

Practicing self-love and self-acceptance is essential for cultivating emotional well-being, which positively impacts our relationships. When we love and accept ourselves, we are less likely to seek validation or approval from others. This emotional independence allows us to enter into relationships from a place of wholeness rather than seeking validation or fulfilling unmet needs. By prioritizing our own emotional well-being, we are better equipped to engage in healthy and balanced relationships.

Respecting and Honoring Others:

Self-love and self-acceptance foster a sense of respect and empathy for others. When we cultivate self-compassion and self-acceptance, we are more likely to extend those qualities to others. By acknowledging and honoring our own unique experiences and journeys, we can recognize and appreciate the individuality and autonomy of others, creating an environment of mutual respect and understanding.

Setting Positive Examples:

Practicing self-love and self-acceptance sets a positive example for others and encourages them to do the same. When we embrace and love ourselves unconditionally, we inspire others to do the same. Our relationships can become spaces where self-love is celebrated and nurtured, creating a ripple effect of positive self-esteem and self-acceptance.

Affirmations for Cultivating Self-Love and Self-Acceptance:

"I love and accept myself unconditionally, just as I am."

"I am worthy of love, respect, and healthy relationships."

"I embrace my unique qualities and celebrate my individuality."

"I forgive myself for past mistakes and embrace growth and self-improvement."

"I prioritize self-care and nurture my physical, mental, and emotional well-being."

"I trust myself to make decisions that align with my values and highest good."

"I release self-judgment and embrace self-compassion in all aspects of my life."

"I deserve to be treated with kindness, love, and respect in all my relationships."

"I let go of comparison and focus on my own journey of self-discovery and growth."

"I am enough, just as I am, and I bring value and joy to my relationships."

By incorporating these affirmations into our daily practice, we strengthen our foundation of self-love and self-acceptance. As we cultivate a healthy relationship with ourselves, we become better equipped to engage in fulfilling, authentic, and meaningful connections with others. Remember that self-love is a journey, and it requires consistent effort, self-reflection, and self-compassion. With time and practice, we can build strong relationships that are built on a solid foundation of self-love and acceptance.

AFFIRMING THE DESIRE FOR MEANINGFUL AND SUPPORTIVE CONNECTIONS.

Human beings are inherently social creatures, seeking connection, belonging, and support from others. Affirming our desire for meaningful and supportive connections is a powerful way to attract and manifest the relationships we long for. By setting positive intentions and aligning our energy with the type of connections we wish to experience, we open ourselves up to the abundance of fulfilling relationships that the universe has to offer. In this section, we will explore the significance of affirming our desire for meaningful and supportive connections and provide a range of affirmations to help you manifest and attract these relationships into your life.

Recognizing Your Worthiness:

Affirming the desire for meaningful and supportive connections begins with recognizing your inherent worthiness of love and positive relationships. Remind yourself daily that you deserve to be surrounded by people who uplift, support, and cherish you.

Affirmation: "I am worthy of meaningful and supportive connections that bring joy, growth, and love into my life."

Intentional Relationship Building:

Setting intentions is a powerful tool for manifesting the connections we desire. By affirming our intention to attract and cultivate meaningful relationships, we align our energy and actions with that desire.

Affirmation: "I am intentional in building relationships that are genuine, supportive, and aligned with my values."

Embracing Vulnerability:

Meaningful connections often require vulnerability. By affirming your willingness to be vulnerable and open in your relationships, you create space for deeper connections and authentic interactions.

Affirmation: "I embrace vulnerability and allow others to see and know the real me, fostering deeper and more meaningful connections."

Expressing Authenticity:

Authenticity is the foundation of genuine connections. Affirm your commitment to being true to yourself and expressing your authentic self in your relationships.

Affirmation: "I embrace and express my authentic self in all my relationships, attracting connections that appreciate and celebrate the real me."

Surrounding Yourself with Positive Energy:

Affirm the importance of surrounding yourself with people who radiate positivity, kindness, and support. By setting this intention, you create a magnetic force that attracts like-minded individuals into your life.

Affirmation: "I attract and surround myself with positive, uplifting individuals who support and inspire me."

Cultivating Mutual Growth and Support:

Meaningful connections are characterized by mutual growth and support. Affirm your desire for relationships that encourage personal and collective growth.

Affirmation: "I attract relationships that foster mutual growth, support, and encouragement on our respective journeys."

Nurturing Deep Connections:

Affirm your desire for deep, meaningful connections that go beyond surface-level interactions. Declare your intention to create and nurture relationships that are built on trust, understanding, and shared experiences.

Affirmation: "I attract and nurture deep connections with others, where we can be vulnerable, share our joys and challenges, and grow together."

Manifesting Healthy and Balanced Relationships:

Affirm your intention to manifest relationships that are healthy, balanced, and respectful. Set the intention to create connections that bring out the best in you and promote your overall well-being.

Affirmation: "I am manifesting healthy and balanced relationships that uplift and support me in all aspects of my life."

Attracting Like-Minded Souls:

Affirm your desire to attract like-minded individuals who share similar values, interests, and aspirations. Set the intention to connect with people who align with your soul's purpose and contribute positively to your life.

Affirmation: "I attract like-minded souls who share my passions, values, and vision, creating meaningful connections and partnerships."

Gratitude for Existing and Future Connections:

Express gratitude for the relationships you currently have and those that are yet to come. Affirm your appreciation for the connections in your life, knowing that gratitude attracts more of what you are grateful for.

Affirmation: "I am grateful for the meaningful connections in my life, and I attract more loving, supportive relationships to cherish and be grateful for."

By incorporating these affirmations into your daily practice and aligning your thoughts, emotions, and actions with the desire for meaningful and supportive connections, you invite the universe to bring forth the relationships that resonate with your highest good. Remember to be patient, open, and receptive to the connections that come your way, and trust that you are on a path to experiencing fulfilling and nourishing relationships in your life.

CULTIVATING OPEN COMMUNICATION AND ACTIVE LISTENING IN RELATIONSHIPS.

Cultivating open communication and active listening is vital for fostering healthy and fulfilling relationships. Effective communication allows us to express ourselves authentically, understand others' perspectives, and resolve conflicts constructively. Active listening, in turn, enables us to fully engage with our loved ones, demonstrating that we value their thoughts and feelings. In this section, we will delve into the transformative potential of affirmations in cultivating open communication and active listening, fostering deeper connections and harmony within our relationships.

The Importance of Open Communication:

Open communication is the foundation of strong and meaningful relationships. It involves expressing oneself honestly, sharing thoughts and feelings without fear of judgment, and actively seeking to understand others. When we cultivate open communication, we create an environment where trust, vulnerability, and emotional intimacy can thrive. By fostering a safe space for honest expression, we can build stronger connections, address issues effectively, and celebrate shared joys together.

Affirmations for Cultivating Open Communication:

Affirmations can serve as powerful tools for cultivating open communication within our relationships. By incorporating these affirmations into our daily lives, we can develop a mindset that promotes openness, authenticity, and effective communication. Here are some affirmations for cultivating open communication:

"I communicate with honesty and authenticity, fostering trust and openness in my relationships."

"I express my thoughts and feelings openly, knowing that my voice matters and is valued."

"I listen attentively to others, giving them my full presence and attention."

"I embrace vulnerability and create a safe space for others to share their truths."

"I choose my words wisely, speaking with kindness and respect to promote understanding."

"I seek to understand before being understood, valuing the perspectives of others."

"I invite open and honest conversations, addressing concerns and conflicts with compassion and empathy."

"I am open to feedback and constructive criticism, recognizing that it fosters personal and relational growth."

"I practice active listening, engaging with empathy and curiosity to truly understand others."

"I encourage open dialogue and create an environment where all voices are heard and valued."

By consistently affirming these statements and integrating them into our communication practices, we can foster a culture of open communication, trust, and respect within our relationships.

Practicing Active Listening:

Active listening is an essential component of effective communication. It involves fully engaging with our loved ones, being present in the conversation, and genuinely seeking to understand their perspective. Here are some practical strategies to cultivate active listening in our relationships:

Give Your Full Attention: Eliminate distractions and give your full focus to the person speaking.

Maintain Eye Contact: Demonstrate your engagement and interest by maintaining eye contact with the speaker.

Show Non-Verbal Cues: Use affirmative nods, smiles, and other non-verbal cues to show that you are actively listening.

Avoid Interrupting: Allow the speaker to express themselves fully without interrupting or interjecting.

Practice Reflective Listening: Reflect back what you have heard to ensure understanding and clarify any misunderstandings.

Ask Open-Ended Questions: Encourage further discussion by asking open-ended questions that invite the speaker to elaborate and share more deeply.

Validate and Empathize: Acknowledge the speaker's emotions and validate their experiences, expressing empathy and understanding.

Be Patient: Allow the speaker to express themselves at their own pace, without rushing or jumping to conclusions.

Set Aside Assumptions: Avoid making assumptions or jumping to conclusions about what the speaker is saying; instead, seek clarification when needed.

Respond with Empathy: Respond with empathy and compassion, offering words of support and understanding.

By practicing these strategies alongside affirmations, we can foster a culture of active listening, create deeper connections, and nurture healthier relationships with our loved ones.

Conclusion:

Cultivating open communication and active listening is essential for building strong, fulfilling relationships. By incorporating affirmations that promote open communication and active listening into our daily lives, we can develop healthier communication habits, deepen our connections, and foster greater understanding and empathy. Remember, effective communication is a continuous practice that requires effort, patience, and a genuine desire to understand and be understood. By embracing these practices, we can create a foundation of openness, trust, and respect within our relationships, leading to greater harmony, intimacy, and emotional well-being.

AFFIRMING EMPATHY AND UNDERSTANDING IN INTERACTIONS WITH LOVED ONES.

Affirming empathy and understanding is essential for nurturing healthy and harmonious relationships with our loved ones. Empathy allows us to connect deeply with others, to understand and share in their emotions, and to offer support and compassion. When we affirm empathy and understanding in our interactions, we create a safe and nurturing space where our loved ones feel seen, heard, and validated. In this section, we will explore the transformative power of affirmations in cultivating empathy and understanding, fostering emotional connection, and building strong bonds with our loved ones.

The Importance of Empathy and Understanding:

Empathy is the ability to put ourselves in another person's shoes, to truly understand and resonate with their experiences, feelings, and perspectives. It is a fundamental aspect of emotional intelligence and a key ingredient in nurturing meaningful and fulfilling relationships. When we practice empathy, we show genuine care and concern for others, fostering deeper connections and building trust. Understanding, on the other hand, involves actively seeking to comprehend the thoughts, beliefs, and motivations of our loved ones. It allows us to see beyond our own perspectives and biases, fostering a sense of acceptance and appreciation for their uniqueness.

Affirmations for Cultivating Empathy and Understanding:

Affirmations can be powerful tools for cultivating empathy and understanding within our interactions with loved ones. By consciously practicing these affirmations, we can develop a mindset that promotes empathy, compassion, and deep emotional connection. Here are some affirmations for affirming empathy and understanding in our relationships:

"I open my heart to truly listen and understand the emotions and experiences of my loved ones."

"I embrace empathy and compassion, offering a safe space for my loved ones to express themselves."

"I seek to understand before seeking to be understood, fostering deeper connections with my loved ones."

"I validate the feelings and experiences of my loved ones, honoring their unique perspectives."

"I let go of judgment and assumptions, allowing space for empathy and understanding to flourish."

"I practice active listening, giving my full attention to my loved ones and their needs."

"I communicate with kindness and empathy, considering the impact of my words on others."

"I recognize and respect the boundaries and emotions of my loved ones, nurturing a sense of safety and trust."

"I celebrate the diversity of thoughts and opinions within my relationships, fostering understanding and growth."

"I choose to respond with empathy and kindness, even in moments of disagreement or conflict."

By integrating these affirmations into our daily lives, we can develop a deep sense of empathy and understanding, creating an environment where our loved ones feel truly seen, heard, and valued.

Practicing Empathy and Understanding in Daily Interactions:

Affirmations are most effective when combined with consistent action. To truly cultivate empathy and understanding in our relationships, it is essential to translate these affirmations into tangible behaviors. Here are some practical ways to practice empathy and understanding in our daily interactions:

Active Listening: Give your full attention to the person speaking, maintain eye contact, and show genuine interest in their words and emotions.

Validate Feelings: Acknowledge and validate the emotions expressed by your loved ones, even if you may not fully understand or agree with them.

Practice Non-Judgment: Let go of judgment and preconceived notions, allowing yourself to be open and receptive to different perspectives.

Empathetic Responses: Respond with empathy and compassion, offering words of support and understanding.

Perspective-Taking: Put yourself in the other person's shoes, imagining how they might be feeling or experiencing a situation.

Seek Clarification: If you're unsure about something, ask for clarification rather than making assumptions.

Emotional Availability: Create space and time for your loved ones to express their feelings and concerns without interruption or judgment.

Respect Boundaries: Honor the boundaries and personal space of your loved ones, allowing them to feel safe and secure in the relationship.

Cultivate Curiosity: Ask questions to gain a deeper understanding of your loved ones' experiences, beliefs, and values.

Practice Self-Reflection: Reflect on your own biases, assumptions, and communication patterns, and make efforts to grow and improve.

By combining these practical strategies with the power of affirmations, we can foster a culture of empathy and understanding within our relationships, creating a strong foundation for love, connection, and emotional well-being.

AFFIRMATIONS FOR BUILDING AND MAINTAINING TRUST IN RELATIONSHIPS.

Building and maintaining trust is crucial for the health and longevity of any relationship. Trust forms the foundation upon which strong and meaningful connections are built. In this section, we will explore the transformative power of affirmations in fostering trust within relationships. Drawing inspiration from various fields such as psychology, relationship counseling, and personal growth, we will delve into the profound impact of positive affirmations on building and maintaining trust, promoting open communication, and creating a safe and secure emotional environment.

The Role of Trust in Relationships:

Trust is the cornerstone of healthy relationships, providing a sense of safety, security, and emotional intimacy. It is the belief that we can rely on our partner, that they have our best interests at heart, and that they will be honest and faithful. Trust enables vulnerability, effective communication, and mutual respect. Without trust, relationships can suffer from insecurity, doubt, and emotional distance. Therefore, consciously nurturing and strengthening trust is essential for cultivating a strong and lasting bond.

Affirmations for Building Trust:

Affirmations can be powerful tools to reinforce trust-building beliefs and behaviors within relationships. By consciously practicing affirmations, we can strengthen the foundation of trust and create an environment that fosters security and openness. Here are some affirmations for building and maintaining trust in relationships:

"I trust my partner completely and unconditionally."

"I am open and honest in my communication, fostering trust in my relationship."

"I believe in the integrity and loyalty of my partner, nurturing trust between us."

"I am trustworthy and reliable, earning and maintaining the trust of my partner."

"I let go of past hurts and choose to trust my partner in the present moment."

"I create a safe and non-judgmental space for open and transparent communication in my relationship."

"I choose to see the best in my partner, building trust and understanding."

"I am committed to building trust through consistent words and actions."

"I honor my partner's boundaries and respect their need for trust and privacy."

"I communicate my needs and concerns honestly, promoting trust and understanding in my relationship."

By integrating these affirmations into your daily practice, you can develop a mindset that supports trust-building behaviors and fosters a secure and loving relationship. Remember, building trust takes time and effort from both partners. Practice patience, understanding, and consistent communication to strengthen the foundation of trust within your relationship.

Maintaining Trust Through Challenges:

Challenges and setbacks are inevitable in any relationship. It is during these times that the strength of trust is tested. Affirmations can provide support and reassurance during difficult moments. Here are some affirmations for maintaining trust during challenging times:

"Even in challenging times, I trust that my partner and I can work through any obstacles together."

"I communicate openly and honestly, addressing any concerns that may arise, and nurturing trust in my relationship."

"I choose forgiveness and understanding, allowing trust to grow and heal after moments of conflict."

"I trust that my partner's intentions are always genuine and loving, even when we face challenges."

"I am committed to rebuilding trust if it has been broken, learning and growing together in the process."

By affirming these statements, you reaffirm your commitment to trust, even in the face of difficulties. Remember that trust is a continuous process, and it requires ongoing effort and commitment from both partners.

Conclusion:

Trust is the bedrock of healthy and fulfilling relationships. Affirmations serve as powerful tools for building and maintaining trust, fostering open communication, and creating a safe emotional environment. By consciously practicing affirmations that promote trust, both partners can cultivate a deep sense of security, intimacy, and understanding. Through consistent effort, open communication, and a willingness to grow together, trust can flourish, leading to a stronger and more fulfilling relationship.

NURTURING LOVE AND AFFECTION IN ROMANTIC RELATIONSHIPS.

Nurturing love and affection in romantic relationships is a vital aspect of creating and maintaining a strong and fulfilling partnership. Love and affection are the building blocks of intimacy, connection, and emotional well-being. In this section, we will explore the transformative power of affirmations in nurturing love and affection within romantic relationships. Drawing inspiration from various fields such as psychology, relationship counseling, and spirituality, we will delve into the profound impact of positive affirmations on deepening emotional bonds, fostering intimacy, and cultivating a loving and affectionate partnership.

The Power of Affirmations in Romantic Relationships:

Affirmations serve as powerful tools to reinforce positive beliefs and intentions in our relationships. By consciously choosing and practicing affirmations, we can strengthen the emotional connection, express love and affection, and create a nurturing and supportive environment for both partners. Affirmations help shift our mindset and thoughts towards love, kindness, and appreciation, allowing us to foster a deeper sense of connection and affection within our romantic relationships.

Affirmations for Expressing Love and Affection:

Affirmations can be used to express love, tenderness, and affection towards our partners. By crafting affirmations that reflect our genuine feelings and intentions, we can communicate our love and appreciation in a meaningful and heartfelt way. Here are some examples of affirmations for nurturing love and affection in romantic relationships:

"I deeply love and cherish my partner, and I express my affection freely and openly."

"Every day, I show my partner how much they mean to me through loving words and actions."

"I am grateful for the love and joy my partner brings into my life, and I reciprocate with equal warmth and affection."

"I am fully present in my relationship, showering my partner with love, attention, and affection."

"I create moments of intimacy and connection with my partner, fostering a loving and affectionate bond."

"I am a source of comfort and support for my partner, offering love and affection unconditionally."

"I delight in expressing my love and affection to my partner, creating a nurturing and loving atmosphere in our relationship."

"I prioritize quality time and affectionate gestures to strengthen the love and intimacy between us."

"I continuously seek new ways to show my partner how much I love and appreciate them."

"I nurture the flame of passion and affection in our relationship, creating a lasting bond of love and warmth."

By integrating these affirmations into your daily practice, you can cultivate a mindset of love, tenderness, and affection, and actively nurture these qualities within your romantic relationship. Remember, affirmations are most effective when spoken sincerely and from the heart. Allow these affirmations to guide your actions and intentions, creating a loving and affectionate atmosphere that deepens your connection and brings joy to both you and your partner.

Conclusion:

In conclusion, nurturing love and affection in romantic relationships is essential for creating a fulfilling and long-lasting partnership. Affirmations provide a powerful means to express love, tenderness, and affection towards our partners. By practicing affirmations that reflect our genuine feelings and intentions, we can foster a deep sense of connection and create a nurturing and loving environment within our relationship. Through consistent practice and heartfelt communication, we can cultivate a relationship filled with love, affection, and emotional intimacy, bringing joy and fulfillment to both partners.

AFFIRMATIONS FOR SETTING HEALTHY BOUNDARIES AND FOSTERING RESPECT.

Setting healthy boundaries and fostering respect are essential elements in maintaining harmonious and fulfilling relationships. Boundaries serve as a means of self-care, protecting our emotional and physical well-being, while respect forms the foundation for mutual understanding and appreciation. In this section, drawing inspiration from various fields such as Witchcraft, Divination, Herbalism, Shamanism, and Ecospirituality, we explore the transformative power of affirmations in establishing and upholding healthy boundaries, as well as fostering respect in our relationships. Through a comprehensive analysis, students will gain insight into the significance of boundaries and respect, understand the principles that guide their establishment, and learn practical strategies and affirmations to nurture these qualities in their interactions with others.

I honor my needs and set clear boundaries that support my well-being and happiness.

I deserve to be treated with respect and kindness in all my relationships.

My boundaries are valid, and I assertively communicate them with confidence and grace.

I trust myself to know what is best for me, and I honor that by setting and maintaining healthy boundaries.

I release the need to please others at the expense of my own well-being. My needs matter too.

I attract and surround myself with people who respect and honor my boundaries.

I am worthy of love and respect, and I give the same in return to others.

I communicate my boundaries assertively, without guilt or fear, knowing that it is an act of self-care.

I value my personal space and time, and I create boundaries to protect and nurture them.

I choose relationships that support my growth and well-being, and I let go of those that do not honor my boundaries.

I listen to and honor my intuition when it comes to setting boundaries in my relationships.

I deserve to be heard and understood, and I communicate my needs and boundaries with clarity and compassion.

I release the need to control others and allow them the space to express their own boundaries and opinions.

I respect the boundaries of others, understanding that everyone has the right to set limits that feel comfortable to them.

I embrace healthy conflict resolution and assertive communication, knowing that it strengthens my relationships and fosters mutual respect.

Remember, affirmations are most effective when practiced consistently and with intention. By integrating these affirmations into your daily routine, you can cultivate a mindset that supports healthy boundaries and fosters respect in all your relationships.

AFFIRMING FORGIVENESS AND LETTING GO OF PAST RESENTMENTS IN RELATIONSHIPS.

Forgiveness is a transformative practice that can bring healing, liberation, and renewed harmony to our relationships. Holding onto past resentments and grievances can create barriers and hinder the growth and depth of our connections with others. By affirming forgiveness and letting go of past resentments, we free ourselves from the burden of negative emotions and create space for love, compassion, and understanding to flourish. In this section, we will explore the significance of affirming forgiveness in relationships and provide a range of affirmations to support the process of letting go and cultivating forgiveness.

Embracing Forgiveness as a Gift to Yourself:

Affirm the understanding that forgiveness is not about condoning or forgetting past hurts but is a gift you give yourself. By releasing the grip of resentments, you allow yourself to experience inner peace, emotional freedom, and the possibility of rebuilding the relationship.

Affirmation: "I choose to forgive as a gift to myself, releasing the heavy burden of resentments and embracing inner peace and healing."

Releasing Attachments to Painful Memories:

Affirm your willingness to let go of attachments to painful memories and experiences that no longer serve your highest good. By releasing the grip of the past, you create space for new possibilities and a fresh start in your relationships.

Affirmation: "I release attachments to painful memories and allow myself to be open to new experiences and positive transformations in my relationships."

Practicing Compassion and Empathy:

Affirm your commitment to practicing compassion and empathy towards yourself and others involved in the past hurts. Recognize that everyone is on their own journey, and by extending understanding and empathy, you create a foundation for forgiveness and healing.

Affirmation: "I cultivate compassion and empathy towards myself and others, recognizing that we are all imperfect beings on a path of growth and learning."

Letting Go of Resentment and Bitterness:

Affirm your intention to release resentment and bitterness that may have been built up over time. By letting go of these negative emotions, you create space for forgiveness, understanding, and the possibility of rebuilding trust in your relationships.

Affirmation: "I release resentment and bitterness, allowing forgiveness and understanding to flow into my relationships."

Healing and Transforming Wounds:

Affirm your commitment to healing and transforming the wounds caused by past hurts. By affirming your willingness to do the inner work necessary for healing, you open the door to renewed connection and growth in your relationships.

Affirmation: "I am committed to healing and transforming the wounds caused by past hurts, allowing for growth, and the deepening of my relationships."

Rebuilding Trust and Restoring Connection:

Affirm your desire to rebuild trust and restore connection in your relationships. Recognize that forgiveness is a stepping stone towards rebuilding and strengthening the bonds of trust and intimacy.

Affirmation: "I am open to rebuilding trust and restoring connection in my relationships, knowing that forgiveness is the bridge that leads to deeper understanding and love."

Releasing the Need for Control:

Affirm your willingness to release the need for control over past events and outcomes. Understand that you can only control your own actions and reactions, and by letting go of the need to control others, you create space for forgiveness and acceptance.

Affirmation: "I surrender the need for control and embrace acceptance and forgiveness in my relationships."

Embracing Growth and Transformation:

Affirm your commitment to personal growth and transformation as you navigate the path of forgiveness. Recognize that forgiveness is a journey that requires patience, self-reflection, and a willingness to evolve.

Affirmation: "I embrace growth and transformation as I navigate the journey of forgiveness, knowing that it is a process that unfolds over time.

Cultivating Self-Compassion:

Affirm your commitment to practicing self-compassion as you forgive yourself for any past mistakes or shortcomings in your relationships. Understand that self-forgiveness is an essential part of the forgiveness process.

Affirmation: "I extend compassion and forgiveness to myself, acknowledging that I am human and deserving of love and understanding."

Embracing a Renewed Vision for the Future:

Affirm your commitment to creating a renewed vision for the future of your relationships, based on forgiveness, love, and mutual growth. Visualize the possibilities of deeper connection, harmony, and joy.

Affirmation: "I envision a future of deep connection, harmony, and joy in my relationships, founded on forgiveness, love, and mutual growth."

By incorporating these affirmations into your daily practice and infusing them with genuine intention and heartfelt emotions, you empower yourself to cultivate forgiveness and let go of past resentments. Remember that forgiveness is a process, and it may take time and effort. Be patient and kind to yourself as you embark on this transformative journey, and trust that the practice of affirming forgiveness will bring about positive changes in your relationships and in your own well-being.

AFFIRMATIONS FOR EMBRACING VULNERABILITY AND FOSTERING EMOTIONAL INTIMACY.

Vulnerability is the key to deepening emotional intimacy and building meaningful connections with others. When we embrace vulnerability, we open ourselves up to authentic and genuine experiences, allowing for deeper emotional connections and a sense of closeness. In this section, we will explore the significance of affirming vulnerability in relationships and provide a range of affirmations to support the process of embracing vulnerability and fostering emotional intimacy.

Embracing Vulnerability as a Strength:

Affirm the belief that vulnerability is not a weakness but a strength that allows for genuine connections and emotional depth in relationships. By embracing vulnerability, you invite others to do the same, creating a safe space for openness and authenticity.

Affirmation: "I embrace vulnerability as a strength, knowing that it fosters emotional intimacy and genuine connections in my relationships."

Allowing Myself to Be Seen and Heard:

Affirm your willingness to be seen and heard in your relationships. Acknowledge that by sharing your true thoughts, feelings, and experiences, you create opportunities for deeper understanding and connection with others.

Affirmation: "I allow myself to be seen and heard, knowing that my authentic self is worthy of love and acceptance."

Trusting in the Power of Vulnerability:

Affirm your trust in the transformative power of vulnerability. Understand that by opening up and sharing your vulnerabilities, you create space for others to respond with empathy, compassion, and understanding.

Affirmation: "I trust in the power of vulnerability, knowing that it deepens emotional intimacy and strengthens the bonds in my relationships."

Honoring My Emotions and Expressing Them:

Affirm your commitment to honoring your emotions and expressing them authentically in your relationships. Recognize that emotional honesty and vulnerability go hand in hand, allowing for deeper connection and a better understanding of each other's needs and desires.

Affirmation: "I honor my emotions and express them authentically, knowing that it fosters emotional intimacy and understanding in my relationships."

Creating a Safe and Non-Judgmental Space:

Affirm your commitment to creating a safe and non-judgmental space for vulnerability in your relationships. Understand that by fostering an environment where vulnerability is met with acceptance and understanding, you invite deeper emotional connections to flourish.

Affirmation: "I create a safe and non-judgmental space for vulnerability in my relationships, allowing for authentic connections to thrive."

Cultivating Empathy and Compassion:

Affirm your commitment to cultivating empathy and compassion towards yourself and others. Understand that by practicing empathy, you create an atmosphere of acceptance and understanding, encouraging vulnerability and emotional intimacy.

Affirmation: "I cultivate empathy and compassion, creating a nurturing environment for vulnerability and emotional intimacy in my relationships."

Embracing Imperfections and Flaws:

Affirm your acceptance of imperfections and flaws, both in yourself and in others. Understand that vulnerability is about embracing our humanness and being open about our imperfections, fostering a sense of authenticity and connection.

Affirmation: "I embrace imperfections and flaws, knowing that vulnerability allows for genuine connections beyond surface-level expectations."

Letting Go of the Fear of Rejection:

Affirm your willingness to let go of the fear of rejection and judgment when embracing vulnerability. Understand that true connections require taking risks and that the rewards of emotional intimacy far outweigh the potential discomfort.

Affirmation: "I release the fear of rejection and open myself up to the possibilities of deep emotional connections and growth in my relationships."

Listening with Empathy and Non-Judgment:

Affirm your commitment to listening with empathy and non-judgment in your relationships. Recognize that by providing a supportive listening ear, you create an environment where vulnerability is met with understanding and acceptance.

Affirmation: "I listen with empathy and non-judgment, creating a safe space for vulnerability and emotional intimacy to flourish."

Celebrating Vulnerability as a Catalyst for Growth:

Affirm the belief that vulnerability is a catalyst for personal and relational growth. Recognize that through embracing vulnerability, you invite transformative experiences and opportunities for deepening connections with others.

Affirmation: "I celebrate vulnerability as a catalyst for growth, knowing that it opens the door to meaningful connections and emotional intimacy in my relationships."

By incorporating these affirmations into your daily practice and embracing vulnerability with a compassionate and open heart, you can foster emotional intimacy and cultivate deeper connections in your relationships. Remember that vulnerability is a journey, and it requires trust, self-compassion, and patience. Allow yourself and others the space to be vulnerable, and watch as your relationships thrive and blossom with emotional depth and intimacy.

AFFIRMATIONS FOR EXPRESSING APPRECIATION AND GRATITUDE TOWARDS LOVED ONES.

Expressing appreciation and gratitude towards our loved ones is a powerful way to strengthen our relationships and deepen the bond of connection. When we express gratitude, we acknowledge the value and importance of our loved ones in our lives, fostering a sense of love, warmth, and appreciation. In this section, we will explore the significance of affirming appreciation and gratitude in relationships and provide a range of affirmations to support the practice of expressing gratitude towards our loved ones.

Acknowledging the Blessing of Love:

Affirm the recognition that love is a precious and valuable gift. Express gratitude for the presence of love in your life and the impact it has on your well-being and happiness.

Affirmation: "I am grateful for the blessing of love in my life and the joy it brings to my heart."

Appreciating the Qualities and Traits of Loved Ones:

Affirm your appreciation for the unique qualities, traits, and strengths of your loved ones. Express gratitude for the positive attributes they possess and the ways in which they enhance your life.

Affirmation: "I am grateful for the remarkable qualities and traits of my loved ones, and I cherish the ways they enrich my life."

Recognizing Acts of Kindness and Support:

Affirm your gratitude for the acts of kindness and support you receive from your loved ones. Express appreciation for their gestures, whether big or small, and the ways they show up for you in times of need.

Affirmation: "I am thankful for the acts of kindness and support from my loved ones. I appreciate their presence and the ways they help me navigate life's challenges."

Expressing Gratitude for Emotional Support:

Affirm your gratitude for the emotional support and understanding you receive from your loved ones. Recognize the comfort and reassurance they provide during difficult times, and express appreciation for their empathy and care.

Affirmation: "I am grateful for the emotional support and understanding of my loved ones. I appreciate their presence and the way they hold space for me."

Thanking Loved Ones for Their Presence:

Affirm your gratitude for the presence of your loved ones in your life. Express appreciation for the joy, laughter, and shared experiences you have together, recognizing the value of their companionship.

Affirmation: "I am thankful for the presence of my loved ones in my life. I cherish the moments we share and the memories we create together."

Grateful for Love's Growth and Evolution:

Affirm your gratitude for the growth and evolution of love in your relationships. Express appreciation for the ways in which your connections deepen, mature, and become more profound over time.

Affirmation: "I am grateful for the growth and evolution of love in my relationships. I appreciate the journey we have embarked on together."

Thankful for the Gift of Understanding:

Affirm your gratitude for the gift of understanding that exists within your relationships. Express appreciation for the ability to communicate and connect on a deep level, fostering mutual understanding and empathy.

Affirmation: "I am thankful for the gift of understanding in my relationships. I appreciate the depth of connection we share."

Expressing Gratitude for Shared Moments of Joy:

Affirm your gratitude for the shared moments of joy and happiness with your loved ones. Express appreciation for the laughter, adventures, and joyful experiences you create together.

Affirmation: "I am grateful for the shared moments of joy with my loved ones. I cherish the laughter and happiness we experience together."

Thanking Loved Ones for Their Unconditional Love:

Affirm your gratitude for the unconditional love you receive from your loved ones. Express appreciation for their acceptance, support, and unwavering presence in your life.

Affirmation: "I am thankful for the unconditional love of my loved ones. I appreciate their acceptance and support, knowing that I am deeply loved."

Grateful for the Growth and Transformation Love Brings:

Affirm your gratitude for the growth and transformation that love brings into your life. Express appreciation for the ways in which your relationships inspire personal growth, healing, and self-discovery.

Affirmation: "I am grateful for the growth and transformation that love brings into my life. I appreciate the ways in which my relationships inspire me to become the best version of myself."

By incorporating these affirmations into your daily practice, you can cultivate a deeper sense of appreciation and gratitude towards your loved ones. Remember to express your gratitude not only through affirmations but also through heartfelt words, acts of kindness, and quality time spent together. As you nurture a culture of appreciation and gratitude, you will find your relationships flourishing with love, connection, and mutual support.

AFFIRMING EFFECTIVE CONFLICT RESOLUTION AND PROBLEM-SOLVING SKILLS.

Conflict is an inevitable part of any relationship. It arises from differences in perspectives, needs, and desires. However, how we approach and resolve conflicts can significantly impact the health and longevity of our relationships. By affirming effective conflict resolution and problem-solving skills, we can cultivate an environment of understanding, collaboration, and growth. In this section, we will explore the significance of affirming these skills and provide a range of affirmations to support the practice of resolving conflicts in a healthy and constructive manner.

Affirming Open and Respectful Communication:

Affirm the importance of open and respectful communication in resolving conflicts. Emphasize the need for honest expression, active listening, and the willingness to understand the perspectives of others.

Affirmation: "I am committed to open and respectful communication in resolving conflicts. I listen attentively and express myself honestly and with kindness."

Believing in the Possibility of Resolution:

Affirm your belief in the possibility of resolving conflicts in a positive and constructive manner. Trust in the power of dialogue, compromise, and finding mutually beneficial solutions.

Affirmation: "I believe in the potential for resolution and growth in conflicts. I approach them with optimism, knowing that we can find common ground."

Affirming Empathy and Understanding:

Affirm your commitment to empathy and understanding in conflict resolution. Recognize the importance of putting yourself in the shoes of others and seeking to understand their emotions and perspectives.

Affirmation: "I cultivate empathy and understanding in conflict resolution. I strive to see the situation from the perspective of others, fostering compassion and mutual understanding."

Embracing Collaborative Problem-Solving:

Affirm your willingness to engage in collaborative problem-solving. Emphasize the importance of working together to find creative and mutually satisfactory solutions to conflicts.

Affirmation: "I embrace collaborative problem-solving in resolving conflicts. I actively seek solutions that honor the needs and concerns of all parties involved."

Affirming Emotional Regulation:

Affirm your commitment to emotional regulation during conflicts. Recognize the significance of managing your emotions and responding calmly and constructively, even in challenging situations.

Affirmation: "I practice emotional regulation in conflict resolution. I remain calm and composed, allowing space for thoughtful and respectful communication."

Cultivating Patience and Understanding:

Affirm your dedication to cultivating patience and understanding during conflicts. Recognize that resolution takes time and effort, and commit to approaching conflicts with patience and a willingness to listen and understand.

Affirmation: "I cultivate patience and understanding in conflict resolution. I allow the necessary time and space for resolution to unfold, fostering a deeper understanding."

Affirming the Power of Compromise:

Affirm the value of compromise in conflict resolution. Acknowledge that finding common ground and reaching a mutually beneficial agreement often requires a willingness to give and take.

Affirmation: "I recognize the power of compromise in conflict resolution. I am open to finding solutions that honor the needs and interests of all parties involved."

Emphasizing Solutions over Blame:

Affirm your commitment to focusing on solutions rather than blame or pointing fingers during conflicts. Shift the focus towards finding constructive ways to address the issue at hand.

Affirmation: "I prioritize solutions over blame in conflict resolution. I let go of the need to assign fault and instead seek productive ways to address the issue."

Affirming the Power of Active Listening:

Affirm the importance of active listening in conflict resolution. Commit to giving your full attention to others' perspectives, validating their feelings, and fostering effective communication.

Affirmation: "I practice active listening in conflict resolution. I give my full attention, validate the emotions of others, and foster a safe space for open dialogue."

Believing in Growth and Learning:

Affirm your belief in the growth and learning opportunities that conflicts provide. Recognize that conflicts can be transformative, leading to deeper understanding, personal growth, and stronger relationships.

Affirmation: "I believe in the growth and learning that conflicts offer. I approach them as opportunities for personal development and building stronger relationships."

By incorporating these affirmations into your daily practice, you can develop and reinforce effective conflict resolution and problem-solving skills. Remember, conflict is a natural part of relationships, and how we navigate it plays a crucial role in the health and well-being of our connections. Through affirming these skills, you can foster an environment of understanding, collaboration, and growth, leading to stronger and more fulfilling relationships.

AFFIRMATIONS FOR EMBRACING AND CELEBRATING DIFFERENCES IN RELATIONSHIPS.

Differences in opinions, backgrounds, and perspectives are a natural part of any relationship. Embracing and celebrating these differences can foster a rich and diverse dynamic that enhances the connection between individuals. By affirming the value of embracing and celebrating differences, we can cultivate an environment of acceptance, respect, and appreciation. In this section, we will explore the significance of affirming these qualities and provide a range of affirmations to support the practice of embracing and celebrating differences in relationships.

Affirming the Beauty of Diversity:

Acknowledge and appreciate the beauty of diversity in all its forms. Affirm the belief that differences enrich our relationships and provide opportunities for growth and learning.

Affirmation: "I embrace and celebrate the diversity within my relationships. I recognize that our differences bring unique perspectives, insights, and experiences."

Valuing and Respecting Differences:

Affirm your commitment to valuing and respecting the differences in others. Recognize that everyone's experiences and perspectives are valid and deserving of respect.

Affirmation: "I value and respect the differences in others. I embrace the uniqueness they bring and treat them with kindness and understanding."

Cultivating Curiosity and Open-Mindedness:

Affirm your willingness to approach differences with curiosity and an open mind. Embrace the opportunity to learn from others and broaden your understanding of the world.

Affirmation: "I cultivate curiosity and open-mindedness towards differences. I seek to learn from others and expand my perspective through their diverse experiences."

Embracing the Power of Collaboration:

Affirm the strength that comes from collaborating with individuals who have different skills, backgrounds, and perspectives. Recognize that diversity enhances creativity and problem-solving.

Affirmation: "I embrace the power of collaboration with individuals who have different strengths and perspectives. Together, we create innovative solutions and achieve greater success."

Affirming Empathy and Compassion:

Affirm your commitment to empathy and compassion when encountering differences. Seek to understand others' experiences and emotions, fostering a deeper connection and mutual support.

Affirmation: "I approach differences with empathy and compassion. I strive to understand others' perspectives and support them with kindness and empathy."

Celebrating Growth and Learning:

Affirm the belief that embracing differences leads to personal growth and learning. Celebrate the opportunities for self-discovery and expanding your horizons that come with encountering diverse viewpoints.

Affirmation: "I celebrate the growth and learning that comes from embracing differences. Each encounter broadens my understanding and helps me become a better version of myself."

Affirming Acceptance and Inclusion:

Affirm your commitment to acceptance and inclusion, creating a safe space for all individuals to express themselves authentically. Encourage an environment where differences are celebrated and cherished.

Affirmation: "I foster acceptance and inclusion in my relationships. I create a safe space where everyone feels welcomed and valued for who they are."

Embracing Cultural Awareness:

Affirm your dedication to embracing and learning about different cultures, traditions, and customs. Embrace the richness of cultural diversity and seek opportunities to deepen your cultural awareness.

Affirmation: "I embrace and celebrate diverse cultures. I actively seek to learn about different traditions and customs, fostering cultural understanding and appreciation."

Affirming Humility and Vulnerability:

Affirm the importance of approaching differences with humility and vulnerability. Recognize that embracing differences requires us to acknowledge our own limitations and be open to new perspectives.

Affirmation: "I approach differences with humility and vulnerability. I am willing to acknowledge my own limitations and embrace new perspectives with an open heart and mind."

Celebrating Personal Growth:

Affirm the belief that encountering differences allows for personal growth and self-reflection. Celebrate the opportunity to learn more about yourself and expand your understanding of the world.

Affirmation: "I celebrate my personal growth through encountering differences. Each interaction provides an opportunity for self-reflection and a deeper connection with others."

By incorporating these affirmations into your daily practice, you can cultivate a mindset of embracing and celebrating differences in your relationships. Remember, diversity is a strength that enriches our connections and expands our understanding of the world. Through affirming these values, you create an environment of acceptance, respect, and appreciation, fostering stronger and more harmonious relationships.

AFFIRMATIONS FOR FOSTERING A SENSE OF PARTNERSHIP AND TEAMWORK.

In any relationship, whether it's a romantic partnership, friendship, or professional collaboration, fostering a sense of partnership and teamwork is essential for creating a strong and harmonious connection. When individuals work together as a team, they can achieve greater success, overcome challenges, and support each other's growth. Affirming the qualities and values that contribute to a sense of partnership and teamwork can strengthen relationships and promote collaboration. In this section, we will explore the significance of affirming these qualities and provide a range of affirmations to support the practice of fostering a sense of partnership and teamwork.

Affirming Collaboration and Cooperation:

Acknowledge and appreciate the power of collaboration and cooperation in building strong relationships. Affirm the belief that working together as a team leads to greater success and fulfillment.

Affirmation: "I embrace collaboration and cooperation in my relationships. Together, we can achieve more and create meaningful outcomes."

Recognizing and Valuing Each Other's Strengths:

Affirm your recognition and appreciation of each other's strengths and unique abilities. Recognize that by leveraging each other's strengths, you can accomplish more as a team.

Affirmation: "I recognize and value the strengths of those I work with. We each bring unique talents to the table, and together, we can accomplish great things."

Embracing Effective Communication:

Affirm your commitment to effective communication as a cornerstone of partnership and teamwork. Recognize the importance of clear and open communication in fostering understanding and collaboration.

Affirmation: "I practice effective communication in my relationships. I listen attentively, express myself clearly, and create a safe space for open and honest dialogue."

Cultivating Trust and Mutual Support:

Affirm the importance of trust and mutual support in building a strong partnership. Recognize that by trusting and supporting each other, you create a solid foundation for collaboration and growth.

Affirmation: "I cultivate trust and mutual support in my relationships. I trust in the abilities and intentions of my team members, and I offer my support wholeheartedly."

Affirming Shared Goals and Vision:

Affirm your alignment with shared goals and vision within the team. Recognize the power of a shared purpose in motivating and inspiring teamwork.

Affirmation: "I am aligned with the shared goals and vision of my team. We work together towards a common purpose, driving us towards success."

Embracing Flexibility and Adaptability:

Affirm your willingness to be flexible and adaptable in the face of challenges and changing circumstances. Recognize that flexibility allows for creative problem-solving and strengthens the team's resilience.

Affirmation: "I embrace flexibility and adaptability in my relationships. I remain open to new ideas and approaches, fostering agility and resilience."

Affirming Respect and Empathy:

Affirm the importance of respect and empathy in creating a supportive and inclusive team environment. Recognize and honor the feelings, perspectives, and boundaries of each team member.

Affirmation: "I approach my team members with respect and empathy. I value their experiences and perspectives, and I create a space where everyone feels heard and valued."

Celebrating Success as a Team:

Affirm the practice of celebrating success as a team, recognizing the contributions of each member. Celebrate milestones and achievements together, fostering a sense of shared accomplishment.

Affirmation: "I celebrate success as a team. We acknowledge and appreciate the contributions of each team member, and we share in the joy of our collective achievements."

Affirming Accountability and Responsibility:

Affirm your commitment to accountability and responsibility within the team. Recognize that each member plays a crucial role and has a responsibility to contribute to the team's success.

Affirmation: "I hold myself accountable and take responsibility for my actions within the team. I contribute my best efforts and support the success of the whole."

Nurturing a Positive and Supportive Team Culture:

Affirm the importance of nurturing a positive and supportive team culture. Foster an environment where everyone feels valued, empowered, and encouraged to grow and succeed.

Affirmation: "I contribute to a positive and supportive team culture. I uplift and inspire my team members, fostering a nurturing and empowering environment."

By incorporating these affirmations into your daily practice, you can cultivate a sense of partnership and teamwork in your relationships. Remember, building strong relationships requires effort, commitment, and a shared vision. Through affirming these values, you can create an environment of collaboration, support, and shared success, leading to fulfilling and harmonious connections.

AFFIRMING COMMITMENT AND LOYALTY IN LONG-TERM RELATIONSHIPS.

Long-term relationships, whether romantic partnerships or deep friendships, often require a strong sense of commitment and loyalty to thrive and endure. Affirming these qualities can help strengthen the bond between individuals and foster a deep sense of trust and security. In this section, we will explore the significance of affirming commitment and loyalty in long-term relationships and provide a range of affirmations to support the practice of nurturing these qualities.

Affirming Devotion and Dedication:

Affirm your devotion and dedication to your long-term relationship. Recognize that commitment requires effort and intentional action to maintain a deep connection with your partner or friend.

Affirmation: "I am devoted to nurturing my long-term relationship. I commit to investing time, energy, and love to strengthen our bond."

Embracing Emotional Intimacy:

Affirm the importance of emotional intimacy in long-term relationships. Recognize that emotional closeness and vulnerability are essential for building a lasting and fulfilling connection.

Affirmation: "I embrace emotional intimacy in my long-term relationship. I am open, honest, and vulnerable, creating a space for deep connection and understanding."

Honoring Trust and Loyalty:

Affirm your commitment to trust and loyalty in your long-term relationship. Recognize that trust is the foundation upon which lasting relationships are built and that loyalty strengthens the bond between individuals.

Affirmation: "I honor trust and loyalty in my long-term relationship. I am trustworthy and loyal, creating a safe and secure space for our love and friendship to flourish."

Affirming Support and Encouragement:

Affirm your commitment to supporting and encouraging your partner or friend. Recognize the importance of being a reliable source of support in their journey, celebrating their successes, and offering a listening ear during challenges.

Affirmation: "I am a source of support and encouragement in my long-term relationship. I celebrate my partner's or friend's successes and provide comfort and guidance during difficult times."

Committing to Growth and Evolution:

Affirm your commitment to personal growth and the growth of your long-term relationship. Recognize that change is inevitable, and embracing growth together fosters a stronger and more resilient connection.

Affirmation: "I am committed to personal growth and the growth of our relationship. We evolve together, embracing change and becoming the best versions of ourselves."

Affirming Open and Honest Communication:

Affirm the practice of open and honest communication in your long-term relationship. Recognize that effective communication allows for understanding, resolution of conflicts, and the deepening of your connection.

Affirmation: "I communicate openly and honestly in my long-term relationship. I listen attentively and express my thoughts and feelings with compassion and clarity."

Nurturing Shared Goals and Dreams:

Affirm your commitment to nurturing shared goals and dreams in your long-term relationship. Recognize that having common aspirations creates a sense of purpose and unity.

Affirmation: "I am committed to nurturing our shared goals and dreams. Together, we work towards our vision, supporting and inspiring each other along the way."

Affirming Resilience in Times of Challenge:

Affirm your resilience and the resilience of your long-term relationship. Recognize that challenges are a natural part of any journey and affirm your commitment to overcoming obstacles together.

Affirmation: "I am resilient in my long-term relationship. We face challenges with courage, adaptability, and unwavering support for each other."

Celebrating Milestones and Anniversaries:

Affirm the practice of celebrating milestones and anniversaries in your long-term relationship. Recognize the importance of marking special moments and expressing gratitude for the time you have spent together.

Affirmation: "I celebrate the milestones and anniversaries in our long-term relationship. I express gratitude for the memories we have created and look forward to a future filled with love and joy."

Affirming Unconditional Love and Acceptance:

Affirm your unconditional love and acceptance for your partner or friend. Recognize that love should be accepting, compassionate, and free from judgment.

Affirmation: "I love and accept my partner or friend unconditionally. I embrace their flaws and celebrate their uniqueness, creating a space of love and acceptance."

By incorporating these affirmations into your daily practice, you can affirm and nurture commitment and loyalty in your long-term relationships. Remember that building and maintaining strong connections require ongoing effort, patience, and a deep understanding of each other's needs. Through affirming these values, you can cultivate a lasting and fulfilling relationship filled with love, trust, and mutual support.

AFFIRMATIONS FOR NURTURING FRIENDSHIPS AND BUILDING A SUPPORTIVE SOCIAL NETWORK.

Friendships play a vital role in our lives, offering companionship, support, and shared experiences. Cultivating and nurturing friendships can contribute to our overall well-being and happiness. In this section, we will explore the significance of affirming friendships and provide a range of affirmations to support the practice of nurturing these connections.

Affirming the Value of Friendship:

Acknowledge the importance of friendships in your life. Recognize the positive impact they have on your emotional well-being and personal growth.

Affirmation: "I cherish and value my friendships. They enrich my life and bring me joy, support, and meaningful connections."

Cultivating Authenticity and Vulnerability:

Embrace authenticity and vulnerability in your friendships. Create a safe space where you can share your true thoughts and feelings, and encourage your friends to do the same.

Affirmation: "I cultivate authenticity and vulnerability in my friendships. I am open, honest, and genuine, allowing for deep and meaningful connections."

Affirming Trust and Loyalty:

Affirm your commitment to trust and loyalty in your friendships. Build a foundation of trust by being reliable, honest, and supportive.

Affirmation: "I am a trustworthy and loyal friend. I honor the trust my friends place in me and provide unwavering support and encouragement."

Nurturing Mutual Respect and Acceptance:

Embrace mutual respect and acceptance in your friendships. Value each other's unique perspectives, strengths, and differences.

Affirmation: "I nurture mutual respect and acceptance in my friendships. I appreciate and celebrate the diversity and individuality of my friends."

Supporting Growth and Personal Development:

Support the growth and personal development of your friends. Encourage their dreams, celebrate their achievements, and provide a listening ear during challenging times.

Affirmation: "I support the growth and personal development of my friends. I am a source of encouragement, inspiration, and guidance in their journeys."

Affirming Active Listening and Empathy:

Practice active listening and empathy in your friendships. Be present, attentive, and compassionate when your friends share their joys, concerns, and struggles.

Affirmation: "I am an active listener and show empathy in my friendships. I offer a compassionate heart and a non-judgmental ear when my friends need it."

Cultivating Quality Time and Shared Experiences:

Make time for quality interactions and shared experiences with your friends. Create lasting memories through meaningful conversations, outings, and adventures.

Affirmation: "I prioritize quality time and shared experiences with my friends. We create unforgettable moments and strengthen our bond."

Affirming Supportive and Encouraging Friendships:

Affirm the practice of being a supportive and encouraging friend. Celebrate your friends' successes, provide comfort during challenging times, and offer guidance when needed.

Affirmation: "I am a supportive and encouraging friend. I celebrate my friends' achievements, offer a comforting shoulder, and provide guidance when asked."

Embracing Flexibility and Forgiveness:

Embrace flexibility and forgiveness in your friendships. Understand that misunderstandings and conflicts are a part of any relationship, and practice forgiveness to maintain harmony and growth.

Affirmation: "I embrace flexibility and forgiveness in my friendships. I am willing to compromise, let go of resentments, and work towards resolution."

Affirming Gratitude for Friendships:

Express gratitude for the presence of your friends in your life. Recognize the blessings they bring and the positive impact they have on your well-being.

Affirmation: "I am grateful for the friendships in my life. I appreciate the love, laughter, and support my friends bring into my world."

By incorporating these affirmations into your daily practice, you can nurture your friendships and build a supportive social network. Remember that friendships require effort, communication, and mutual care. By affirming these values, you can cultivate meaningful connections that bring joy, support, and fulfillment to your life.

AFFIRMATIONS FOR STRENGTHENING PARENT-CHILD RELATIONSHIPS.

Parent-child relationships are among the most important and influential connections we have in our lives. These relationships shape our upbringing, impact our self-esteem, and contribute to our overall well-being. Nurturing a strong and loving bond with your child is crucial for their emotional and social development. In this section, we will explore affirmations that can support and strengthen parent-child relationships.

Affirming Unconditional Love:

Affirm your unconditional love for your child. Let them know that your love is unwavering, regardless of their successes or challenges.

Affirmation: "I unconditionally love my child. My love is constant, supporting them through every step of their journey."

Building Trust and Open Communication:

Foster trust and open communication with your child. Create a safe and supportive environment where they feel comfortable expressing themselves and sharing their thoughts and feelings.

Affirmation: "I cultivate trust and open communication with my child. We have a strong foundation of honesty and understanding."

Affirming Respect and Mutual Understanding:

Affirm respect and mutual understanding in your relationship with your child. Treat them with respect, listen to their perspectives, and validate their feelings.

Affirmation: "I respect and value my child's thoughts and feelings. I strive to understand their unique perspective and foster a harmonious connection."

Nurturing Emotional Connection:

Focus on nurturing an emotional connection with your child. Show empathy, validate their emotions, and provide a safe space for them to express themselves.

Affirmation: "I nurture a deep emotional connection with my child. I am attuned to their emotions and offer comfort and support when needed."

Affirming Support and Encouragement:

Affirm your role as a supportive and encouraging parent. Provide guidance, celebrate achievements, and offer reassurance during challenging times.

Affirmation: "I am a supportive and encouraging parent. I provide guidance, celebrate my child's successes, and offer reassurance when they face difficulties."

Embracing Patience and Understanding:

Embrace patience and understanding in your interactions with your child. Recognize that they are growing and learning, and allow them the space to make mistakes and grow from them.

Affirmation: "I approach parenting with patience and understanding. I give my child room to learn, grow, and develop at their own pace."

Affirming Quality Time and Shared Activities:

Make quality time and shared activities a priority in your relationship with your child. Engage in activities that foster connection, laughter, and meaningful moments together.

Affirmation: "I prioritize quality time and shared activities with my child. We create cherished memories and strengthen our bond."

Emphasizing Positive Reinforcement:

Focus on positive reinforcement to encourage your child's growth and development. Acknowledge their efforts, strengths, and achievements to boost their self-esteem.

Affirmation: "I provide positive reinforcement to my child. I recognize and celebrate their strengths and accomplishments, nurturing their confidence."

Affirming Boundaries and Discipline:

Affirm the importance of setting boundaries and providing appropriate discipline. Teach your child about responsibility, accountability, and the importance of respectful behavior.

Affirmation: "I establish healthy boundaries and provide loving discipline for my child. I guide them towards making responsible choices and treating others with kindness."

Affirming Uniqueness and Individuality:

Celebrate and affirm your child's uniqueness and individuality. Embrace their interests, passions, and talents, and encourage them to express themselves authentically.

Affirmation: "I affirm and celebrate my child's uniqueness. I encourage them to embrace their individuality and pursue their passions."

Promoting Independence and Autonomy:

Support your child's independence and autonomy. Give them opportunities to make decisions, learn from their experiences, and grow into confident individuals.

Affirmation: "I empower my child to become independent and autonomous. I trust their judgment and support them in their journey of self-discovery."

Cultivating Empathy and Kindness:

Teach and model empathy and kindness towards others. Encourage your child to be considerate, compassionate, and understanding towards people from all walks of life.

Affirmation: "I cultivate empathy and kindness in my child. They embrace compassion and understanding, spreading love and positivity."

Affirming Gratitude and Appreciation:

Instill gratitude and appreciation in your child. Encourage them to express gratitude for the people and things in their lives, fostering a positive and thankful mindset.

Affirmation: "I teach my child the importance of gratitude and appreciation. They cultivate a grateful heart, finding joy in the blessings around them."

Encouraging Self-Love and Self-Acceptance:

Encourage your child to love and accept themselves. Teach them the value of self-care, self-compassion, and embracing their unique qualities.

Affirmation: "I encourage my child to love and accept themselves fully. They appreciate their strengths and embrace their beautiful, authentic selves."

Affirming Unbreakable Bond:

Affirm the unbreakable bond you share with your child. Reassure them that you will always be there for them, providing love, support, and guidance throughout their lives.

Affirmation: "The bond between my child and me is unbreakable. I am their constant source of love, support, and guidance."

By incorporating these affirmations into your daily life, you can strengthen and nourish your parent-child relationship. Remember that building a strong bond takes time, effort, and consistent love. Through affirmations and intentional actions, you can create a loving and nurturing environment that fosters your child's growth and well-being.

AFFIRMATIONS FOR FOSTERING HEALTHY CO-WORKER RELATIONSHIPS AND COLLABORATION.

In the professional world, cultivating healthy relationships with your co-workers is essential for creating a positive and productive work environment. Strong co-worker relationships contribute to better collaboration, increased job satisfaction, and overall success within the organization. In this section, we will explore affirmations that can help foster healthy co-worker relationships and encourage collaboration.

Affirming Respect and Professionalism:

Affirm respect and professionalism in your interactions with co-workers. Treat them with courtesy, listen actively, and value their opinions and contributions.

Affirmation: "I approach my co-workers with respect and professionalism. I appreciate their expertise and perspectives, fostering a harmonious work environment."

Building Trust and Support:

Focus on building trust and support among your co-workers. Be reliable, keep your commitments, and offer assistance when needed. Trust is the foundation for effective collaboration.

Affirmation: "I build trust and support among my co-workers. We rely on each other and work together towards shared goals."

Affirming Open and Transparent Communication:

Affirm open and transparent communication in the workplace. Encourage honest and constructive dialogue, fostering an environment where ideas can be freely shared and discussed.

Affirmation: "I engage in open and transparent communication with my co-workers. We value diverse perspectives and communicate effectively to achieve our objectives."

Embracing Collaboration and Teamwork:

Embrace collaboration and teamwork as key values in your work relationships. Foster a culture where colleagues support each other and work together towards shared goals.

Affirmation: "I embrace collaboration and teamwork with my co-workers. Together, we achieve greater success and create a positive work environment."

Affirming Empathy and Understanding:

Affirm empathy and understanding in your interactions with co-workers. Seek to understand their perspectives, show compassion, and support them during challenging times.

Affirmation: "I approach my co-workers with empathy and understanding. I offer support and compassion, fostering a caring and inclusive workplace."

Nurturing Positive Relationships:

Nurture positive relationships with your co-workers. Celebrate their successes, express appreciation, and create opportunities for camaraderie and team bonding.

Affirmation: "I nurture positive relationships with my co-workers. We celebrate each other's achievements and create a supportive and enjoyable work environment."

Affirming Conflict Resolution Skills:

Affirm your ability to handle conflicts constructively. Develop strong conflict resolution skills, promoting open dialogue and finding mutually beneficial solutions.

Affirmation: "I approach conflicts with my co-workers as opportunities for growth. I communicate respectfully, seek common ground, and find resolutions that benefit all."

Valuing Diversity and Inclusion:

Value diversity and inclusion in the workplace. Embrace the unique perspectives and backgrounds of your co-workers, fostering a culture of acceptance and appreciation.

Affirmation: "I value diversity and inclusion in my workplace. I embrace the richness of different perspectives and create an environment where everyone feels valued."

Affirming Professional Growth and Development:

Affirm the importance of professional growth and development within your co-worker relationships. Support and encourage each other's professional aspirations and celebrate individual accomplishments.

Affirmation: "I support the professional growth and development of my co-workers. We inspire each other to reach new heights and celebrate our achievements together."

Promoting Work-Life Balance:

Promote a healthy work-life balance among your co-workers. Encourage self-care, time off, and work-life integration, fostering a culture that values well-being.

Affirmation: "I promote work-life balance among my co-workers. We prioritize self-care and create an environment that supports overall well-being."

AFFIRMATIONS FOR ATTRACTING AND MANIFESTING A LOVING AND FULFILLING PARTNERSHIP.

Finding a loving and fulfilling partnership is a desire many people hold close to their hearts. Affirmations can be powerful tools to help you align your thoughts, beliefs, and intentions with the manifestation of a loving relationship. In this section, we will explore affirmations that can support you in attracting and manifesting a healthy and fulfilling partnership.

Affirming Self-Worth and Deservingness:

Affirm your self-worth and deservingness of a loving partnership. Recognize that you are deserving of love and that you have unique qualities to offer in a relationship.

Affirmation: "I am worthy of a loving and fulfilling partnership. I deserve a relationship that brings joy, support, and growth into my life."

Embracing Love and Vulnerability:

Embrace love and vulnerability in your affirmations. Open yourself up to the possibility of deep emotional connection and allow yourself to be vulnerable in sharing your authentic self.

Affirmation: "I embrace love with an open heart. I allow myself to be vulnerable, knowing that true intimacy and connection come from authenticity."

Affirming Alignment with Your Ideal Partner:

Affirm that you are aligned with your ideal partner energetically and emotionally. Visualize yourself in a relationship that brings out the best in both partners and fosters mutual growth.

Affirmation: "I am in perfect alignment with my ideal partner. Together, we support and inspire each other to reach our highest potential."

Cultivating Positive Beliefs About Relationships:

Cultivate positive beliefs about relationships and love. Affirm beliefs that relationships can be nurturing, fulfilling, and based on mutual respect and understanding.

Affirmation: "I believe in the power of love and relationships. I attract and manifest a partnership that is nurturing, fulfilling, and built on mutual respect and understanding."

Affirming Clarity in Your Relationship Intentions:

Affirm clarity in your relationship intentions. Clearly state the qualities and values you desire in a partner and the type of relationship you wish to create.

Affirmation: "I am clear in my relationship intentions. I attract a partner who shares my values, aligns with my vision, and supports my personal growth."

Embracing Patience and Trust in Divine Timing:

Embrace patience and trust in divine timing. Affirm that the right partner will come into your life at the perfect time, and trust that the universe is guiding you towards your ideal relationship.

Affirmation: "I trust in divine timing. The universe brings the right partner into my life when the time is right, and I embrace patience in my journey."

Affirming Self-Love and Self-Care:

Affirm self-love and self-care as essential foundations for attracting a loving partnership. Prioritize self-care and nurture a loving relationship with yourself, knowing that it sets the tone for the relationships you attract.

Affirmation: "I practice self-love and self-care. By loving and caring for myself deeply, I attract a partner who also values and cherishes me."

Affirming Openness and Willingness to Receive Love:

Affirm your openness and willingness to receive love. Release any barriers or fears that may be blocking love from entering your life, and affirm your readiness to welcome love with open arms.

Affirmation: "I am open to receiving love. I release any fears or barriers that block love and embrace the abundance of love that flows into my life."

Affirming Compatibility and Harmonious Connection:

Affirm compatibility and a harmonious connection with your ideal partner. Visualize yourself in a relationship where you share mutual understanding, compatibility, and a deep sense of connection.

Affirmation: "I attract a partner who is compatible and in harmony with me. We share a deep connection, understanding, and a joyous journey together."

Gratitude for the Relationship Manifestation Process:

Express gratitude for the process of manifesting a loving partnership. Embrace gratitude for the lessons, growth, and opportunities that come along the way, knowing that each step brings you closer to your desired relationship.

Affirmation: "I am grateful for the journey of manifesting a loving partnership. I embrace the lessons and growth that come along the way, knowing that my desired relationship is on its way."

Remember that affirmations are most effective when practiced consistently and accompanied by aligned actions. Combine these affirmations with a mindset of openness, self-awareness, and active participation in your own growth and personal development. By affirming your intentions and beliefs, you can attract and manifest a loving and fulfilling partnership that aligns with your deepest desires and values.

AFFIRMATIONS FOR SELF-WORTH AND ATTRACTING HEALTHY LOVE INTO YOUR LIFE.

Self-worth is the foundation for attracting and cultivating healthy love in your life. When you have a strong sense of self-worth, you create a magnetic energy that draws in love that aligns with your highest good. In this section, we will explore affirmations that can support you in recognizing your inherent worthiness and attracting healthy love into your life.

Affirming Your Inherent Worthiness:

Affirm your inherent worthiness and value as a person. Recognize that you are deserving of love and that your worth is not determined by external factors or validation from others.

Affirmation: "I am inherently worthy of love. I recognize my value and know that I deserve healthy and fulfilling relationships."

Embracing Self-Love and Self-Care:

Embrace self-love and self-care as essential practices in attracting healthy love. Prioritize your well-being, nurture yourself, and establish healthy boundaries that honor your needs and values.

Affirmation: "I love and care for myself deeply. I prioritize self-care and set healthy boundaries, attracting love that respects and supports my well-being."

Affirming Positive Self-Talk:

Affirm positive self-talk and cultivate a loving and compassionate inner dialogue. Replace self-criticism and negative beliefs with empowering affirmations that uplift and inspire you.

Affirmation: "I speak to myself with kindness and compassion. I affirm my worth and embrace my unique qualities, attracting love that recognizes and cherishes them."

Recognizing and Releasing Limiting Beliefs:

Recognize and release limiting beliefs that undermine your self-worth and hinder the attraction of healthy love. Challenge beliefs such as "I am not deserving of love" or "I am unworthy of a healthy relationship" and replace them with empowering alternatives.

Affirmation: "I release limiting beliefs about my worthiness of love. I replace them with empowering beliefs that affirm my deservingness of healthy and loving relationships."

Affirming Boundaries and Self-Respect:

Affirm boundaries and self-respect in your relationships. Set clear boundaries that honor your values, needs, and well-being, attracting love that respects and supports your boundaries.

Affirmation: "I establish and communicate my boundaries with confidence and self-respect. I attract love that honors and respects my boundaries."

Affirming Authenticity and Vulnerability:

Affirm your authenticity and embrace vulnerability in your relationships. Be true to yourself and express your needs, desires, and emotions authentically, attracting love that appreciates and values your true self.

Affirmation: "I embrace my authenticity and vulnerability in relationships. I attract love that values and cherishes my true self."

Affirming Healthy Communication:

Affirm healthy communication in your relationships. Practice open and honest communication, actively listening and expressing yourself with kindness and clarity, attracting love that fosters understanding and emotional connection.

Affirmation: "I communicate with love, kindness, and clarity. I attract love that values open and honest communication, fostering deep emotional connection."

Affirming Trust in the Process of Love:

Affirm trust in the process of love. Believe that the right person and the right love will come into your life at the perfect time, trusting in divine timing and the alignment of energies.

Affirmation: "I trust in the process of love. The right person and the right love come into my life when the time is right, aligning with my highest good."

Affirming Gratitude for Love's Presence:

Express gratitude for the love that is already present in your life. Cultivate an attitude of gratitude for the love you receive from friends, family, and yourself, attracting more love and abundance into your life.

Affirmation: "I am grateful for the love that surrounds me. I attract more love and abundance into my life, celebrating and cherishing the love that is already present."

Affirming Self-Reflection and Growth:

Affirm self-reflection and personal growth as ongoing processes in attracting healthy love. Continuously explore and develop yourself, learning from past experiences and embracing opportunities for growth.

Affirmation: "I am committed to self-reflection and personal growth. I attract love that supports and encourages my journey of self-discovery and transformation."

By incorporating these affirmations into your daily practice, you can cultivate a strong sense of self-worth and attract healthy love into your life. Remember to practice self-love, set boundaries, communicate effectively, and embrace your authentic self. Trust in the process and express gratitude for the love that already exists. Through affirmations and aligned actions, you create an environment that magnetizes healthy and fulfilling love, inviting it to flourish and thrive in your life.

AFFIRMATIONS FOR HEALING FROM PAST RELATIONSHIP WOUNDS AND OPENING UP TO LOVE.

Healing from past relationship wounds is crucial for opening up to love and creating healthy and fulfilling relationships. When we carry unresolved pain and trauma from past experiences, it can hinder our ability to trust, connect, and fully embrace love. In this section, we will explore affirmations that can support you in healing from past relationship wounds and opening yourself up to love again.

Acknowledging and Honoring Your Healing Journey:

Acknowledge and honor your healing journey. Recognize that healing takes time and that it is a process of self-discovery and growth.

Affirmation: "I honor my healing journey. I am patient and compassionate with myself as I heal from past relationship wounds and open myself up to love."

Releasing Resentment and Forgiving:

Release resentment and cultivate forgiveness towards yourself and others. Free yourself from the burden of holding onto past grievances, allowing space for love and healing to enter your life.

Affirmation: "I release resentment and forgive myself and others. I choose to let go of past hurts and create space for love and healing in my heart."

Affirming Self-Love and Self-Acceptance:

Affirm self-love and self-acceptance as you heal from past relationship wounds. Embrace yourself fully, including your strengths, vulnerabilities, and imperfections.

Affirmation: "I love and accept myself unconditionally. I embrace all aspects of who I am as I heal and open myself up to love."

Cultivating Trust in the Process of Healing:

Cultivate trust in the process of healing. Believe in your ability to heal, grow, and attract healthy love into your life.

Affirmation: "I trust in the process of healing. I am open to the transformative power of love and believe in my capacity to attract healthy and nurturing relationships."

Rebuilding Self-Confidence and Self-Worth:

Rebuild self-confidence and self-worth as you heal from past relationship wounds. Recognize your value and the unique qualities that make you deserving of love.

Affirmation: "I am confident and worthy of love. I recognize my value and embrace my worthiness as I heal and open myself up to love."

Affirming Boundaries and Self-Protection:

Affirm boundaries and self-protection as you navigate new relationships. Set clear boundaries that protect your emotional well-being and honor your needs and values.

Affirmation: "I set healthy boundaries and protect my emotional well-being. I attract love that respects and supports my boundaries."

Opening Your Heart to Love:

Open your heart to love, allowing yourself to be vulnerable and receptive to new connections. Embrace the possibility of experiencing deep love and connection again.

Affirmation: "I am open to love. I courageously open my heart, trusting that love will find its way to me in the most beautiful and fulfilling ways."

Affirming Your Deservingness of Love:

Affirm your deservingness of love. Recognize that you are worthy of a loving and fulfilling relationship, free from past wounds and limitations.

Affirmation: "I deserve love and happiness. I release the past and step into a future filled with love, joy, and fulfillment."

Cultivating Self-Compassion:

Cultivate self-compassion as you heal from past relationship wounds. Be gentle with yourself, offering kindness and understanding during moments of pain or triggers.

Affirmation: "I am compassionate with myself. I extend kindness and understanding to myself as I navigate the healing journey and open myself up to love."

Embracing Positive Affirmations for Love:

Embrace positive affirmations that reinforce your belief in love and your ability to attract a healthy and loving relationship.

Affirmation: "Love flows effortlessly into my life. I am deserving of a deep, authentic, and nurturing love. I attract and manifest a loving and fulfilling relationship."

By incorporating these affirmations into your daily practice, you can support your healing process and open yourself up to love. Remember that healing is a personal journey, and it takes time and patience. Be kind to yourself, honor your emotions, and embrace the transformative power of love. Trust that as you heal and let go of past wounds, you create space for love to enter your life in beautiful and meaningful ways.

AFFIRMATIONS FOR EMBRACING AUTHENTICITY AND BEING TRUE TO YOURSELF IN RELATIONSHIPS.

Embracing authenticity and being true to yourself is essential for building healthy and fulfilling relationships. When you are authentic, you attract like-minded individuals who appreciate and accept you for who you truly are. In this section, we will explore affirmations that can support you in embracing authenticity and staying true to yourself in your relationships.

Embracing Your True Self:

Embrace your true self and honor your unique qualities, values, and beliefs. Celebrate the authentic essence that makes you who you are.

Affirmation: "I embrace my authentic self. I am worthy of love and acceptance just as I am."

Trusting Your Intuition:

Trust your intuition and inner wisdom to guide you in your relationships. Listen to your gut feelings and honor the messages they bring.

Affirmation: "I trust my intuition. I listen to my inner voice and make choices that align with my authentic self."

Expressing Your Needs and Desires:

Express your needs and desires openly and honestly in your relationships. Communicate your boundaries and preferences with clarity and respect.

Affirmation: "I confidently express my needs and desires. I communicate my boundaries and expectations with love and respect."

Embracing Vulnerability:

Embrace vulnerability as a strength and a pathway to deeper connection. Allow yourself to be seen authentically and share your true thoughts and emotions.

Affirmation: "I embrace vulnerability. I am open and honest in my relationships, allowing for deeper connection and intimacy."

Setting Boundaries:

Set healthy boundaries that protect your well-being and honor your values. Respect your own limits and communicate them with love and assertiveness.

Affirmation: "I set clear and healthy boundaries. I honor my needs and create space for authentic connections."

Honoring Your Values:

Honor your values and live in alignment with them. Make choices and engage in relationships that resonate with your core principles.

Affirmation: "I honor my values. I attract relationships that align with my authentic self and support my personal growth."

Practicing Self-Care:

Prioritize self-care and self-love in your relationships. Nurture your own well-being and ensure that your own needs are met.

Affirmation: "I prioritize self-care. I give myself the love and care I deserve, creating a solid foundation for authentic connections."

Embracing Imperfection:

Embrace your imperfections and let go of the need for perfection. Allow yourself to make mistakes and learn from them in your relationships.

Affirmation: "I embrace my imperfections. I am worthy of love and acceptance, even with my flaws and mistakes."

Speaking Your Truth:

Speak your truth with courage and authenticity. Express your thoughts, feelings, and opinions honestly and respectfully.

Affirmation: "I speak my truth with love. I express myself authentically and confidently in my relationships."

Embracing Growth and Evolution:

Embrace personal growth and evolution in your relationships. Allow yourself and your loved ones to change, learn, and grow together.

Affirmation: "I embrace growth and evolution. I am open to learning and evolving in my relationships, embracing positive change."

Celebrating Individuality:

Celebrate your individuality and the individuality of others in your relationships. Appreciate and value the unique qualities that each person brings.

Affirmation: "I celebrate individuality. I embrace the diverse perspectives and qualities that enrich my relationships."

Respecting Differences:

Respect and honor the differences in your relationships. Embrace diversity and learn from each other's unique perspectives and experiences.

Affirmation: "I respect differences. I cultivate an inclusive and accepting environment in my relationships."

Trusting Your Authentic Magnetism:

Trust in your authentic magnetism to attract the right people into your life. Believe that by being true to yourself, you naturally draw in those who resonate with you.

Affirmation: "I trust in my authentic magnetism. I attract genuine connections by being true to myself."

Releasing the Need for Approval:

Release the need for external validation and approval. Find validation from within and trust in your own worthiness.

Affirmation: "I release the need for approval. I validate and honor myself, knowing that I am worthy of love and acceptance."

Embracing Unconditional Self-Love:

Embrace unconditional self-love as the foundation of your relationships. Love yourself unconditionally, and attract relationships that reflect this love.

Affirmation: "I love myself unconditionally. I attract relationships that mirror the love and acceptance I have for myself."

By incorporating these affirmations into your daily practice, you can cultivate a strong sense of authenticity and stay true to yourself in your relationships. Remember, genuine connections thrive when built on the foundation of authenticity and self-love. Trust in yourself, honor your true essence, and embrace the beautiful journey of building authentic and fulfilling relationships.

AFFIRMATIONS FOR PRACTICING PATIENCE AND UNDERSTANDING IN RELATIONSHIPS.

Practicing patience and understanding is crucial for nurturing healthy and harmonious relationships. It allows us to cultivate empathy, compassion, and a deeper sense of connection with our loved ones. In this section, we will explore affirmations that can support you in developing patience and understanding within your relationships.

Cultivating Patience:

I cultivate patience in my relationships, allowing space and time for growth and understanding.

Empathy and Compassion:

I approach my loved ones with empathy and compassion, seeking to understand their perspectives and emotions.

Active Listening:

I am an active listener, fully present and attentive to the needs and concerns of my loved ones.

Non-judgmental Attitude:

I release judgment and embrace a non-judgmental attitude, accepting others for who they are without imposing my own expectations.

Responding, Not Reacting:

I respond to situations with thoughtfulness and understanding, rather than reacting impulsively.

Seeking Common Ground:

I actively seek common ground with my loved ones, focusing on shared values and goals to foster understanding and connection.

Respecting Differences:

I respect the differences in opinions, beliefs, and perspectives within my relationships, allowing space for diverse viewpoints.

Practicing Forgiveness:

I practice forgiveness, letting go of past hurts and resentments, and allowing space for healing and growth.

Stepping into Others' Shoes:

I consciously put myself in the shoes of my loved ones, seeking to understand their experiences and emotions.

Emotional Intelligence:

I nurture my emotional intelligence, recognizing and managing my own emotions while being sensitive to the emotions of others.

Giving Space:

I respect the need for personal space and independence within my relationships, allowing each person to grow and thrive individually.

Communicating with Patience:

I communicate with patience and understanding, expressing myself in a calm and respectful manner.

Embracing the Learning Process:

I embrace the learning process within my relationships, understanding that growth and understanding take time and effort.

Practicing Self-Reflection:

I engage in regular self-reflection, examining my own thoughts, feelings, and behaviors to promote understanding and personal growth.

Cultivating Gratitude:

I cultivate gratitude for the presence of my loved ones in my life, recognizing their unique contributions and expressing appreciation.

By incorporating these affirmations into your daily practice, you can develop patience and understanding within your relationships. Remember, building strong and meaningful connections requires effort, empathy, and a willingness to grow together. Embrace the power of patience and understanding, and watch as your relationships flourish and deepen in a nurturing and harmonious way.

AFFIRMATIONS FOR FOSTERING A SENSE OF FUN AND ADVENTURE IN RELATIONSHIPS.

Fostering a sense of fun and adventure in relationships is essential for creating joyful and fulfilling experiences together. It allows us to break free from routine, explore new possibilities, and deepen our bond with our loved ones. In this section, we will explore affirmations that can support you in embracing a sense of fun and adventure within your relationships.

Embracing Spontaneity:

I embrace spontaneity in my relationships, inviting excitement and surprises into our shared experiences.

Embodying Playfulness:

I embrace my inner child and bring a spirit of playfulness into my interactions with my loved ones.

Seeking Novelty:

I actively seek out new and novel experiences with my partner, keeping our relationship fresh and exciting.

Letting Go of Expectations:

I release expectations and allow myself and my loved ones to explore and enjoy each moment without judgment or pressure.

Embracing New Experiences:

I am open to trying new activities, adventures, and hobbies with my partner, expanding our horizons together.

Creating Shared Adventures:

I actively participate in creating shared adventures and experiences, fostering a sense of togetherness and shared memories.

Embracing Laughter:

I invite laughter and humor into our relationship, finding joy and lightness in even the simplest moments.

Celebrating Milestones:

I celebrate milestones and accomplishments in our relationship, recognizing and acknowledging the growth and progress we have made.

Seeking Thrills Together:

I actively seek thrilling experiences with my partner, whether it be exploring new destinations, trying adventurous activities, or embracing adrenaline-pumping challenges.

Nurturing a Spirit of Play:

I prioritize play and recreation in our relationship, creating space for lightheartedness, fun, and enjoyment.

Exploring the Outdoors:

I embrace the beauty of nature and enjoy outdoor adventures with my loved ones, connecting with the world around us.

Cultivating Curiosity:

I cultivate curiosity and a sense of wonder, exploring new interests and ideas together with my partner.

Embracing Surprise and Spontaneity:

I welcome surprises and spontaneous gestures of love and adventure, adding excitement and unpredictability to our relationship.

Making Time for Play:

I prioritize and make time for play and leisure activities in our busy lives, recognizing their importance in fostering a sense of fun and adventure.

Embracing the Present Moment:

I fully immerse myself in the present moment, savoring the experiences and creating lasting memories with my loved ones.

By incorporating these affirmations into your daily practice, you can foster a sense of fun and adventure in your relationships. Embrace the joy of spontaneity, laughter, and shared experiences, and watch as your relationship becomes a playground of love, growth, and cherished memories.

CONCLUSION: ENCOURAGEMENT TO PRACTICE DAILY AFFIRMATIONS FOR BUILDING AND NURTURING LOVING RELATIONSHIPS.

Building and nurturing loving relationships is a lifelong journey that requires continuous effort, intention, and growth. Throughout this discussion, we have explored the power of affirmations in fostering positive, fulfilling connections with oneself and others. Affirmations serve as powerful tools for shifting our mindset, cultivating self-love, and attracting and manifesting healthy relationships into our lives. In this concluding section, we offer encouragement and guidance on the practice of daily affirmations to build and nurture loving relationships.

Embrace Consistency:

Commit to incorporating affirmations into your daily routine. Consistency is key in reinforcing positive beliefs and creating lasting change in your mindset and relationships.

Set Intentions:

Before starting your day, set intentions for the kind of relationships you want to cultivate. Use affirmations to align your thoughts and actions with these intentions, paving the way for loving and fulfilling connections.

Cultivate Self-Love:

Nurture a strong foundation of self-love and self-acceptance. Affirmations that promote self-worth, self-compassion, and self-care are essential in creating a healthy sense of self and attracting loving relationships.

Practice Gratitude:

Express gratitude for the relationships you have and the love that exists in your life. Affirmations of gratitude foster appreciation and help you focus on the positive aspects of your relationships, deepening your connection with your loved ones.

Visualize Your Ideal Relationships:

Use affirmations to visualize and manifest your ideal relationships. Envision the qualities, dynamics, and experiences you desire, and affirm them as already present in your life.

Embrace Vulnerability:

Affirmations that embrace vulnerability and openness help create an environment of trust and emotional intimacy in your relationships. Allow yourself to be authentic and encourage your loved ones to do the same.

Communicate with Love and Respect:

Use affirmations to remind yourself to communicate with love, respect, and active listening. Affirm your commitment to understanding and validating the feelings and perspectives of your loved ones.

Set Healthy Boundaries:

Affirmations can help you establish and maintain healthy boundaries in your relationships. Reinforce your self-worth and affirm your right to set boundaries that promote mutual respect and emotional well-being.

Resolve Conflicts Constructively:

Affirmations that support effective conflict resolution and problem-solving skills are invaluable in nurturing loving relationships. Affirm your commitment to resolving conflicts with empathy, compassion, and a focus on finding mutually beneficial solutions.

Embrace Growth and Evolution:

Affirmations that embrace personal growth and evolution foster resilience and adaptability in relationships. Affirm your commitment to continuous growth, both individually and together with your loved ones.

Show Appreciation and Affection:

Express appreciation and affection through affirmations and heartfelt gestures. Affirm your love, admiration, and gratitude for your loved ones, reinforcing the positive energy and connection in your relationships.

Practice Forgiveness and Letting Go:

Affirmations that promote forgiveness and letting go of past resentments are crucial for healing and fostering loving relationships. Affirm your willingness to release grudges and embrace a future free from the burdens of the past.

Cultivate Mutual Support:

Affirm your commitment to being a supportive partner, friend, or family member. Affirmations that emphasize your willingness to offer encouragement, assistance, and understanding help create a strong support system within your relationships.

Embrace Balance and Flexibility:

Affirmations that prioritize balance and flexibility in relationships encourage harmony and understanding. Affirm your willingness to adapt, compromise, and seek solutions that honor the needs and desires of all involved.

Trust in the Process:

Finally, affirm your trust in the process of building and nurturing loving relationships. Trust that the affirmations you practice consistently and wholeheartedly will manifest positive change and bring forth the love and connection you seek.

In conclusion, daily affirmations have the power to transform your mindset, enhance your self-worth, and attract and nurture loving relationships. By integrating these affirmations into your daily practice, you can create a foundation of love, trust, and understanding within yourself and extend it to your relationships with others. Embrace the journey of growth, be patient and compassionate with yourself and your loved ones, and watch as your relationships flourish with love, joy, and fulfillment.

We hope that this book, "Affirmations for Building and Nurturing Loving Relationships," has served as a valuable resource on your journey towards cultivating and sustaining meaningful connections. The power of affirmations lies in their ability to transform our thoughts, beliefs, and actions, ultimately shaping the quality of our relationships and our overall well-being.

As you continue your exploration of personal growth and self-discovery, we invite you to delve deeper into the realm of positive affirmations by picking up our second book, "Empowered Affirmations: Cultivating Happiness and Joy in Everyday Life." In this next installment, we will embark on a new chapter focused on success and achievement, exploring various aspects of life where affirmations can empower and uplift.

Within the pages of "Empowered Affirmations," you will find an abundance of affirmations to nurture happiness and joy, inviting positivity and fulfillment into your daily experiences. You will discover affirmations that foster inner peace and calmness, helping you navigate life's challenges with serenity and grace. Additionally, you will explore affirmations that awaken your creativity and inspiration, igniting a spark within to bring forth your unique gifts and talents.

Moreover, "Empowered Affirmations" will guide you on a journey of spiritual growth and mindfulness, providing affirmations that deepen your connection to the divine and cultivate a sense of presence and purpose in your life. Through this exploration, you will uncover the power within you to create a life filled with joy, abundance, and meaning.

We encourage you to continue your practice of affirmations, to embrace the transformative power they hold, and to unlock the infinite possibilities that lie within you. May your path be illuminated with love, happiness, and success as you embark on this empowering journey.

Remember, the journey towards self-empowerment and personal growth is ongoing. As you turn the last page of this book, we invite you to open the next chapter of your life and continue your exploration with "Empowered Affirmations: Cultivating Happiness and Joy in Everyday Life." May it be a companion on your path to realizing your fullest potential.

Wishing you love, happiness, and abundant blessings on your journey of growth and fulfillment.

With warm regards,   *M. L. Ruscsak*

GLOSSARY

Abundance: The state of having more than enough of something, often associated with wealth and prosperity.

Affirmations: Positive statements or phrases used to challenge and overcome self-limiting beliefs, promote self-empowerment, and manifest desired outcomes.

Authenticity: The quality of being genuine, true to oneself, and aligned with one's values, beliefs, and emotions.

Boundaries: Personal limits and guidelines that define acceptable behavior and protect one's physical, emotional, and mental well-being in relationships.

Communication: The process of exchanging information, ideas, and emotions through verbal and non-verbal means to foster understanding and connection.

Conflict resolution: The process of addressing and resolving disagreements or conflicts in a peaceful and constructive manner.

Empathy: The ability to understand and share the feelings, thoughts, and experiences of others, often accompanied by compassion and non-judgment.

Forgiveness: The act of letting go of resentments, grudges, and negative emotions towards oneself or others, promoting healing and peace.

Gratitude: The practice of acknowledging and appreciating the blessings, experiences, and people in one's life, cultivating a positive outlook and emotional well-being.

Healthy habits: Behaviors and routines that contribute to physical, mental, and emotional well-being, such as regular exercise, balanced nutrition, and adequate rest.

Inner peace: A state of calmness, tranquility, and harmony within oneself, often achieved through mindfulness, meditation, and self-reflection.

Listening: The act of actively and attentively hearing and comprehending what others are communicating, without judgment or interruption.

Love: An intense feeling of deep affection, care, and connection towards oneself and others, characterized by kindness, compassion, and support.

Resilience: The ability to bounce back and adapt in the face of adversity, challenges, or setbacks, often accompanied by personal growth and strength.

Self-acceptance: The practice of embracing oneself fully, including one's strengths, weaknesses, flaws, and imperfections, with kindness and compassion.

Self-belief: The confidence and trust in one's abilities, qualities, and potential to achieve personal goals and overcome challenges.

Self-love: The unconditional regard, care, and compassion towards oneself, prioritizing self-care, self-acceptance, and self-empowerment.

Trust: The firm belief in the reliability, honesty, and integrity of oneself and others, forming the foundation of healthy and strong relationships.

Vulnerability: The willingness to be open, honest, and authentic, exposing one's true thoughts, feelings, and emotions, often leading to deeper connections and intimacy.

Well-being: The state of being in good physical, mental, and emotional health, experiencing a sense of balance, fulfillment, and contentment in life.

www.ingramcontent.com/pod-product-compliance
Lightning Source LLC
Chambersburg PA
CBHW052109020426
42335CB00021B/2684